WITH MY TROUSERS
ROLLED

WITH MY TROUSERS ROLLED

Familiar Essays by

JOSEPH EPSTEIN

W. W. NORTON & COMPANY

NEW YORK   LONDON

First Edition

The text of this book is composed in 11/14 Janson Alternate with the display set in
Weiss Initial. Composition and manufacturing by the Haddon Craftsmen, Inc.

Library of Congress Cataloging-in-Publication Data
Epstein, Joseph, 1937–
With my trousers rolled : familiar essays / Joseph Epstein.
p. cm.
I. Title.
PS3555.P6527W57   1995
814'.54—dc20   94-36706

ISBN 0-393-03757-6

W. W. Norton & Company, Inc., 500 Fifth Avenue, New York, N.Y. 10110
W. W. Norton & Company Ltd., 10 Coptic Street, London WC1A 1PU

1 2 3 4 5 6 7 8 9 0

For Jean Stipicevic and Sandra Costich,
Kindest and Best of Comrades

I grow old . . . I grow old . . .
I shall wear the bottom of my trousers rolled.

—T. S. Eliot
"The Love Song of J. Alfred Prufrock"

Contents

WITH MY TROUSERS ROLLED

Livestock

"My young friend," Aldous Huxley once instructed an aspiring novelist, "if you want to be a psychological novelist and write about human beings, the best thing you can do is keep a pair of cats." Whether this is good advice or not I do not know, but for me, a simple if more than occasionally pretentious essayist, one cat has done nicely. In recent years I have spent more time in the company of such a creature than I have with any human being, and, speaking for myself and not the creature in question, I find that it has its subtle compensations. It took me a long while to understand that a cat is the animal best suited to my talent and temperament. Since I have shown no talent whatsoever for training either children or dogs, having a cat, which is by nature intractable, has been a great relief. As for temperament, my cat and I share a penchant for being left alone for long stretches; neither of us is overly demonstrative in our emotions; and we are both quite good at gaining attention when we need it. Before leaving the matters of talent and temperament, I should add that cats generally tend to be cleaner, better athletes, and on the whole more suited for the contemplative life than I.

I realize that owning up to a serious admiration for cats puts me in slightly odd company. Whenever I take my own cat to the veterinarian, at a place called the Chicago Cat Clinic, I feel myself in a somewhat unusual crowd. I will not be more specific than to say that, as a group, my fellow cat lovers show marked differences from the regular Sunday-afternoon National Football League audience. Yet the admiration of cats does have a lengthy literary lineage. Ever since Montaigne struck off his famous sentence about his cat—"When I play with my cat who knows whether she diverts herself with me, or I with her!"—the link between literary men and women and cats has been forged. It has been notably strong in France. From Montaigne through Chateaubriand through Sainte-Beuve through Huysmans through Colette—ailurophiles all—cats have been on the scene to note some interesting literary composition. The literary history of France, it has been said, could be written through the nation's cat lovers.

They order these things differently in England. The English are most famously keen on dogs. Of all creatures great and small, to coin a phrase, the English seem most partial to their dogs. The pleasures of a small garden, the companionship of a dog, and most Englishmen, at least of recent past generations, felt life paradisical enough. To gain some flavor of the English love of dogs, I have just read for the first time the English writer J. R. Ackerley's *My Dog Tulip,* his account of life with his Alsatian bitch hound, a book that has long had the status of "one of the greatest masterpieces of animal literature," according to Christopher Isherwood. It does not have that status with me; much too much talk in it for my taste of micturition, defecation, impregnation, gestation, and parturition. Ackerley really wallows in all this, can't seem to write enough about it, but when he isn't doing so he does make vivid some of the strange enchantment that animals have for us, if not necessarily we for them. "How wonderful to have had an animal come to one to communicate where no communication is," he writes, "over the incommunicability of no common speech, to ask a personal favor." It is exactly so; and so, too, that "the only way to avoid the onus of responsibility for the lives of animals is never to traffic in them at all." This many of us cannot bring ourselves to do.

To avoid all such traffic is the perhaps sensible policy of the majority of men and women. With what cheerful disdain they are able to look upon those of us who have chosen to share our lives with animals. Gazing out a sixth-story window upon an ice-laden street on a below-zero morning at a shivering man waiting for a small Yorkshire terrier to do what is euphemistically called its "business" fills one with a reassuring sense of one's own prudence and the comic imbecility of advanced civilization. I have been both the man with that dog and the man in the window, and, while I can testify that life is more comfortable behind the window, I do not in retrospect regret my mornings with that Yorkshire terrier.

My only regret in this line has to do with another terrier I once owned, this one a wirehair, Sigmund by name, an affable fellow who one otherwise sunny afternoon was struck by a passing car. Great damage was done to the dog's leg. Many X-rays were required and no fewer than three operations and resettings of a pathetic cast that made a heartrending sound upon wooden floors. Expenses piled up; I have blocked the figures from my mind. A non-animal-owning friend with a cruel sense of humor suggested that there was a good man in Zurich to whom I ought to send the dog. After a lengthy and costly convalescence, Sigmund, I am pleased to report, regained full use of his injured leg—sufficient use, I am less pleased to report, to be able to run away, permanently and without so much as a by-your-leave. Farewell, ungrateful voyager.

I neglected to mention Sigmund's perfidious behavior to

the Warden of an Oxford college who one night, awash with champagne, launched into a powerful and unrelenting attack on dogs in general. "So sycophantic," he exclaimed, "so hopelessly uncritical. Nothing more odious than a large dog, its tongue extended, drooling for its master's or anyone else's attention. Pathetic creatures, dogs, the playthings of those men and women who wish unqualified admiration and derive contentment from acting the part of lord over an ignorant, generally slobbering beast." On and on he went, warming to his subject with increasing intensity, so that toward the end of his tirade ownership of a dog seemed roughly comparable to membership in the Nazi Party through the war years. A dog owner myself at the time—the aforementioned Yorkshire terrier, named Max, was then in my possession—I felt I must at least bring this up, if not offer a full defense of dogs.

"Before you go further," I said, "I must report to you that I myself own a dog. He is a very small dog, true, but I am much enamored of him."

"Is he old?" the Warden inquired through a champagne-induced lisp.

"Nine years old."

"I see," said the Warden. "My advice is to keep him till he dies. But, pray, do not replace him."

As it happens, I never did. In the fullness of time—and not so full as all that—the charming and beloved Max departed the scene. We later moved to an apartment where dogs were not permitted. Below-zero mornings I remained smugly indoors; returning late at night I felt a distinct relief at not having to brave the dark neighborhood streets. For a longish period I settled in without the company of animals. Without livestock, I won't say it was the good life, but it was a less-encumbered, a much simpler, life than I had become accustomed to.

Evidently I cannot stand too much simplicity. With children grown and gone, the element of tumult and even human traffic much diminished from daily life, I must have felt the want of a little additional complication. I began to notice myself considering other people's pets admiringly. A relative in San Francisco with whom I visited had a cat of such sweet temper, playfulness, and courtesy that I determined that I should begin to look for a cat of my own.

"A cat," said Edith Wharton, who all her adult life kept highbred small dogs, "is a snake in furs." Many people—technically known as ailurophobes—feel likewise. I never did, but I was for many years, given a choice, partial to dogs. Cats, though, have much to recommend them, especially for city living. A cat does not need to be walked; a cat is the only domestic animal I know who toilet trains itself and does a damned impressive job of it. A cat's requirement for attention is of an utterly different order from that of a dog. My cat seems to like my company but does nicely without my conversation. As I write, for example, she is asleep on my desk, atop correspondence I am late in answering and behind a small stack of books. Apart from her dubious value as a paperweight, I like her company, too, when she chooses to give it, though why it pleases me—no, make that comforts me—to have this sleeping creature on my desk is itself a mildly interesting question.

Before going any further, before I begin to give the false impression of vast sensitivity to all forms of animal life, I had better make it quite clear that you are a long way from reading an urbanized, Jewish, modern-day Saint Francis. Many are the animals I wish had never made the ark. I have never met a rodent I liked; and rats drive me, as they did George Orwell, nearly ill with revulsion. Slobbering dogs are not my idea of a good time, either; I cannot see a Doberman pinscher without thinking of the gestapo; and Pekingese, of the kind that appear in several of Evelyn Waugh's novels, always suggest to me the possibility of furious nips at the back of one's ankles. Rabbits I can take or leave alone. Birds cannot be topped aesthetically, but I have never longed to own an aviary. Snakes I do not despise, though I much prefer them out of the grass and in zoos. Giraffes and penguins I adore for their lovely, elegant oddity. Monkeys and apes come too close to home.

Everyone can put together a similar list of zoological sympathies and antipathies—love iguanas, hate gophers—but some among us believe in something akin to a special, I hesitate to say mystical, perhaps the best word is romantic, relationship with animals, or at any rate with one animal. Sentimental, even sappy though I know this to be, I fear that, however tenuously, I myself hold this belief. In my case, I think it derives from a strong diet when young of animal movies and literature combined with an absence of any opportunity during these same years to live in a natural way with animals.

Walt Disney, with his fine anthropomorphizing hand, started me off nicely with Bambi, Dumbo, Jiminy Cricket, and other animal adorables now lost to memory. In the short subjects then known as serials, I recall being much taken with the high intelligence of Rin Tin Tin. The Lassie movies—*Lassie Come Home* and others—were even more affecting, for a collie, to a child's moviegoing eye, is incontestably more beautiful than a German shepherd. And the horses, the splendid, muscular, many-hued horses: my friend Flicka, Black Beauty, the dazzling palominos, the dangerous white stallions, the frisky pinto ponies, almost all of them ready to answer to the right human whistle, to count with their hooves, to gallop empty-saddled to the nearest town to bring back help.

Sabu, the Indian boy who could communicate perfectly with elephants, fed the belief not only in friendship between human and animal, but in their near-perfect understanding, given sufficient patience and kindness on the part of the human. This was greatly reinforced by the ever-ineloquent Tarzan, whose own unmelodious diction and brutish syntax, it occurs to me now, may have been formed by too much converse with apes, elephants, and other jungle denizens. Perhaps the only movie of my youth containing a heavy dose of truth about the relationship between man and beast was *The Yearling*, made from Marjorie Kinnan Rawlings's novel, about the sad consequences of a boy who, through love, wishes to domesticate a creature meant to live in nature.

It would be nice to be able to report that I have gotten over my infatuation with this sort of fare, but, alas, it is not so. Another boy-and-horse movie, this one titled *The Black Stallion* (1979), did it to me again. The movie contains a roughly twenty-minute sequence of an eight- or nine-year-old boy riding upon the bare back of a Leonardoesque black horse plunging powerfully through the azure waters of the Mediterranean, lushly filmed from all possible angles, which I can only say, not very analytically, sends me each time I see it; and, owing to cassette tape, I have seen it four or five times. I gulp, I gush, I am a goner.

Perhaps only a city kid could fall so hard. In the solidly middle-class neighborhood in Chicago where I grew up, I have no recollection of any neighbors with dogs or cats, or scarcely any remembrance of animal life at all. World War II was on. It may well be that, with a scarcity of apartments, our building and those around it did not permit pets. Food was rationed, and meat for dogs and cats was not readily available. I was sent off to an expensive summer camp in Wisconsin when I was eight, but, owing to the war, we were told that the camp had had to cancel horseback riding. Meanwhile, all those movies, along with a fair amount of reading, stoked my untested regard for the companionship of living, non-human creatures. Pathetic to report, even grasshoppers interested me, and I tried to keep a few alive in a jar with a perforated top. I don't think I went so far as to name them; at least I hope I didn't.

When we finally acquired a pet, a dog, it seemed to come too late. We had moved to more spacious quarters, I was well into my adolescence, and the once powerful fantasy of an abiding friendship with an animal could not compete with rivaling fantasies about sports and girls. It was the early 1950s, and our dog was the popular dog of its day, a cocker spaniel. Cocker spaniels came in three colors, black, tan, and auburn, and were usually named, with extraordinarily unimaginative repetitiveness, respectively, Inky, Taffy, and Rusty. Ours was a Rusty. He wasn't a puppy but five or six years old when we acquired him. Whatever the animal equivalent to personality is, Rusty's, near as I could make out, was singularly without interesting idiosyncrasy. A dull guy, Rusty. He was rather sniffy about food, and my mother, who had hitherto evinced no special sympathy for animals, cooked for the dog. The aroma of veal and hamburger sizzling in a heavy black skillet returns to me now; it and other viands were set before him. The result was a diet too rich for his system, and it threw off his toilet training habits. This vastly abbreviated Rusty's tenure with Swiss Family Epstein. In less than a year's time he was farmed out to the man who picked up and delivered our laundry, who lived in the country with a family of ten children. I hope Rusty lived out his days in dull contentment, but "Rusty come home" was never a cry that passed my lips.

Irving followed Rusty, at the goodly distance of some seven years. Irving was a black poodle, who was sold to me as a toy but turned out to be a standard. Nothing about poor Irving was quite licit, including my owning him in an apartment where dogs were strictly verboten. I had acquired Irving in the first place to please a woman with whom I was much taken, who was herself quite mad about domestic animals. She had earlier presented me with a hamster to whom, frankly, I was never quite able, as they say, to relate. Owing to Irving's precarious position in the apartment as, in effect, a stowaway, through no fault of his own he was never able to get the business of doing his business down pat. He had to be taken out at odd hours—when, specifically, the coast was clear—or often rushed out just before he was no longer able to control himself. Consequently, all his days he relieved himself nervously, never quite stationary in the act, always shuffling about slightly. Irving was eventually turned over to a childless aunt of mine who already owned a Chihuahua whom she hand-fed and had named—so far as I could make out, without a trace of irony—Caesar. She treated Irving with surpassing kindness, for which I was immensely grateful, since I felt it let me off the hook a bit for what I had put him through.

The woman for whom I bought Irving and I went on to live in a state of holy matrimony and a condition of impressive chaos for nearly a decade. At one point we had three dogs (a mongrelized sheepdog named Luv, the feckless Sigmund, and dear Max) and two Siamese cats (Ralph and Clara were their names), not to speak of a thirty-gallon antique tank stocked with tropical fish. The Siamese cats had two different litters of kittens. (Ralph will always remain memorable to me for using a bathroom toilet to make water, a trick he must have picked up from the example of the boy children in the house.) One day I came home to discover an enormous collie that had been left at the Anti-Cruelty Society by a young man going off to Vietnam; it proved to be too much, and a few days later the collie was returned to the society whence it came. At various times during this marriage I felt less like a husband and father than a rancher.

"Divorced, no kids, no cats," with a few touches of anatomical description thrown in, is not an uncommon shorthand for one man formulating the situation of a woman to another, interested and eligible, man. My second (my current, my final, my dear and irreplaceable) wife was neither divorced nor had children, but she did have a cat, Ursula, when we married. I still had my main man, the Yorkshire terrier Max. Max and Ursula, Ursula and Max—either way it sounded like a delightful German film. Ursula was very black, very elegant, very independent, and not one to bestow affection thoughtlessly. Even now I recall the first time she climbed onto my lap, after I had been around her for some two years, and the enormous compliment I felt in the gesture.

Max, charming and not entirely resourceless, Max, always desirous of friendship, put his best moves on Ursula. When she was sitting on a couch he would gently sidle up; when she was stretched out upon a rug he with tactful caution would approach. But it was no go; for his efforts, he got a hiss and a spit, or sometimes a declawed paw in the *punim*. We were pulling for Max all the way, hoping Ursula would relent, aching to witness the lion lie down with the lamb. Alas, he had no more chance than a fellow with a few gold neck chains and a lot of cheap astrology talk setting out to seduce Greta Garbo. Another animal fantasy blown out of the air.

But I wish to report a reformation of character, at least in this particular regard, with the entry into my life, some six years ago, of our cat Isabelle. I am not ready to go so far as those authors who, in their acknowledgments to their books, wish to thank their husbands or wives for making them warm and open and caring persons, but this cat has, I believe, taught me a thing or two about the proper relationship between human beings and animals. She has given me much quiet pleasure and no pain whatsoever. I am pleased to have earned her toleration and continue to be delighted by her not infrequent gift of affection. Her demeanor is a reminder that it is possible to get through life without having to be in the least obsequious. Her longish tail, which forms itself at its tip into a question mark when she walks with a certain confident gait, reminds me, when I note it, of the value of skepticism. To gaze upon her in certain of her moods, especially when she is sleeping, can render me almost instantly tranquil. I have decided that this little animal is for me the cat of cats, the long-awaited one, the animal who will mean most to me in my life and who is likely never to be replaced in my affection.

A cat, I realize, cannot be everyone's cup of fur. Alexander the Great, Napoleon, and Hitler are all said to have been ailurophobes. Scarcely shocking, this, for if one has a taste for command and a potent will to power, one does better without a cat for company. Cats resist compulsion and are by nature unpunishable; a grown man or woman yelling at a cat makes a ridiculous spectacle. It may be that you can't teach an old dog new tricks, but, unless one is fanatical, one cannot hope to teach a new cat old tricks. Besides, they have such interesting tricks of their own. You must either take a cat as she is or leave her alone. "A cat's game," a phrase from tic-tac-toe, means standoff, stalemate, forget about it. Even the notion of *owning* a cat seems faintly absurd; better to say that one is living with a cat and paying the bills.

When not long ago, after recounting how much pleasure Isabelle's company has given me, I advised a friend to consider acquiring a cat, he shook his head and replied, "I consider cats furniture." An amusing remark, and not without its quotient of truth. A cat can sit in the same place, awake yet supremely supine, longer than any breathing creature going. (As pure furniture, I should add, perhaps nothing surpasses the cat as the most decorative domestic item the world has thus far pro-duced.) To admire this extreme talent for repose in cats, one must oneself have a certain aspiration for repose in one's own life. Schopenhauer spoke to this point of torpid contentment in certain animals—surely cats must have been uppermost in his mind, since he said that neither dogs nor apes had it—this enjoyment of life as simple existence, claiming that those animals command it who live outside anything beyond immediate motivation. "That is why," Schopenhauer writes in one of his aphorisms, "they find complete contentment in simple existence and why it suffices to fill their entire lives; so that they can pass many hours completely inactive without feeling discontented or impatient, although they are not thinking but merely looking."

I once remarked of William Maxwell, some of whose novels I admire, that if he had any serious flaw it was that he tended to anthropomorphize children. I am rather sorry I said that, for I now intend to anthropomorphize our cat. I often try to imagine what, if Isabelle had human speech, she would say. I assume that for the most part she would keep her own counsel, using language only with great precision and never needing to avail herself of words that end in "ism." Comparing hers to a human life, I sometimes envy her the leisure of her days and all the things she doesn't have to do: work her way through the turgid fatuity of a *New York Times* editorial, make a quarterly tax payment, meet a deadline, believe in progress, feign interest. She need give no thought to owning a fax machine or computer; she need not have anything to do with technical advances. "So that's the telephone," said Degas to Forain, when the latter was so proud of having had one installed in his house. "It rings, and you run." When my telephone rings, Isabelle doesn't even blink. Let us not speak of "call waiting."

When I leave the apartment, I generally say goodbye to Isabelle, even if she is asleep. If this isn't anthropomorphizing, I'm not sure what is. Yet when I return, she generally walks to the door to greet me. (Felinomorphizing, perhaps?) Isabelle is a house cat; she only leaves the apartment in a carrying case—lined, to be sure, with a thick yellow towel—either to see a veterinarian, or to go off with us on a weekend visit, or to board with a relative when we are traveling. You probably ought to know, too, that her front claws have been removed; and she has been—a much less than apt word—"fixed." The declawing and the desexing were done more for my convenience than for hers. Letting her run free in our urban neighborhood carries less moral complication; to do so would be to invite her quick departure if not demise. Still, to put the question anthropofelinosophically, would I give up the right to claw and fornicate at will for a reasonable amount of security, food, and comfort? Don't look now, folks, but I believe I already have. In modern life, it is apparently civilization and its discontents for cats, too.

But enough of discontents, of which the world provides sufficient to go round. I don't think many are evident in Isabelle, who, at seven years old, is a cat full of fire, which is the way I prefer a cat. When the mood is upon her, she goes galloping down the long hall of our apartment, leaping onto the top of the back of a high wing chair. Or she will jump from my desk to a nearby file cabinet, thence to hop atop a bookcase. She has a lovely way of suddenly appearing—on my desk, on our bed, behind my reading chair—with an effortless little Balanchinian hop that I think of as her "star turn." When she does this, the impression I always get is that of a great ballerina suddenly emergent from the wings. All this while, with all this galloping, leaping, hopping, in a fairly tchotchke-laden apartment, Isabelle has never broken a single item.

This cat has given us no trouble over diet, having none of the finickiness about food for which domestic cats are infamous. She even defies the standard generalizations in this line. The essayist Agnes Repplier has remarked that she has "never known a cat that would touch ham": Isabelle relishes it, but then shows little interest in a bowl of milk. The cat, write Frances and Richard Lockbridge, two popular writers on the subject, "is a great victim of the human inclination to generalize." Quite true; and her use to the essayist may be precisely that, in her conduct, she generally tends to defy all generalizations applied to her.

"We cannot," remarked the scientist St. George Mivart, "without becoming cats, perfectly understand the cat mind." Carl Van Vechten, author of *The Tiger in the House,* in my opinion the best of all books about cats, puts it rather better: "Faith is needed to comprehend the cat, to understand that one can never comprehend the cat." Whether cats "think" at all is, among ethologists, apparently a matter of serious debate. Yet if it is not thoughtfulness, what is it in Isabelle that has allowed her to become so keen—and she grows steadily keener—at sensing the moods of those into whose hands her fate has rather arbitrarily been tossed? She does not always come when wanted—and never on demand—yet she never arrives when unwanted, and, as it happens, is always wanted when she arrives. And why not? She has brought me, variously, tranquillity, companionship, an enhanced sense of life's possibilities. All she in her turn asks is that I never impugn her independence.

Carl Van Vechten writes that the cat ought to serve as an inspiration to the writer, since the cat suggests grace, power, and beauty, and "the perfect symmetry of his body urges one to achieve an equally perfect form" in one's work.

The sharp but concealed claws, the contracting pupil of the eye, which allows only the necessary amount of light to enter, the independence, should be the best models for any critic; the graceful movements of the animal who waves a glorious banner as he walks silently should stir the soul of any poet. The cat symbolizes, indeed, all that a good writer tries to put into his work.

Van Vechten goes on to say that the cat, with his reserves of dignity and urbanity, his magisterial calm overlaying his bountiful energy, "is as nearly as possible what many a writer would like to be himself." There's something to it.

There's something also to Van Vechten's adding that the cat can inspire literary creation on nearly any subject—"any subject, mind you, not necessarily on the cat himself." Part of the problem is that cats are a good deal more difficult to describe than are men and women. They are not so easily drawn or painted, either, at least in a way that captures the true individuality that anyone who has lived with a cat knows that his own cat possesses. Here it strikes me that the cat has been better drawn than painted, perhaps because in a drawing the element of character—or, more precisely, caricature—comes through more lucidly.

Close readers will have noted that thus far along I have shied away from describing anything about my own cat except the charming question mark that the end of her tail sometimes forms. Isabelle, you should know, is a tabby, with dark stripes predominating over a taupe background on her long, rather slender body. On her forehead she has the traditional M-shape marking of the tabby; and black lines, which shape themselves into slightly exotic wings, flare out in perfect (as opposed to William Blake's "fearful") symmetry along both her cheeks. Her whiskers are white and emerge from near a dotting or freckling along and just beneath her nose. Plenty of taupe plays about her face; her underbody is a mélange of different shades of taupe; her only white fur is under her chin. She has a small

head, an extremely elegant one, in my opinion. I much prefer
a cat with a small head, for too large a head not only seems
indelicate in itself but is a bit too tigerish for my taste. I read
into a large-headed cat the tableau of a tiger ripping the entrails
of a gazelle near a brackish pond: red tooth of nature and all
that, whereas my own clear preference runs to white tooth of
dental floss and a warm bathrobe.

I have spent a fair amount of time gazing into Isabelle's face
and must confess that I have not found there the least trace of
what the French poet Charles Cros suspects, in a white cat of
his acquaintance, to be what we should nowadays call a hidden
agenda: *"Je te demande dans ces vers / Quel secret dort dans tes
yeux verts / Quel sarcasme sous ta moustache."* Nor, peering into
Isabelle's blue-green eyes, have I ever discovered what it was
that caused George Eliot to ask: "Who can tell what just criticisms the cat may be passing on us beings of wider speculation?" The great French draftsman Grandville claimed to have
discovered seventy-five different expressions on the faces of
cats. I have never counted those I have discovered on Isabelle,
but among them have been neither uncritical adoration nor
secret contempt, which seems to me fair enough.

Lots of music plays in this apartment, nearly all of it so-
called "serious" music, much of it coming from radios dialed
to classical music stations. This music seems further to becalm
the already quite calm Isabelle, who appears especially taken
with baroque music, with, I believe I detect, a particular par-
tiality for woodwinds. So utterly content does she seem when
lying on a bed or on my desk with music playing that when
I have to leave the apartment briefly, I often leave the radio
playing for her. Anecdotes about the enjoyment of music by
cats are not uncommon. Théophile Gautier wrote charmingly
about one of his cats' reactions to hearing singers whom Gautier accompanied on the piano in his apartment. The cat of the

composer Henri Sauguet was bonkers for the music of Debussy. For a time I thought Isabelle quite gone on Bach's Cantata 147, "Jesu, Joy of Man's Desiring," in the Dame Myra Hess transcription. Desmond Morris, the zoologist, claims that "the musical sense of cats is just another feline myth." I am sure he is correct, but I prefer to cling, ever so lightly, to the myth. "Human kind," a certain lover of cats named T. S. Eliot once remarked, "cannot bear very much reality." Perhaps ailurophiles can bear just a jot less.

What may be at work here is the naive hope that a creature who has given me so much comfort and pleasure can herself take comfort and pleasure in some of the same things I do. For a long while I felt similarly about feline companionship for Isabelle and contemplated acquiring a second cat. She, Isabelle, spent the first months of her life in a bookshop—"Cat-free Bookstore" reads the sign in the window of an old *New Yorker* cartoon, suggesting that there aren't all that many of them— and the first time I saw her she was asleep entwined with a large, gentle marmalade-colored cat named Gingy. Two cats are said to be better than one, or so the current received wisdom has it, especially if one goes off to work and leaves a cat alone most of the day. Isabelle is not alone in this way, yet I have felt that in installing her in our apartment, perhaps I have cruelly deprived her of the company of her own kind.

Perhaps. Yet every time I have seen Isabelle with other cats, she has appeared either bored or put off by them. Feline sociability does not seem to be, as they said in the sixties, her "thing." Which leads me to wonder if perhaps it was I who really wanted yet another cat. Adding cats is not difficult to do. Ernest Newman, the music critic of the *Times* in London, longed for the day he could settle into a house and have a cat. He ended up with three. (Those cats must have heard some splendid music.) The decisive jump, I have always thought, is from two cats to three. If three cats, after all, why not five? And if five, why not eight? I would say that family therapy is strongly indicated somewhere around six cats, at least for apartment dwellers.

I hope that I have not given the impression that Isabelle is a genius among cats, for it is not so. If cats had IQs, hers, my guess is, would fall somewhere in the middle range; if cats took SATs, we should have to look for a small school somewhere in the Middle West for her where discipline is not emphasized. Isabelle eats flowers—though for some reason not African violets—and cannot be convinced to refrain. We consequently don't keep flowers in the apartment. Although my wife and I love flowers, we have decided that we love this cat more, and the deprivation of one of life's several little pleasures is worth it.

I am, then, prepared to allow that Isabelle isn't brilliant but not that she isn't dear. She is, as I have mentioned, currently seven years old, yet already—perhaps it is a habit of my own middle age—I begin to think of the shortness of her life, even stretched to its fullest potential. Owing to the companionship of this cat, I have begun to understand friends who, having lost a dog or cat through age or illness, choose not to replace it, saying that they can't bear to go through it all again.

Solzhenitsyn remarks in one of his novels that people who cannot be kind to animals are unlikely to be kind to human beings. A charming sentiment but far, I suspect, from generally true. ("I wanted you to see why I work with animals," says a female veterinarian in a novel by Jim Harrison. "I can't stand people.") Yet genuine kindness to animals is always impressive. One of the finest stories told about Mohammed has to do with his having to answer the call to prayer while a cat is asleep on the hem of his cloak; with scissors he cuts off the hem, lest he wake the cat, and proceeds on his way.

Searching for the cat who turned out to be Isabelle, I met a woman who had converted two of the three stories of her house in a working-class neighborhood over to the care of injured and deserted animals: three-legged cats, a blind German shepherd, an aged St. Bernard in a body bandage are among the animals I recall roaming the first floor. Something like eighty cats lived in the basement. The smell, expense, sheer trouble of it all overwhelmed me and I didn't hang around long. The existence of Heaven, though, suddenly made a good deal of sense, for nothing less can be a just reward for such a woman.

Cats are said to be notably deficient in gratitude. Certainly they are nowhere near so efficient at sending thank-you notes as, say, members of the Junior League. But they have their own extraordinary ways of repaying such trivial debts as they accrue: through their example of repose, through the sensuous harmony of their elegant movements, through their gift of unpredictable but always welcome affection. I need call in no auditor to inform me that my debts to Isabelle vastly exceed hers to me, and that there is no way to pay them off except with a mute gratitude and an occasional privately uttered toast: "Here's to you, kid, than which few things give more pleasure."

The Ignorant Man's Guide to Serious Music

My title is a bit askew. The ignorant man, it turns out, *is* the guide, and that benighted fellow is I. I have been listening to serious music—the traditional word, *classical*, seems to me inept—for a number of decades and with increasing interest and intensity as I grow older. I have also begun to read more and more about music, in the form of criticism, memoirs, letters, biographies, and autobiographies of composers and performers. I currently read more about music than about any other single subject. When I go into a used-book store, I go directly to the music section. I attend probably some twenty or so concerts a year. The four radios in our apartment are preset to our city's two serious-music stations. So, too, is the radio in our car, though in the car I more often listen to music on cassette tapes. (The other day I came very close to getting a speeding ticket when carried away by a Herbert von Karajan recording of the *Eroica*.) I have become passionate about music, really quite bonkers about it, but—and here's the catch—without becoming particularly intelligent or sophisticated about it. My condition resembles that of an adolescent greatly stirred by love without in the least understanding it. The difference is that the adolescent figures eventually to grow out of his condition, but I don't figure, ever, to grow out of mine.

It may be that I came to music too late. The home I grew up in was not one in which music had much part. My deprivation was not so drastic as that of President U. S. Grant, who claimed to know only two tunes: "One of them is 'Yankee Doodle'; and the other isn't." But I cannot recall my mother ever singing or humming a tune. My father would occasionally sing, while shaving, a song from his youth called "Anybody Here Seen Kelly?" ("Kelly," I believe the second line went, "of the Emerald Isle"). My father was also partial to the songs of Stephen Foster, and we owned an album of Bing Crosby singing Stephen Foster songs. But the height of musical culture in the milieu in which I grew up was musical comedy. My parents went to their share of these. They were not, however, fanatical about them, as some of my friends' parents were, traveling to New York to see a musical comedy, then seeing it again when it played in Chicago, then buying the record to play at home, often over and over again. Men who worked very hard at very tough businesses seemed to be able to derive immense pleasure out of what seemed to me, even as a boy, an astonishingly trivial entertainment. Yet there they would be, at considerable cost and no small inconvenience, after a day battling in the marketplace, watching for the second or third time such shows as *The Most Happy Fella* or *Pajama Game*, smiles of almost idiotic contentment on their faces.

If I had any genius, or even a spark of talent, for music— and I had neither—it would doubtless have shown itself, whatever the conditions of my upbringing. Alongside the intensely musical families of the Bachs, the Haydns, the Mozarts, there have been musicians—Handel, Debussy, Myra Hess—who were the sole members of their families to show musical ability, and they proceeded quite nicely, thank you very much, to make their way without family understanding or guidance.

In the Chicago public school system, when I was a boy in the 1940s, there were opportunities for musical talent to show itself. In the early grades—second perhaps, or possibly third—a man came around offering lessons for various instruments; the lessons were twenty-five cents each, and one could rent the instruments (save a piano) until such time as one cared to buy one's own. (Tap dancing lessons were also offered, at the same price.) I informed my mother that I wouldn't mind playing the piano (an instrument we did not have) or the trumpet (an instrument that would have been cause for eviction). My mother suggested the violin—the Jewish instrument *par excellence*, as the pianist Artur Schnabel was once told by an Israeli in explanation of the merely mildly enthusiastic response that Schnabel's own playing received in Israel. Even then, at age seven or eight, I did not see myself playing the violin (today I see myself playing any instrument but the bassoon), and so the conversation was dropped. Dropped, too, was the prospect of my getting a grounding in music, which I now, in my keen yet bumbling appreciation of serious music, greatly regret.

I endured without anything like sustained contact with serious music for at least the following decade. In my circle of friends and classmates, piano lessons seemed to be chiefly for girls and represented, as near as I could make out, a pretense of culture and an attempt to instill breeding. Those boys among my friends who, as the phrase was, "took" piano, had "put it back" by early adolescence. I attended no concerts, though once I was taken, by my mother, to a puppet opera, with a full puppet orchestra, the ingenuity of which so impressed me that I never bothered to learn who wrote the opera and scarcely heard the music. We had a high school chorus, but it held no attraction for me. I listened to the popular songs of the day—a less illustrious day than that which produced George Gershwin, Cole Porter, Irving Berlin, and Jerome Kern—and owe a small debt of gratitude to Messrs. Nat King Cole and Frank Sinatra for helping me to attain what little success I had with girls in my adolescence. I used to pride myself on knowing the current top ten or twenty songs, until the age of rock descended, locust-like, over the land, replacing the sentimentality, triviality, and self-pity of most popular songs with the unintelligible violence of primitive rhythms funneled through heavy electrical amplification. "Roll over Beethoven and tell Tchaikovsky the news," one early rock tune had it, and the news, for those of us not brought up on it, was not good: it was that rock and roll was here to stay, which in fact, in various permutations, it has.

Apart from some grammar school teaching of scales and keys, the first, and only, instruction in music I had came in a university course in the humanities that sought to demonstrate the affinities among the arts of literature, painting, and music. I say "sought" advisedly, for I never found any of these affinities very cogent. In the study of painting, slides of great masterworks were shown, and the instructor, pointer in hand, told us where, owing to the composition of the painting, our eye purportedly went. Only my eye never seemed to go where his did. In music, he would earnestly point out the statement of a theme, then note its recurrence. Only my ear never heard it. Where exactly my eye went, or what roughly my ear heard, I am not at all certain. But with the sinking heart that was a standard side effect of so much of my formal education, I knew that I should have to find my own way in music and art as I had already begun to do in literature and politics and love and everything else of interest and importance in life.

The one thing this course did was to inspire me to buy my

first album of serious music. It was a recording of Haydn's *Surprise* Symphony. I spent a fair amount of time listening to it, doubtless missing its theme and the recurrences of its theme each time, but nonetheless feeling an immediate and immense pleasure merely hearing it and allowing the music to wash over me. I'm quite sure I never asked what the music meant, how close to the truth it came, or even if it was well played. I was along for the ride, and it was a lovely one.

But the hook wasn't really in. I spent little time listening to music after college, apart from a passing interest in jazz and an even more fleeting interest in folk singing. As for serious music, I could take it or leave it, and apparently found it much easier to leave it. I went to a concert every now and then, though more for social than musical reasons. Once or twice I drove out to the Ravinia summer music festival outside Chicago, and on one occasion, at a free concert in Grant Park while on a date, I fell asleep on the grass, awaking with a portion of that day's *Chicago Tribune* front page imprinted on my right cheek and forehead—a condition from which not even Frank Sinatra or Nat Cole could redeem me.

I am someone for whom his twenties remain a blur. Army, marriage, children, living in three different cities, having six different jobs, on fire with ambition, it all flew by, *allegro agitato*. Serious music played no part in it. Such music, after all, requires time—or, more precisely, repose—which I didn't seem to have. The only music I had time for was that which comes under the category of noise pollution, the popular songs of the kind that one has to live a life of some purity in America not to know. Such songs still permeated my consciousness, for I recall, out of the blur of this time, standing up at my desk in the office of a small New York magazine, about to edit the prose, sadly convoluted by a stroke late in life, of Reinhold Niebuhr, and singing, "C'mon, Reiny, let's do the twist."

In my thirty-third year I had half-season tickets, in the mezzanine, to the home games of the Chicago Bulls and full-season tickets, in the balcony, to the Chicago Fine Arts Quartet. About the quintet in shorts I knew much more than I did about the quartet in dinner jackets. The moves of the latter, though less spectacular than those of the former, were nonetheless more intricate and, in the fullness of time, came to seem to me more interesting. A taste for chamber music generally began to develop in me. Limited though my musical experience was, I found chamber music more pleasurable than symphonic music—and also, somehow, purer. This was partly because I found it much easier to concentrate on music played by fewer instruments; and partly because music is better imbibed, at least for me, without the mediation of one of "those good dancers," as the conductor Roger Désmorière described conductors in the exhibitionist style of the late Leonard Bernstein. But in the main I found chamber music more enjoyable because I could follow it more readily; for, as Homer Ulrich puts it in his book *Chamber Music: The Growth and Practice of an Intimate Art:* "In chamber music there is room only for essentials, all mere padding is avoided. One is aware of the musical essence, of the composer's inmost intentions."

But now that I have just quoted this, it occurs to me that I have only the foggiest notion of what the key phrases "musical essence" and "the composer's inmost intentions" can possibly mean. Yet I want to believe in them. I am all for the notion that music has an "essence" and that composers have "inmost intentions." The problem is that some of the most serious musicians appear to argue otherwise. Stravinsky, the most impressive of modern composers, has remarked of his methods of composition: "Something comes into my ear and I write it down." Stravinsky also said that all literary descriptions of musical form are misleading, and he was, after all, in a position to know. And yet I find myself struggling against the notion that music is without meaning—is, as Santayana says, "essentially useless, as life is." If I believed with Santayana that life is useless, I suppose I should have to agree that so is music. It would remove a certain amount of pressure from daily living if one could believe such things—"If that's all there is, my dear," as a popular song, sung by Peggy Lee, has it, "then let's keep dancing"—but I cannot.

Someone authoritative—an important composer, perhaps a great music critic, I don't recall—once said that every other word a literary man writes on the subject of music is almost certain to be wrong. Maybe the reason I do not recall who said it is that, as they say in the head trades, I am blocking it out, for I have grave suspicions that it may indeed be true, and this is more than a little daunting to a literary man setting out to record even his confusions about the subject. Some esteemed literary men and women found that they did better to take a pass on music altogether. Charles Lamb, allowing that he had a tin ear, wrote that a carpenter's hammering on a summer day was to him as nothing compared to "the measured malice of music." Yet Lamb must have had doubts, the feeling that he was perhaps missing out on something extraordinary if not glorious, for the first lines of his poem "Free Thoughts on Several Eminent Composers" read:

> Some cry up Haydn, some Mozart,
> Just as the whim bites. For my part,
> I do not care a farthing candle
> For either of them nor for Handel.
> Cannot a man live free and easy,
> Without admiring Pergolesi?

Samuel Johnson appears to have had no such compunction. Music, he said, "excites in my mind no ideas, and hinders me from contemplating my own." The Reverend Sydney Smith had no taste for long musical evenings, and he particularly detested oratorios: "Nothing can be more disgusting than an Oratorio," he wrote. "How absurd to see 500 people fiddling like madmen about the Israelites in the Red Sea!" Rather more surprising—at least it was to me—is George Eliot, who I should have thought would have been delighted by the majestic mysteries of music, but who, as it turns out, pronounced that "music sweeps by me like a messenger carrying a message that is not for me." My own position, and situation, is closer to that described by Coleridge: "An ear for music is a very different thing from a taste for music. I have no ear whatever; I could not sing an air to save my life; but I have the intensest delight in music, and can detect good from bad."

At least I think I can detect the difference between good and bad music, though sometimes I have my doubts. I like so much music, and—worse news yet—am regularly finding still more to like. The other night, for example, at a concert of baroque music, I heard a Sinfonia for Two Trumpets in D Major by Giuseppi Torelli. It was too brief, but what there was of it was, to use an elevated critical term, swell. I had not hitherto heard of Torelli (1658–1709), a Bolognese not to be confused with Gasparo Torelli, a Paduan who worked more than a century earlier. It seems that Giuseppi wrote some 150 instrumental works—I am lifting all this from *The Norton/ Grove Concise Encyclopedia of Music*—that show "experimental steps towards concerto scoring and ritornello form." This Torelli was, musically, apparently no ordinary Giuseppi. Yet, I am reasonably certain, a month from now I shall have quite forgotten his name. And how many Torelli-like composers are there in other nationalities?

One of the first things the aspiring music amateur—aspiring, that is, to gain some modest grasp upon the general subject—is confronted with is the sheer vastness of music. Ernest Newman, the fine English music critic, noted that when he set out to fill in his own musical education, he gave himself three or four years to complete the job. "I did not realize," Newman wrote, "that of all students the student of music has the heaviest task." Apart from the continuous flow of contemporary music, he discovered, he was unaware of how much interesting music lay off the beaten track: what I think of as the Torelli factor. As Newman went on to recount, students of literature are generally required to know the literature of their own and perhaps one other country along with a smattering of that of other European countries. "But the student of music has to know the music of at least half a dozen countries as well as he knows the music of any one of them." This is in part owing to the obvious point that music, having no language, has no geographical boundaries. Yet it is also owing to the unprovable but I believe true point that there is in the world a great deal more good music than there is good literature or painting. Painters and writers roughly equivalent to Giuseppi Torelli probably aren't worth reading or looking at to the same degree that he is worth listening to.

Despite the current academic ruckus about what works ought to be taught in the college curriculum—the debate, as it is charmingly termed, over "canonicity"—wake even a true-believing Marxico-hystericist-structuralesque critic at 3:00 A.M., put a cold gun to his temple, inform him that you ain't fooling around, and he is likely to be able to deliver on demand a fairly sensible list of books that a person ought to read who wishes to consider himself educated. The list is likely to be one to which, with a qualification here and there, most people would agree. But I doubt if a similar list can be composed for music. For one thing, to have heard a work of music isn't comparable to having read a work of literature; certainly not having heard it only once or twice, it isn't. For another, one can say one has read Homer, Dante, Shakespeare, and it means something; but to say one has heard Bach, Mozart, Beethoven doesn't seem to carry anything like the same weight. It even sounds a bit stupid; something about their music seems bottomless, endless (and I do not speak of the vast quantities of it), subject neither to convincing final interpretation nor to true intellectual possession.

Still, I suppose people who know music well could agree on what constitutes the musical equivalent of what today we wrongly call "literacy" when we really mean proficiency. A reasonable proficiency in musical knowledge would doubtless include the major works of Beethoven (did he write any minor ones, it occurs to me naively to inquire), much of Bach, Mozart, Haydn, Handel, Schubert, Berlioz, Chopin, Brahms, Schumann, Tchaikovsky. Less but still substantial amounts would need to be added of Debussy, Ravel, Rachmaninoff, and Stravinsky. Palestrina, Telemann, Vivaldi, and Scarlatti, Bruckner, Mahler, and Schönberg, and the immense array of impressive composers in between and the interesting ones who came after—these, too, would be in the musical core curriculum. I have not mentioned composers who wrote chiefly for opera—and the always special case of Wagner—but then one has only to mention the name of one composer for three others whose music is possibly better to spring to mind. It's a thick jungle of notes, a rolling sea of sound out there in which one can get so easily lost, or drowned—that is, if one comes to it fairly late in life, greedy to hear, enjoy, understand it all.

Not that it really takes that much to make me feel musically lost, drowned, completely overwhelmed. I have, to begin with, an astonishing musical memory—there is no piece of serious music, I have discovered, that I am incapable of mis-identifying or forgetting altogether. This power seems to grow in me. The other morning it was a large portion of Vivaldi's *Four Seasons* heard over the radio that I could not identify. A week or so before, I had pressed my fists against my forehead as an aid to recalling what turned out to be a segment of Schubert's *Trout*, which I have heard countless times and adore. No doubt I shall end up by not recognizing the opening notes of Beethoven's Fifth Symphony. It goes without saying that I cannot call up musical passages whenever I wish either, although they do have an odd way of showing up when not required. I shall be sitting in a concert listening to a Schumann piano work when my mind suddenly fills with the dramatic third movement *(allegro giocoso)* of Brahms's Violin Concerto. More often, though, I hear something I have heard several times before, am really quite fond of—Mendelssohn's entirely distinctive *Italian* Symphony, to cite another recent example—and cannot call up title or composer. Why is this? Why should this be? I begin to believe that the joke here is that I am uniquely unfit for something I so much love, a charmless and not particularly intelligent dwarf in pursuit of Sophia Loren.

Not only do I not remember music, except inconveniently, but I do not talk about it at all well. In fact, I talk about it very little. Music is a sonic event, air in motion, sounds neatly timed; and I find that after I have heard it I have little to say—and the more moved I am by a piece of music, the less I seem to have to say. The composer Ned Rorem has remarked that "the effect [of the best music criticism] is accomplished by description, not opinion. If description is accurate, opinion cannot but simmer through and not be strained for." To describe music one must fall back fairly fast on metaphor; certainly this is true for those of us unfitted for talking about music technically. Rorem is himself not bad with musical metaphor, as when he writes about the pianist Paul Jacobs: "Of the three innately good piano sounds, steel and gold and silver, Paul Jacobs's is silver, as befits the *Études.* " Virgil Thomson claimed that his method in writing about music "was to seek out the precise adjective," which he could do with nearly unfailing deftness. I am generally not a bad metaphor man myself, and I don't recall ever feeling wanting in the realm of adjectives. Yet in attempting to describe music I have only to open my mouth and such metaphorical power as I have departs the room and I find myself adjectivally costive. Music leaves me, otherwise a fairly garrulous character, strangely silent.

If I believed in reincarnation, I should like to return to earth as Donald Francis Tovey, the English composer, pianist, and critic, who could do musically all those things I can only dream of doing: make music, play music, discuss music divinely well. As with so many greatly talented musicians, Tovey (1875–1940) came into the world loaded down with gifts. Mary Grierson's admiring biography of Tovey begins with the following anecdote:

There was a sound of clapping in the next room, and Miss Weisse went to the door to look in. A small boy of 10 was applauding vigorously, and the score of a Haydn Quartet which he had just finished reading was lying on the table in front of him. He looked up in confusion and said, "Oh, I beg your pardon, I thought I *heard* it."

Even for a musician, Donald Tovey had an unusually musical mind. "It is doubtful," Miss Grierson writes, "whether to the end of his life he ever realized that the faculty which he already possessed at the age of 12 for reading a musical score as easily as the average person reads a book (and generally with a much more accurate memory of its contents) is a faculty which, if acquired at all, costs most musicians years of practice." So musical was Tovey that, when reading philosophy as a student at Balliol College, Oxford, he once regretted that he could not read Plato as simply as he read Bach, but added that he frequently caught himself solving some problem of a philosophical nature "in, say, the key of A minor, where I had utterly failed to reason it out in words." As for musical memory, a Cambridge don once asked Tovey how long it would take him to play every composition he knew by heart, playing eight hours a day. "Oh, about four weeks," Tovey said at first, then revised the figure: "No, I think it would take eight weeks, or seven at least." Never known as a braggart, or for being even mildly boastful, Tovey, one must conclude, truly did have seven or eight weeks of music stored in his head.

Donald Tovey was not, I suppose, all that wildly precocious, given the astonishing youthfulness at which many musicians brought off extraordinary accomplishments. Mozart is of course the most famous, if not a slightly freakish, case. But there is also Schubert, about whom it is written, in the *Pelican Book of Chamber Music,* that "from the age of thirteen he wrote, or at any rate started, two or more chamber works every year until 1817, when he achieved full mastery of the medium." In 1817 Schubert was twenty; when I was twenty I am not certain that I had mastery over my hair. But then musicians seem to be on different clocks and calendars than the rest of us. In reading the memoirs of such performers as Artur Rubinstein and Artur Schnabel and Nathan Milstein, one cannot help but be impressed by how early they were on their own and how little they received in the way of formal education. Rubinstein and Schnabel and Milstein were loosed on the world while still essentially children, under the most minimal supervision, playing in backwater towns, often under extremely crude conditions, making their own way, and somehow coming through it intact, highly intelligent, and often with a clear perspective on the human comedy.

The early maturity conferred on musicians is another of the

mysteries of music. If there are no Mozarts in literature—no one has produced at so high a level so young—there are Goethes in music (one thinks right off of Beethoven's late quartets). What music doesn't seem to have is any Joseph Conrads—that is, men or women who come to it only fairly late in life, as Conrad came to literature, publishing his first novel at age thirty-nine, and who begin to succeed in early middle age. In literature one almost always has to wait until one's talent ripens; painting, I gather, is not so very different. But in music one generally knows, and knows early, whether or not one has it—the magic *it*—before one is twenty. One can be good and get better, obviously, but one is quite unlikely suddenly, at the age of forty, to become good.

Hard work, as in all the arts, means a great deal. "How do you get to Carnegie Hall?" a tourist asks a New Yorker in an old joke. "Practice, practice, practice" is the response. A friend of mine, once a piano prodigy, recalls as a small boy listening to President Roosevelt speak over the radio at the beginning of World War II on the need for every American to do his job for the war effort, and his mother afterwards remarking to him that his job during the war was to practice piano even harder. But hard work is not fundamental—talent is. Somerset Maugham's magnificent story "The Alien Corn" illustrates the point unforgettably. "What is it you want me to tell you?" asks the pianist in the story who is called in to judge the talent of George Bland, the young man who, against his family's wishes, is staking everything on his musical prospects. "I want you to tell me whether I have any chance of becoming in time a pianist in the first rank." Then Maugham—quickly, cleanly— delivers the *coup de grâce:* "Not in a thousand years," she answers. At the story's end the young man goes off and shoots himself.

Yet another side to the youthfulness of musical creation is

the number of major composers who left the game too soon—blazing comets that tailed off much too early. Mozart (1756–1791) was thirty-five at his death; Schubert (1797–1828) only thirty-one; Chopin (1810–1849) was probably lucky, given his bad health, to have made it to thirty-nine; Schumann (1810–1856) was forty-six; Tchaikovsky (1840–1893) was immensely productive up until his death at fifty-three; and even at fifty-seven, Beethoven (1770–1827), given his furious energy, seems to have died before his time. Did Mozart, did Schubert, did other of these men compose at the astounding clip that they did with some premonition that they would be short-lived? Without the least evidence to back it up, one is inclined to think that perhaps they did. Or does it make more sense to consider Hugo Wolf's darkly deterministic opinion that artists die when their work is complete? More mystery; music, it sometimes seems, is all mystery.

What has become less mysterious to me is why my own love for music remains so hopelessly bumbling. Maurice Baring, the English essayist, has in part helped explain my own case to me. Baring was a man who in his day claimed to "have heard some very nice noises," among them Piatti and Casals playing the violoncello, Donald Tovey playing Beethoven and Bach, Paderewski playing Chopin, Chaliapin singing through an entire opera at the piano in his own home, Caruso scores of times. Baring defined and ranked persons who are really musical as "those happy few who have an absolute ear and who can detect and distinguish any key that is being played"; then those who can read a full score with profit and pleasure; then those who can read music at sight; and finally "those who cannot read at sight, but who can play by ear." Baring himself could do none of these things; and neither, at this point will it scarcely shock anyone to learn, can I. My guess is that if I could I would remember music much better than I now do;

that I would be able to hum great stretches of it, like the music critic who is the narrator of Kingsley Amis's *Girl, 20* and who, to control his temper, hums "the openings of all the movements of Beethoven's string quartets"; that I might just curl up of a wintry evening with the score of the *Jupiter* Symphony on my lap. As it is, having neither natural gifts nor training, without knowing either the grammar or the syntax of music, I continue to muddle along, my taste and hunger for music unabated by my ignorance of it.

Maurice Baring was not fond of concerts and claimed that he had never been to one that he didn't think too long. Here we part company, for I do look forward to concerts, even though I often have a tough time keeping my mind on the music and sometimes even in the room. Much in the room, though, usually does interest me. The crowds at concerts, especially chamber music concerts, tend not to be composed of glittering people; and the more serious the music, the less glittering they are. Music, it does not take much imagination to grasp, is for many of these people consolation. Consolation for what? Natural disadvantages in life, personal tragedies, a thousand different sadnesses. As consolation, it seems to work remarkably well. "When people listen to music," wrote the young Ben Hecht, "it always reminds me we are descended from fish." I disagree. Rapt in music, many faces take on an impressive serenity, even beauty. Others, evidently at the concert under domestic duress, hit the deck hard and are snoozing away, *adagio sostenuto,* early in the proceedings.

My own mind often floats off during a concert—to thoughts about my work, or petty troubles, or grandiose plans for the future. I urge myself to return mentally to the music, but I'm not always successful, or at least not for the nearly two hours that most contemporary concerts take. Oddly, the place where I seem to have the greatest power of concentration for music is in my car. There I am in an enclosed place, with no distractions arising other than those supplied by the road, and I am able to command full attention to the music playing on tape or on the excellent car radio. But what I miss is watching the musicians, which not only offers its own fascinations but is helpful to someone of my own lack of sophistication, who cannot always dependably identify, on radio, tapes, records, or CDs, the exact instruments he is hearing.

I condemn the star system in serious music, yet the truth is that I am also caught up in it and go to my share of performances by today's greatly publicized concert performers. From my own less than comprehensive reading about these matters, I gather that it was Paganini and Liszt who, in the nineteenth century, gave the concert soloist his current high status. It was Liszt in particular who lifted the concert performer from the class of paid servant, not alone with his virtuosic playing but with his hauteur. During a concert in St. Petersburg, playing before Tsar Nicholas, Liszt stopped cold and walked away from the piano when the Tsar was speaking loudly with a female companion. "Why have you stopped playing?" the Tsar asked. "When the Tsar speaks," answered Liszt, "one ought to be silent." Still, Liszt could do nothing to abate the interior pressures of musical performance at the highest level, where every time one plays one is putting one's reputation on the line, where one is regularly being judged and compared, and where one is laying bare before large audiences one's emotional life through the performance of music.

In Marian McKenna's biography of Dame Myra Hess I was interested to learn that even after she had performed in hundreds of concerts, Myra Hess's nervousness, which was always considerable, did not lessen with time. In some ways it became even greater, so that later in her career she returned to playing with musical notation before her. It was Clara Schumann who first put solo performers under the obligation of playing lengthy works from memory, when, in 1837, she played the *Appassionata* in Berlin without music. Over a period of a few months, I have seen Daniel Barenboim play both the *Goldberg Variations* and the *Diabelli Variations* without the music before him; piece, apparently for Barenboim, of cake. But Myra Hess had come to believe that playing from memory was "an artificial fetish," and she later said that "it suddenly seemed quite senseless to give oneself the extra 'tight rope' strain of always playing from memory." Whether she was right or wrong about this, having the music before her when she played was thought to have cost Myra Hess with certain critics. They play rough out there in the musical world.

I admire the discipline and the courage that have gone into the careers of the superior musical performers, but above all I feel that they are in on an important secret from which I am excluded. Perhaps it is possession of this secret that gives these performers their magical quality. After her concerts, Myra Hess frequently used to ask, "Did I come nearer the truth?" What truth, exactly, did she have in mind? The truth inherent in the music, doubtless. But why do I sense that this truth is unavailable to me? Is it because I am a writer? "Writers, in general, have not such a spontaneous relation to music as painters and scientists," said Artur Schnabel. "Writers are more self-conscious, inclined to translate every experience into words. This cannot be done with music; therefore their reactions are not pure enough." I fear there may be much to what Schnabel says. How is musical enjoyment related to musical understanding? That is a question I ask with ever greater insistence and puzzlement. And, in my own case, I wonder how I am able to enjoy music so much while understanding it so little. Dimly, off in the background, I can hear a voice whispering, "Only a writer could ask such questions. Only a writer could be so stupid."

Artur Schnabel goes on to say that music ought to be

listened to with a purely musical attentiveness, "in a state of physical passivity, and intellectual passivity too, so far as association of ideas is concerned, but with a spiritual and emotional activity which awaits its release." Dame Myra Hess offers a gentler but perhaps not less true perspective, saying: "For anybody who wants to think, music gives them all they need; for anybody who wants to forget, it will give them that, too. And both kinds of people will be refreshed for having heard some music." Even Schopenhauer, a man who did a bit of writing in his time, notes that music "speaks so much to the heart, while it has nothing to say *directly* to the head and it is a misuse of it to demand that it should do so."

The advice implicit in all those remarks is clear enough: sit down, shut up, and listen to the music, lots of it. Good advice. Time, perhaps, I took it, *presto affectuoso,* and no kidding around, before the doors close and I miss the concert altogether.

A Bonfire of My Vanities

Ayoung woman with not a sexy but a very earnest voice telephones, announcing that she is a producer from the local public radio station. She wants to tell me about something that has been troubling her for quite a while. What has been troubling her, it turns out, is political labels. The way people use such words as *liberal* and *radical* and *conservative* and especially *neo-conservative* seems to her so imprecise, slovenly, confusing. She would like to do a radio show about it. What, she wants to know, do I think of the idea? Not very much, I reply, for my sense is that such a subject would make for deadly dull radio. To go into all the permutations of meaning that the word *liberal* has acquired since it surfaced in the nineteenth century seems to me, I tell her, up there with juggling, fire eating, and bake-offs as activities that radio does best to leave alone. She answers that she doesn't think so, adding that her instinct about these matters is pretty good. Besides, she says, I talk so well about the subject. Would I agree to go on an afternoon public radio show, during which I would be interviewed for roughly half an hour and then answer telephone calls from listeners for the other half hour?

I asked if there was any fee, though I was fairly certain that there would be none, and there wasn't. I said my time was very tight just now, for I was under the lash of a number of dead-lines. I was told that this was no problem—along with "Have a nice day" and one of the several variations for "Kiss off," "No problem" is one of only three phrases an immigrant nowadays needs to make his way in this country—no problem, since the show would not have to be aired for another three or four weeks. My other objections were met with this same gentle but firm resolve on this young woman's part. Arrangements could be made, things worked out, nothing was impossible. Our conversation ended with my saying that I would think it over. She said she would call me early in the following week.

Once off the phone I began to feel that it might be useful if I—calmly, lucidly—set out a few important distinctions about these political labels and their derivations for an interested audience. A job was to be done here, a service delivered. Given the time it would take to travel down and back to the radio station and to organize my thoughts on the subject, it would no doubt mean the loss of a full day's work. I was not myself a regular listener of public radio, but it occurred to me that perhaps its audience is also my audience. I was, when I came to think about it, much impressed with this young producer's earnestness.

What I should have been impressed with, of course, was my own vanity. What made me think that I was in a position to instruct anyone, not to speak of a fairly large general audience, on a subject about which I had myself only a tenuous grasp? Apart from killing a little time for a radio station, what purpose would be served by trotting out my clichés—"Of course, the terms *Left* and *Right* derive from the division of seating arrangements in the French Assembly after 1848 (or was it 1789?), and the Left, partisan observers have been fond of pointing out, is the side of the heart, the Right that of the liver, heh, heh, heh"—except perhaps freshly to impress myself with my good-natured unwillingness to accept any intellectual limits on my learning this side of dividing fractions?

A day or so later, I came as near as a man with my size ego can come to his senses and decided that public radio could survive nicely without my wobbly pontifications and that only my really quite astonishing vanity had impelled me to consider prattling on in public in the first place. I was prepared to tell the earnest young producer when she called back, in the gentlest way, that it was a problem and so to kiss off and have a nice day. But I have to report that she never did call back. Clearly, she had found someone better for the job. If vanity had kidneys, mine could be said to have taken a furious rabbit punch thereat.

Vanity, vanity, vanity—vain, empty, and valueless, Webster calls it, and yet who is without it? Let him who is cast the first comb. Samuel Johnson spoke, iambic pentametrically, of "The Vanity of Human Wishes." Schopenhauer, raising the stakes, wrote "On the Vanity of Existence." Schopenhauer makes a fine distinction between vanity and pride in the book of essays called *Wisdom of Life*, where he writes that "*pride* is an established conviction of one's own paramount worth in some particular respect; while *vanity* is the desire of rousing such a conviction in others and it is generally accompanied by the secret hope of ultimately coming to the same conviction oneself."

Vanity, as with amusingly wicked accuracy Schopenhauer defines it, was the sole motive behind my readiness to go on public radio to discuss political labels. But what about two other invitations that I have recently been offered and have accepted? One is to appear on a panel sponsored by a university to discuss government support for the arts that is to meet in San Diego. The other is to be a moderator for a two-hour session in a conference on the arts sponsored by a foundation.

In both cases I was offered a fee, though not a staggering one (given a choice, I prefer to be staggered). But the prospect of a visit to San Diego in the month of February to a man living in the fastness of the Middle West is itself a temptation to which it is easy to surrender. At the foundation's conference there was the prospect of seeing many friends who would also be there. Sunshine, renewed friendships, a bit of cash, none of these things preclude vanity playing a part in accepting these invitations, but because of them at least I can claim mixed motives. Or—another, slightly more complicated point to consider—is my bringing up these various invitations in the first place itself an act of vanity?

I must be watched very carefully in this essay. Suspend any goodwill I may have earned with you. It is one thing for a writer to take up the subject of vanity generally; it is quite another for him to offer to consider his own. Be suspicious. Get the intellectual radar out and humming. Although everyone has vanity, I think it not unfair to state that writers figure to have rather more than other people; and if they are any good at all, they should be expert at disguising it. Don't be fooled. W. H. Auden put the case, if not the argument behind it, in the last stanza of his poem "At the Grave of Henry James," where, asking James to pray for still-living writers, he remarks that "there is no end to the vanity of our calling." No end? Well, none that I have ever seen.

"On the whole," the critic Desmond MacCarthy has written, "I rather suspect that the mainspring of the initial literary impulse is vanity." He goes on to say that he refuses to believe that most people set out to become writers because of an urgent sense of the significance of what they have to write. "They wish to assert themselves and impress others," he writes, "and if they believe otherwise, they deceive themselves." I hope this isn't universally true; I doubt that it's true of, say, Chekhov or

Solzhenitsyn. I'm afraid, though, that it is altogether true of me. What I most remember about the emotions connected with my decision—it was more like a wish than a decision—to write was an eagerness bordering on lust to see my name in print. I envisioned my name appended to subtle stories in *The New Yorker,* to elegant poems in *Poetry,* to penetrating cultural criticisms in the old *Partisan Review.* What these stories, poems, and criticisms were about, I envisioned less lucidly. I was not aware of anything in particular that I wanted to write; I had no obsessions that needed to be worked out in print, no messages for mankind (let alone for Garcia), not even anything resembling a pressing urge for expression. My name in print in the right places would have done it. What I wanted was to be among the fraternity of good writers—and I wanted this tremendously.

Not all human wishes are vain; nor is vanity behind all human wishes. My own heat to see my name in print had behind it a genuine if still largely inchoate love of literature. But my desire to be accepted as a good—more than a good, an elegant—writer was owing to a quality I have had for as long as I can remember: that of being self-regarding. I have always attempted to maintain a clear view of how I appear to other people—and, for the most part, I care considerably how I come off in their estimate. That I might seem coarse or insignificant would trouble me, perhaps inordinately. I say "perhaps" because I am uncertain if others are quite as vain as I. All human beings fall into one of two categories, I have heard it said: the vain and the extremely vain. Some people, disagreeing, say there is only one category into which we all fall: the extremely vain. About this I am less than sure, though I am ready to concede that I myself no doubt fall into it.

Clothes, haircuts, the way I look generally have never been a negligible matter to me. I do not need to be, and never have been, got up in the fashion of the moment. But it would pain me to wear clothes that I thought were ugly, shabby, or even drab. I am a man who feels a little worse for needing a haircut, and a lot worse for having got a bad one. When my shoes are not shined I feel, if not mildly depressed, at least a schlepper. But more is entailed in all this than merely wishing to avoid schlepperosity. Evidence of this resides in the fact that I have lately taken to buying Charvet bow ties, at nearly seventy dollars a throw. Seventy bones to show a bit of color at my throat is, I realize, ridiculous. Since it is bow and not four-in-hand ties we are talking about, I cannot even see these ties when I wear them. I wear them, apparently, not for myself but for everyone else. The price of seventy dollars frankly appalls me. I am not a rich man—only a vain one.

I assume that these French bow ties quietly announce me as a man of good taste and interesting style, that they help to separate me from the obviously coarse and insignificant. I say "quietly" because these extravagantly priced ties are rather understated. This is as I like it. If there were a machine that could measure vanity, as a polygraph is said to measure lying, I believe I could make such a machine hop and whirl and do as many mechanical gyrations as any man living. But my vanity, which is of a kind not at all uncommon among men, takes the form of pretending not to be vain. I want to appear subdued, not as some dude. I do not wish to stand out—except, decisively, a little.

In the 1960s, during the so-called Peacock Revolution in men's clothes, I went about disguised as a sparrow. Long hair, beards, denim, flowery shirts, great flapping bell-bottoms, boots, I eschewed them all, and without the least touch of regret. Instead of letting it all hang out, as the spirit of the day called for, I carefully tucked it all in. If there is a hell, and if I am assigned to it, as part of my punishment I suspect that I shall be required to dress for eternity in the standard getup of an assistant professor of English at the University of California (Berkeley) in 1969. My headband will bind, my beard will itch, the denim will chafe my skin, my boots will pinch, and I shall regularly trip over the generous expanse of my bell-bottomed jeans. All this will be hell enough, but what will really hurt will be my vanity. Why shouldn't there be vanity in hell, too? Vanity Fair, says Thackeray, who wrote the book, "is a very vain, wicked, foolish place, full of all sorts of humbugs and falsenesses and pretensions."

Male vanity, though it may be no more intense than female vanity, is rather more complicated, if only for its having no agreed-upon outlet. Women can choose either to dress for the attack or not. But men who are also on the attack do not always do well to dress for it. (I use the word *attack*, as does the novelist Anthony Powell, in connection with the attempt to conquer the attention of the opposite sex.) Pandemic feminism to the contrary notwithstanding, great vanity in a woman, at least about outward appearance, appalls not and neither does it infuriate in the way that obvious great vanity in a man does. The resources open to women—in costume, in cosmetics, in conniving with one's physique generally—are well known and for the most part not disapproved. Less in this line is available to men, though they are striving to catch up: see here the men's fragrance section in any large department store.

Still, a too evidently vain man is a pathetic thing, subject to scorn and contempt, and generally receiving both. Something about a man fussing too greatly about his appearance is repellent. One shouldn't too easily be able to imagine a man standing before his mirror, manipulating the strands of his hair under the gale force of a blow-dryer. The working assumption is that a serious man ought to be more concerned about serious matters. Elegance, good looks, an agreeable appearance in a

man ought to come easily or not at all. "A man of my limited
resources cannot presume to have a hairstyle," Churchill once
told his barber, hitting exactly the right masculine note. "Get
on with it."

Fewer and fewer men nowadays are Churchillian in the
sense of wishing to get on with it. They prefer instead to linger
over it. Male vanities of recent decades have widened; much
more leeway is allowed. Yet the chief item upon which masculine vanity is given exercise is the hair of head and face. A
future historian of male vanity—what, one wonders, will he
look like?—will want to discover the exact date on which the
term *hairstyling* entered the language. I cannot make even a
rough guess when it did, though I do recall, in the early 1960s,
passing a barbershop on Lexington Avenue in New York and
sighting men seated inside wearing hair nets. At the time it
seemed remarkable to me that men would allow barbers to put
hair nets on them and even more remarkable that they didn't
mind being seen in this condition by people passing the shop
on a heavily trafficked street. Men were not always so shameless.

The shift from getting one's hair cut to getting it styled was
decisive, for it turned one's appearance over to a professional
for what was in effect exterior decoration. Before, one combed
one's hair as seemed most comely; and if comely wasn't a
possibility, then as it appeared most seemly. One worked, as
Churchill suggested, with the resources at one's disposal.
"Don't take too much off the back," one might tell a barber.
Or, "I like it full on the sides." Under the regime of hairstyling,
your barber tends to tell you how he plans to cut your hair.
And these fellows—many among them are women—have extraordinary ideas. It is owing to hairstyling that a vast number
of men today walk the streets looking as if they are wearing
someone else's hair. The results are frequently (unconsciously)

comic, so that one sees a man with the body of Oliver Hardy wearing the hair of General George Custer, or a man with the natural refinement of a power lifter wearing the pompadour of the Comte Robert de Montesquiou. The Comte, it will be recalled, was the principal model for Proust's Baron de Charlus, and it was to him that Degas declared, "Watch out, M. de Montesquiou, taste is a vice." Montesquiou, France's most perfect dandy, represented male vanity to the highest power. He had himself photographed more than two hundred times and painted by Whistler, Boldoni, Helleu, and others. He wore astonishing getups and amazing ties, and he put more care into his mustache than most men do into their careers. Montesquiou's exorbitant aestheticism—Proust referred to him as Professor of Beauty—set him apart from all other men, even in that outrageously vanity-ridden day.

In our day, every man can be his own Montesquiou, at least from the neck up. Ours has been a time of great creativity in the fashioning of mustaches and beards. While women have cosmetics to alter their looks, men have facial hair. They have been availing themselves of this resource for some time now. I know men of my own age—all of them, it is true, academics—who have been wearing beards for more than a quarter of a century, so that I can scarcely remember what they looked like clean-shaven. I can recall, though, a time when a beard seemed a strange peculiarity, worn only by elderly Orthodox Jews, Monty Woolley, George Bernard Shaw, and the baseball team from the House of David. As for mustaches, they seemed a genuine masculine oddity—rare, rather European, and requiring a certain gravity of mien to bring off. They also presented rich comic possibilities, as Charlie Chaplin and Groucho Marx but not Adolf Hitler recognized.

In his autobiography, Carl Zuckmayer, the German poet and playwright who was born in 1896, recollects of his father's generation "how splendidly self-assured, vital, and conscious of success mustaches were in those days." Balanchine, in an interview published in *The New Yorker* not long before he died, said that he thought that the beards of his father's generation were quite authentic but that all contemporary beards were fakes. I think what both Zuckmayer and Balanchine had in mind is that the mustaches and beards of an earlier time were integral to personality; they had to do with more than fashion, served a purpose greater than cosmetic; they in fact expressed inner conviction. Carl Zuckmayer said of his own father's mustache that "it reflected that naive faith in progress, that still unalloyed delight in the results of enterprise, which marked the period between the war of 1870 and the war of 1914." Today's mustaches and beards, where they are not grown to camouflage a long upper lip or a weak chin, seem more than anything else a form of fantasy. "Who the devil are you supposed to be," said a candid friend of mine to a London editor who had grown long thick sideburns to go along with his goatee, "Brahms or Trotsky?"

Great bushy muttonchops, subtle little imperials, lengthy rabbinicals, food-catching Nietzsches, chaste Amish-Solzhenitsyns, droopy Fu Manchus (or is it Fus Manchu?)—the possibilities in mustache and beard wear are considerable and tempting to the vain. As one of the vain, here I must confess that one summer, vacationing by a lake in the countryside of Wisconsin, I attempted a mustache. I had something rather English in mind: something on the order of a recently mustered-out World War I British cavalry officer now a fellow in classics at Trinity College, Cambridge. This mustache was envisioned as a piece of work at once aristocratic, debonair, intellectual. What in fact in ten or so days grew across my lip was something rather more Latin American in its effect; and I don't mean Cesar Romero Latin American, either. Instead I had the all-too-prominent beginnings of a mustache that looked as if it belonged to one of those anonymous *federales* in the movie *The Treasure of the Sierra Madre.* "No," as I once heard a young professor of English declare upon returning from an MLA meeting, "it wasn't what I had in mind." That mustache never left Wisconsin.

But even if it had appeared to work, if the mustache had been a perfect little objet d'art, it wouldn't really have worked. I am not a man who can grow a mustache one day, a beard a month later, and pop on an earring on Saturday night. I am what I am. From the age of roughly twenty my personal style, such as it is, has remained much the same. With only small variations, I wear the same kind of clothes now as then; I have my hair cut short and I brush it in the same undramatic style as I have since college. (A friend recently likened my hair, in its immutability, to AstroTurf, which I took as a compliment.) A little dull I may be, but, as Napoleon must have thought when he was made emperor, I can live with that. Meanwhile my distinction resides in my being, as I like to think myself, the least likely man in America to show up in a ponytail.

But my vanity about my appearance is small-time stuff next to my vanity as an author. The vanity of authors is by now famous, or at least it ought to be. "But enough talk about me," the caption of a cartoon in *Publishers Weekly* ran, "what do you think about my new book?" Perhaps the reason behind authorial vanity has to do with writers working a good bit alone, often with doubt, not to say extreme dubiety, about the outcome. Perspective gets lost. The two quite contradictory notions that every writer must keep in balance in his mind at all times—that what he is writing at the moment is of thunderous importance and that it is most unlikely to have a long life— frequently get muddled. Add to this that in some circles—

generally quite small ones—writers are greatly revered and hotly overpraised. All of which combines to make for a problem in self-esteem for many of us who write; the problem is that we have too much of it—self-esteem, that is.

At least I know I do, and not very deep down, either, but right up there near the surface. The other day, for example, I received in the mail a most friendly notice of a forthcoming book of mine; the notice begins by saying that I am "one of a handful of living Americans who have mastered the familiar essay." Nice, no? You would think that might please me. If you do, you show how little you know about the vanity of writers. I stopped upon reading that opening clause; I was "brought up by it," as used to be said. A handful who have mastered the familiar essay, I thought. I didn't know there were others. Who, I wondered, might they be? I hope nobody thinks I am making this up.

As with appearance, so with authorship: my vanity is the vanity of, above all, wishing not to seem vain. (If nothing so improves the appearance as a high opinion of oneself, it occurs to me that I ought to be better-looking than I am.) When it comes to my writing, I prefer not to blow my own piccolo or, at any rate, not to be caught blowing it. "But it is more agreeable to preserve the modesty," says Agatha Christie's M. Hercule Poirot after explaining to still another ignorant Englishman that he is the world's greatest detective. Something about playing the great author—on television and radio chat shows, at bookshop signing parties—goes against my peculiar kind of vanity. So I do not promote my books, even though I could find uses for the additional money that promotion might bring in—visions of a closet filled with French bow ties dance in my head—and I am eager to have as many intelligent readers as possible.

My anti-vanity vanity, which begins to sound like reverse

snobbery, runs to the details of book publication. I don't, for example, like to have my photograph appear on the dust jacket of my books. Better, in my view, to let readers imagine what the author they are reading looks like, better a vague apparition than the locked-in, visible definiteness of photography. In my own case, I find I don't particularly enjoy being photographed by professional photographers. Like barbers, tailors, and plastic surgeons, they live day in and day out with other people's vanity, and in their presence I find I grow anxious lest I expose mine. "That's good. Hold it. In this shot you look just like Camus," a photographer once told me. "And you look just like Henri Cartier-Bresson," I replied, just to show him that two could play at this liar's game.

Then there is the matter of blurbs, which calls for asking other writers to indite a few promotional sentences on behalf of one's new book. I do not myself give blurbs and have never wanted them. When asked to write a blurb for someone's book by his publisher, I respond by saying that I only write blurbs for authors who have died and that my blurbs truly aren't worth dying for. I am embarrassed—which may be only another way of saying "too vain"—to ask other writers to supply blurbs for my books and have always chosen not to do so. But when I was about to have a collection of short stories published, and my editor, whose views I much respect, informed me that it would be immensely helpful to my little volume to have a few blurbs written in support of it, I agreed to go along. I am grateful enough that convincing blurbs were found, but the vainglorious truth is that there are only a few living writers of fiction from whom I should genuinely be pleased to have blurbs—Aleksandr Solzhenitsyn, V. S. Naipaul, Andrei Sinyavsky—and none of them, like me, so far as I know, dispenses blurbs.

But, then, truth to tell, I should prefer most of all to have blurbs from writers who are no longer blurbistically feasible, so to speak, because they are long dead. As for the blurbs I have in mind, they would read something like the following:

"He is a writer I take very seriously indeed." —*T. S. Eliot*

"Il est un écrivain exquis." —*Marcel Proust*

"This guy cracks me up." —*Franz Kafka*

"Penetration and subtlety have never, in my experience, been so elegantly suffused with irresistible charm." —*Max Beerbohm*

Now these are blurbs I can go with.

Koved is what the Jews call honor and glory, and I have not won enough of either to be vain about my own *koved.* I have been given an honorary doctorate from a university whose president would, I believe, be ready to allow that it is not yet first-class, and one of my books has won a regional prize. The only other award I have won is for tossing in twenty-one of twenty-five free throws at Green Briar Park in Chicago at the age of thirteen, for which I was supposed to receive a trophy but never did. All three of these awards have been immensely pleasing to me. Greater ones might have meant less. Such is my vanity that I don't think I care much to win honors that have been given to people before me who I don't think are fundamentally very honorable. By now, of course, nearly every prize in this nation has gone to someone or other whom your normally vain man is likely to find not only beneath him but also a touch beneath contempt. It is a problem, but not a deep one. "A man who pursues *koved,*" I am told it says in the Talmud, "from him *koved* runs away." Let it run has become my view. I am for winning all possible prizes and awards, but at the same time I have reached an age where no prize or award will quell my doubts or satisfy my vanity.

"It is not possible," says La Rochefoucauld, "to enumerate all the kinds of vanity." Yet I feel I would be remiss if I didn't mention my vanity about what I take to be my general savvy about the world. There is no compelling evidence for my holding this belief, but hold it I do, quite in defiance of much experience to the contrary. Wary of being made a fool of—in modern life, my view is, paranoia is the better part of valor—I have not infrequently attempted to ward this condition off by attempting, ever so delicately, to fool others. Never shall I forget taking in a car to be repaired and telling the mechanic, lest he take me for a man entirely ignorant about cars (which of course I am), that I wasn't quite sure what was wrong, for I had only recently put in a throw-out bearing, faintly suggesting that I had done the job myself. In fact, I once had a throw-out bearing replaced in a car I owned, but what I didn't realize, and only later learned, was that a throw-out bearing is only required in a car with a clutch, and the car I was now bringing in for repair, having an automatic transmission, had no clutch. How the mechanic, over whose eyes I was attempting to pull the polyester, must have laughed and said confidently to himself, "Gotcha, buster!" "The surest way to be taken in is to think oneself craftier than other people," says (again) La Rochefoucauld. Thank you, my dear Duc, but if I want your advice, I shall ask for it.

One form of vanity I thought I was free of is family vanity. I hope my parents will forgive my saying so, but I come of a most non-distinguished family—if distinction be determined by achievement in public life, the arts, science, or commerce. In all these lines, we have, I can say without hesitation, done diddly. Not only did we fail to come over on the *Mayflower*, but we were lucky to have missed the *Lusitania*. I have often been at some confusion about describing my precise social class, until a short while ago when, reading an account of the life of Mrs. Humphrey Ward, I noted Mrs. Ward described as being of "the cultivated middle class." On the spot I concluded that I come from the "uncultivated middle class," or that class which lives in a certain comfort made possible by money but hasn't the least interest in culture. I have never had any shame about that, though no special pride in it either. Life without ancestors, at least in twentieth-century America, is scarcely a hardship. But then I recalled a remark of Freud's, one doubtless intended to describe his own social condition, which was that better than having ancestors is to be an ancestor. Just so, *mais oui*, and Eureka: I concluded that I, with a lot of luck, may just one day turn out to be an ancestor. Vanity, once more, finds a way.

When I was much younger, a famous novelist told me I was very worldly, and I have ever since been secretly vain about this. I have long thought myself a man of fastidious taste—"fastidiousness is the most pardonable of vices," said Chesterton, "but it is the most unpardonable of virtues"—and yet with a wide tolerance for taste less chaste than my own. A world where everyone dressed or felt about matters of taste as I did would be very dull. But so would a world where I couldn't make fun of those who don't, or they of me. Vanity is nothing if not invidious; nor is it known to obey the law of contradictions. My own vanity allows me to be tolerant yet hypercritical, reasonable yet perverse, worldly yet contemptuous of mere worldlings. Most convenient. I shouldn't know how to live without it.

"Vanity of vanities, saith the Preacher, vanity of vanities; all is vanity." That of course comes from Ecclesiastes, the book in the Old Testament that addresses itself to the question of vanity with rather depressing results, concluding over and over again: "Behold, all is vanity and vexation of spirit." The author of Ecclesiastes is not alone in his bleak views. As I have mentioned, Samuel Johnson wrote in rhyming couplets of "The Vanity of Human Wishes," and Schopenhauer, who could take all the smiles out of Christmas, upped the ante in writing about "The Vanity of Existence," by which he meant all of it. Yet I wonder if it isn't closer to the truth to say not that human existence is vain but that vanity is part of human existence. I prefer Montaigne on this subject. In his essay "Of Vanity," he writes: "If others examine themselves attentively, as I do, they would find themselves, as I do, full of inanity and nonsense. Get rid of it I cannot without getting rid of myself. We are all steeped in it, one as much as another; but those who are aware of it are a little better off—though I don't know." I particularly like that final clause: "though I don't know." I don't, either, though I remain hopeful that awareness might make one perhaps a touch better off.

Montaigne's lengthy essay on vanity is highly digressive, even for him, who averred that his "ideas follow one another, but sometimes it is from a distance, and look at each other, but with a sidelong glance." In fact, Montaigne's essay seems to be chiefly about death. Perhaps it is right that it should be so, for vanity, for all its inanity, at its best speaks to an avidity for the world; and it is in the light of death, as the author of Ecclesiastes well knew, that all seems vain. Yet anyone who is confident that vanity is purged by a recognition of death, even a very close recognition, may find himself surprised. I recall Sir William Haley once telling me that, when he was editor of the *Times* of London, he one evening received a call from the butler of Lord X informing him that his lordship did not expect to make it through the night. What Lord X was doing in having his butler call was to give the *Times* a chance to get his obituary in good order, which strikes me as less astonishing than all too human.

Arthur Schopenhauer, Samuel Johnson, Edward Gibbon—I have a distinct taste for these vanity-oh-all-is-vanity boys. They seem to have put so much energy into demonstrating that life is all a scam, a shuck, a silly if rather large-scale cosmic joke. Yet, if what they say was true, why did they themselves embark on such careful, monumental, furiously impressive works? I think it is because they didn't finally believe it. What they all knew and believed is that men and women are wondrous in their ability to take their eyes off the ball, to become wildly distracted, to believe astonishing nonsense, to let things get so badly out of hand that there can be little arguing with Henry James when, in an essay on Turgenev, he wrote: "Evil is insolent and strong, beauty enchanting but rare; goodness very apt to be weak; folly very apt to be defiant; wickedness to carry the day; imbeciles to be in very great places, people of sense in small, and mankind generally unhappy."

Schopenhauer, who was himself a meticulous dresser and who seemed to get so much pleasure out of showing why men are so miserable, may be quite right when he writes that vanity is "the appropriate term for that which has no solid or intrinsic value," but how much bleaker life would be without it. From Schopenhauer's perspective, we would all go under but for the agency of two simple impulses, hunger and the sexual instinct, "aided a little, perhaps, by the influence of boredom." Ought not vanity to be tossed in there, not only as a form of assuaging boredom (your vain man or woman is rarely bored, having him- or herself perpetually to contemplate) but in helping the world to go round, and for many of us to keep it spinning in the most amusing way.

Suggesting this redeeming social value for vanity is not intended as a provocation, a piece of intellectual perversity, like arguing that Mozart died too late or that we owe the invention of blood plasma to Hitler. I quite mean it. Much of the little

I have been able to accomplish thus far in life I find is owed in good part to vanity—with most of the remainder owed to guilt. Look to your own life to discover if it is much different. My bet is that it isn't. As for stakes, what about two of my French bow ties against your blow-dryer?

Knocking on Three, Winston

Those new institutions of popular and mobile learning, bumper stickers, at least a number of them that show up in my neighborhood, ask me to Visualize World Peace. I try, but I do not find this easy to do. Some advice, I suppose, is more easily taken than other advice. The bitter bumper stickers, unlike the more utopian ones, seem more readily to gain my assent: "Eat well, stay fit, and die anyway," read one such sticker on a car I recently rode behind. It announced this sad truism next to a decal denoting a Teamsters local. A friend reports a car passing him in Colorado whose sticker read not, as many do, "If you love Jesus, honk," but instead, "If you *are* Jesus, honk"—certainly a more interesting proposition. "Have you hugged your kid today?" was one of the first of the popular bumper stickers, one no doubt meant to give all parents a bit of a bad conscience. If I were in the bumper-sticker business, I wouldn't mind running off a few thousand stickers that read, "Have you kicked your role model today?" Now here is a question that gives one something to think about on longish drives. It also gives fine vent to my antagonism to the notion of a role model.

Difficult though world peace may be for me to visualize—if I strain, I think I can see it, though I am saddened to report that it appears duller even than paradise—I can visualize it more easily than a world without such words as *role model.* Such spongy words that don't seem to absorb much truth figure to be around forever. My specific grudge against the term *role model* is, as the best grudges often are, a bit complicated and a touch personal. The term itself comes of bad origins; if it were a racehorse, the tout sheet on it would read: Role Model, by Sociology out of Modern Education. But my chief problem with it isn't its origin so much as it is the people off whose lips it comes so happily tripping. When they say "role model" they seem to feel that they have said something not merely felicitous and penetrating but quite magical. What this boy (student, school, ethnic group, country—fill in the subject for yourself) needs is better role models, they smugly say. Sure he does, I generally say to myself, like my cat needs hubcaps.

My first encounter with the term was an indirect and mildly depressing one. It occurred in the late 1960s, when it came to my attention that one of my stepsons, who was bright, good-natured, and with nothing of the rebel or the recalcitrant about him, was not doing very well in high school. I met with his guidance counselor, an obviously well-meaning woman who, I sensed as we began to talk, was herself perhaps in need of a bit of guidance—as was everyone in those days who had to help run a high school of middle- and upper-middle-class kids that was filled with drugs, racial bad feeling, and lots of hopeless educational theory. "Maybe the boy's problem," the guidance counselor suggested, "is that he is *role* instead of *goal* oriented." Role instead of goal, thought I, rolling the phrase around on my tongue; clearly, I was in a place where they let the rhyme fit the crime. If this were true, I asked, in what role does this put me, who is chiefly responsible for his education? No answer. Having thought about this further on my own, in the end I decided to stay on the boy's case, ready to accept the *role* of villain, nag, and less than fully understanding parent. It was no easy thing, but it seems finally to have worked out all right.

I do not have a very exact sense of when *role model* came into vogue, but my guess is that it slipped in the back door just as the word *hero* was escorted out the front. The feeling against heroes had been building for some time. One of the chief tasks of the modern biographer, beginning with Lytton Strachey, seems to be, on the way to revealing the subject's dirty little secrets, to show that putatively great men and women are, even as you and I, puny and fallible and, when the biographer's truth is told, really much worse than that. In contemporary fiction, the anti-hero—from Joseph Heller's Lieutenant Yossarian to Philip Roth's Alexander Portnoy—was the dominant character type through much of the 1960s and showed up in novels more frequently than losers at singles dances. All those institutions that used to provide heroic figures—the military, the clergy, politics at the higher levels—no longer did so. *Au bloomin' contraire*, they seemed the most mocked, the most scorned and spat upon of all. Heroic action, heroic lives, did not seem a real possibility. As Thomas Carlyle wrote of the eighteenth century, "the very possibility of Heroism had been, as it were, formally abnegated in the minds of all." Or, as they put it in the pages of *Women's Wear Daily*, heroism was out.

As someone who was a young boy during World War II—I was eight years old at its end in 1945—I grew up with heroism forming a good part of my daily psychic diet. The majority of the movies I saw were war movies, and hence movies about heroes, and the rest seemed to be about priests, who were themselves pretty damned—not quite the right word, I realize—heroic, too. The Bible stories that most excited my imagination were those that told of heroic behavior: David taking on and knocking off Goliath, Joseph making his way among the Egyptians, Moses leading that trek of all treks across the desert. Then there were all those fairy tales, with handsome and supremely good princes showing up just when the going got tough, which, as is well known, is precisely when the tough get going. Robin Hood, whose adventures were read to me when I was quite young, also much impressed me. He was a terrific athlete, took from the rich and gave to the poor, had a swell-looking girlfriend, and threw lavish outdoor parties.

So hyped on heroes was I that I can recall feeling a slight disappointment that my father, who was too old to be drafted, was not a soldier during the war. It took a bit away from his heroic status in my eyes. World War II seemed a war without ambiguities—certainly a seven-year-old could find none—and to be able to wear a uniform was automatically to be a figure deserving of respect, not only in my view but in nearly everyone's. When we traveled on vacation during the war, we always picked up servicemen, and so did a great many other people. One of my first heroes in the flesh was Ozzie Bryer, son of Rose and Frank Bryer, who lived upstairs and who was in the navy. When he was discharged, he gave me one of his white gob's hats, which I wore with pride and pleasure. Men who had survived heavy fighting in World War II seemed to me immensely impressive. They still do.

War heroes were soon replaced in my small pantheon by athletic heroes. I grew up in neighborhoods where, if one wasn't a good athlete, one had better be witty or extremely wily or then at least fleet of foot. "Very problematic," I can hear a certain kind of psychologist muttering as he reads this, but it never seemed at all problematic to me, who was a respectable if never a first-class athlete and a kid who had a hardy appetite for games. A block behind the apartment building in which we lived, down along Lake Michigan, the football team of Sullivan High School practiced. Sullivan's was not a winning team. Its coach was a barrel-chested, short-legged man named Ralph Margolis, who used to swear at his players with Yiddish expletives. The word *shtunk*—denoting an ungrateful fool, an unpleasant schlemiel—was easily his favorite. The only players the coach never called *shtunk,* at least while I was watching, were two brothers named Gordy and Ronnie Green.

The Green brothers were so heavily muscled that it seemed to me that they must have lifted weights with their faces, for their cheeks, their foreheads, even their hair seemed powerful. Gordy Green was a fullback, his younger and somewhat smaller brother Ronnie a halfback. They were Jewish tough guys of the kind that appear in Isaac Babel's Benya Krik stories: true brutes, or so it seemed to a small boy of eight or nine standing on the sidelines watching them crash into the line, tossing up clouds of dust, trotting back into the huddle unharmed from crushing collision after crushing collision. I admired them without qualification.

What made a young boy admire two such older boys— boys who then seemed to him men—when he had been told time and again, and in fact quite believed, that it wasn't muscle but brains that counted in life? The first qualification for a hero, in the eyes of a small boy—and not, I suspect, in those of a small boy alone—is the ability to fend off fear. The Green brothers, Gordy and Ronnie, seemed beautifully equipped for this, or so it seemed to me. Far from seeming in any way fearful, they, it occurred to me then, were themselves worth fearing. At that time, without the least hesitation, I should have traded whatever chance I might have had for a good mind for one of their powerful bodies.

It was not long after my admiration for the Green boys had set in that my interest in athletes went national. This came about through my reading a monthly magazine called *Sport*, which I began to do with great intensity around the age of eleven or twelve. The magazine was devoted to the subject of its title, but even more, in those days, to uncomplicated hero worship. *Sport* had nothing to do with criticizing athletes; its editors and writers were as far as possible from being, as a long and justly defunct statesman once put it, "nattering nabobs of negativism." If you were written about in *Sport*, you were, ipso facto, written about as a hero. Nor, best as I can remember, did the magazine go in much for personalities, and certainly never for the dissection of them. A characteristic line, from a piece on the Yankee catcher Yogi Berra, that has rattled around in my head all these years had it that "Yogi likes plenty of pizza in the off-season, when he can generally be found hanging around his friend Yankee shortstop Phil Rizzuto's bowling alley." The same article, written today, might inform us that its subject, with the aid of kin-network therapy, had survived his second divorce in fairly good shape, though he greatly regrets an unfortunate deal on a condominium complex in Acapulco, a leveraged buy-out, in which he had invested heavily.

To *Sport*, too, I owe my first interest in history, for the magazine ran a series of articles under the rubric "The Sport Classic" about great athletic heroes of the past. I recall being much moved by articles on such figures as Jim Thorpe, Bill Tilden, Lou Gehrig, and Red Grange. The theme of these articles was that the great athletes were great-hearted; even famous horses—Man o' War, Whirlaway, Sea Biscuit—were great-hearted. How one acquired a great heart on one's own was a bit less than clear. Sometimes it seemed one was born with it. But more often you worked hard, faced adversity straight on, didn't let life in its harsher aspects defeat you, and if you came through often enough under pressure-laden cir-

cumstances, lo!, you made it—you were a hero. This still seems
to me not so dumb.

A boy's hero worship almost invariably latches onto heroes
whose accomplishments are essentially physical, warriors and
athletes chief among them. Not only do these men—they have,
historically, overwhelmingly been men—choose to disregard
pain but many of them risk premature destruction, which, as
Maupassant says in his story "The Horla," is "the source of all
human dread." The most rudimentary form heroism takes is
that of defying death; and for this reason we honor as heroes
those men and women who have knowingly risked—and frequently lost—their lives for a cause they deemed larger than
their own lives. One of the reasons that one tends to admire
heroes is that they have qualities that one does not have, or at
least that one is uncertain about having. Here is yet another
distinction between heroes and role models. The former are
worth admiring because they are (almost certainly) better than
you; the latter aren't truly that much better—that is, apparently, the utility of them—so that it should be no great trick
to emulate them.

"I understand the large hearts of heroes," said the garrulous
Walt Whitman, "the courage of present times and all times."
If so, then you're a better man than I, Gunga Whitman. As a
worshiper of heroes, I feel less certain of understanding them.
Perhaps this is in good part owing to the fact that I have so
seldom in my life been called upon to act heroically. Luck of
the draw, I have danced merrily betwixt and between wars, too
young for World War II and Korea, too old for Vietnam and
those wars that followed it. I have never been called upon to
save anyone from drowning—a good thing, too, for I am a
poor swimmer—or to pull anyone from a fire, or to fight off
an attacker. What the sports announcers call "crunch times,"
those moments in the game when the pressure is at its greatest,

are times that thus far in the game of life I have never known.

Whenever I have been cited for courage, it has been only for expressing forthright opinions on mildly controversial intellectual matters. The first thing to be said about this is that these matters never seemed all that controversial to me—they seemed, in fact, rather commonsensical—or I should not have been able to be so jollily forthright about them. The second thing to be said is that expressing any opinion in our country doesn't really require anything like courage; in the Soviet Union, in Nazi Germany, in China, saying what one thought had meant courting death. The only penalty one pays here is to be excluded from certain parties, which, to someone who prefers to stay home anyhow, is no penalty whatsoever. Speaking your mind in America is not my idea of courage and nowhere near my idea of heroism.

High school provided lean pickings for hero worship, though a wealth of unimpressive role models were available. One older boy in our school came near to holding hero status in my mind. His name was Roger Berlin. I remember him as being very handsome, though very little interested in girls; not so much a great or graceful as a fearless athlete; and very kind. I don't recall his ever using profanity, which the rest of us boys then used in place of punctuation. There were mildly mythic stories about him: one was that he played tackle football on concrete; another was that after a high school basketball game, he burst into the visiting team's locker room and took on all ten or twelve visiting players and had eventually to be dragged out, still swinging. The book on Roger was that he was a very nice guy whom you didn't want to get angry; and in my high school, one could not have a better book. What happened to Roger Berlin is, in my mind, a bit vague, a bit misty, as all heroes' post-heroic periods ought perhaps to be. He must at some point have become interested in school, for the word was that, after some rocky years, he shored up as a psychiatrist somewhere in Kansas.

At college I turned in heroes of physical courage for heroes of culture. Although I was much impressed by many of my teachers at the University of Chicago, none came anywhere near qualifying as heroic. Oddly, though it never occurred to me to think myself potentially a poet, poets around this time became heroic figures to me. In *On Heroes, Hero-Worship and the Heroic in History,* which I read for the first time only the other day, Thomas Carlyle remarks on the naturalness of the poet as a hero. His claim is that the poet has much in common with the prophet in "that they have penetrated both of them into the sacred mystery of the Universe; what Goethe calls 'the *open* secret.' " I was nowhere near intelligent enough to formulate my hero worship of poets thus, but I did instinctively, and inchoately, worship them. This took the form of my becoming something of a mild great-poets groupie. When a famous poet came to campus, I went to his or her reading, much as other people go to church: with genuine reverence in my heart. I heard and saw in this way E. E. Cummings, Marianne Moore, and Carl Sandburg. I wish now that I had heard and seen Robert Frost and especially T. S. Eliot, who had become rather a widespread hero of culture around this time, or Wallace Stevens, who gave very few readings.

Today, however, I would leave my couch to hear Carl Sandburg only if he read the exact date of my own death and gave an account of my funeral, so little do his mind and talent interest me. My point, though, is not to put down Carl Sandburg, but to show how, with age, one's heroes change. With the passing of years, I have had to smash twenty or thirty busts in my personal pantheon, for the reason that many of the heroes I once much esteemed now seem unworthy of it. As a literary boy and young man, for example, I was a perfect patsy for the writer who was also a man of action. I was never so foolish as to think Ernest Hemingway a hero; I knew that if one was a hero one didn't go around claiming one was a hero, as Hemingway, relentlessly, boringly, did. But I did admire Leon Trotsky, even though I knew enough to abhor Communism, and what I admired him for was his ability both to lead the Red Army and to write the *History of the Russian Revolution*.

Along with Trotsky, two other men whom I admired, because they seemed to make moot the question of whether the pen was mightier than the sword by possessing both, were André Malraux and T. E. Lawrence. But they, too, have shrunk a good bit over the years in my eyes. Malraux, I now see, was intellectually rather muddled and a subtle yet altogether too sedulous self-promoter. Lawrence, though his military achievement remains impressive, is perhaps too meshuga to stand in as a genuine hero. Besides, I tend to think there may be something to Max Beerbohm's remark that he would rather *not* have led the Arab Revolt than have written Lawrence's translation of the *Iliad*.

The older one gets, the fewer the busts left in one's pantheon. And many of those that are left seem to acquire sadly disfiguring chips. T. S. Eliot has come very close to being a culture hero of mine. I don't think there is much question but that his poetry retains much of its power and is among the deepest and most memorable written in English in the twentieth century. His criticism retains a dignified authority that no other critic in our time has been able to equal; it is interesting and usefully provocative even when wrong. The sad events of Eliot's life—chiefly, those surrounding his first marriage—do not, to my mind, detract from his stature; suffering traversed and understood only makes one more sympathetic and dignified.

No, the real chip in Eliot's bust is his anti-Semitism, which is made all the more dreary by the fact, revealed in the first volume of his letters, that he was capable of the kind of very careful careerism that he would have condemned had it appeared in anyone Jewish. When Eliot, at the age of thirty-two, writes to his mother, "Having got this off, we spent the weekend at Eastbourne, visiting some friends called Schiff—very nice Jews," my heart sinks at the sad thought that a man able to rise above his time in so many ways was not able to do so in this way, too. But it is too late: "very nice Jews," as opposed to all those other Jews, has been written and is out in the world. I still think Eliot a great figure in the history of culture, as impressive as any other cultural figure in this century. Yet although I know he had a kindly side to him, I wish he had allowed for my feelings and stowed the anti-Semitism.

The fact is, I prefer my heroes unflawed. This is tough on them, I realize, but it isn't so easy on me, either. To show you the lengths to which I am prepared to go in making demands of my heroes, I prefer my heroes and heroines to be nice people, people I shouldn't mind taking to a concert or a ball game, having over for Thanksgiving dinner, or playing a little gin rummy with. In literature this leaves out Baudelaire, I realize, also Thoreau and Dostoyevsky. But I can, given these criteria, still nicely accommodate Sydney Smith, Turgenev, Chekhov, Willa Cather, Max Beerbohm, and a few others.

To ask that one's hero be, along with heroic, a nice person may seem an unreasonable demand, and probably is. No one ever asked that Alexander the Great also be a great guy. It is far from clear that Pericles was a nice fellow, and Catherine the Great was in no quarter known as Catherine the Pussy Cat. Schopenhauer, another guy no one ever called nice, said that geniuses, which many world-historical heroes turn out to be, aren't very comfortable in the world. "This," writes Schopenhauer, "explains the animation, amounting to disquietude, in men of genius, since the present can seldom satisfy them, because it does not fill their consciousness. This gives them that restless zealous nature, that constant search for new objects worthy of contemplation, and also that longing, hardly ever satisfied, for men of like nature and stature to whom they may open their hearts." In talking about genius, Schopenhauer is in good part here describing himself. It was Nietzsche, for whom Schopenhauer was a personal hero, who said that every idea has its autobiography. It is I who now say that playing a little gin with Schopenhauer or Nietzsche isn't easily imagined, though I suppose I would do better at gin than at argument with either of them.

The gin rummy test, the demand that a hero be rather a decent and companionable person, almost straightaway eliminates most politicians from the sphere of heroism. The only politician in this century whom I think I should have cared to spend much time with, and whom I also consider heroic, is Winston Churchill. In *The Hero in History*, Sidney Hook remarks that "particularly in politics, a medium in which virtues and vices, reason and stupidity, have an entirely different specific gravity than in the clear waters of personal relations and scientific activity, is it difficult to evaluate genius." Hook adds, interestingly, that democratic societies tend not to offer too many political heroes, and that it is part of their own specific genius that they don't. In fact, the only unarguable hero in American political life has been Abraham Lincoln, and I suppose that there are still Southerners who would wish to argue against his status as a hero.

Abraham Lincoln was no hero in his own lifetime, which corroborates Sidney Hook's point that democratic societies "usually refuse to glorify their leaders until they are dead." William Hazlitt, complementing Hook, wrote that "mankind are so ready to bestow their admiration on the dead because the latter do not hear it, or because it gives no pleasure to the objects of it. Even fame is the offspring of envy." In recent years in the United States we have had two men put up for heroism immediately after their deaths, John F. Kennedy and Martin Luther King, Jr., and because of modern methods of research—also known as prying—neither has fared at all well. John F. Kennedy should never have been considered a hero to begin with, and it is only owing to his early death and even more to his Harvard panegyrists, Schlesinger, Galbraith, & Co., that it was possible to stake out a claim for his heroism in the first place; in the second place, with sex scandals and other revelations, he looks smaller and smaller all the time. A charming man, he would have made a fine partner at gin rummy, but as a hero he simply doesn't cut it. Martin Luther King, Jr., whose posthumous reputation has also been besmirched—by sex scandal and by reports of plagiarism—nonetheless in my mind retains heroic status for having conquered fear under seriously fearful conditions. German police dogs, Southern sheriffs, low-grade but truly vicious bullies, none either daunted King or otherwise deterred him from his profoundly moral mission. Yet why do I think he would be a lousy gin rummy partner?

Staking out a claim to be a hero in public life has grown more and more difficult. Consider General H. Norman Schwarzkopf, leader of the successful Desert Storm operation in the Middle East. A solid character, General Schwarzkopf, a man who knows his business, suffers fools not at all, dignified and serious, the best type of the modern military man. Have we a hero here, the real article, I wondered, as I saw him easily conquer those most pestiferous of menaces, the modern journalists? Yet one night I learned that he, General Schwarzkopf, was to be interviewed by Barbara Walters. My dubiety was piqued. Why subject oneself to the depthless inanity of the mawkish Wawa-ian grilling? Barbara—I feel certain she wouldn't want me to call her by anything but her first name—Barbara didn't ask the General what sort of tree he thinks he most closely resembles, or how he wished to be remembered (perhaps, after Desert Storm, as a palm tree). But at one point the television camera played over General Schwarzkopf's modest personal quarters: his bed, his footlocker, his few uniforms, and then the camera came to rest on a Bible and a copy of—oh dear, I wish I had never seen it—*The Prophet* by Kahlil Gibran. What is a man like the General, an earnest, highly intelligent, non-quiche-eating warrior, doing reading such a sententious, sentimental, stuffed-animal sort of book as *The Prophet?* Shuffle the cards, General, while I reconsider your case.

The larger point here is that no one in contemporary life can remain a hero under the ghastly light of modern publicity. One of the chief reasons many of us had so high a regard for the past generation of movie stars—Cary Grant, Gary Cooper, Fred Astaire, Edward G. Robinson; Susan Hayward, Claudette Colbert, Greer Garson, Rosalind Russell—was that they came upon and managed to depart the scene before the advent of the television talk show. Owing to this lucky piece of timing, we were permitted to imagine them as reasonably intelligent human beings. Once we have seen an actor on a talk show or two, there is very little chance of considering him as in some even rough sense admirable. Even so elegant a woman as Katharine Hepburn, after a talk-show shot or two, cannot sustain her magic. "Give her," a small voice whispers, "a velvet, gentle, but nevertheless firm hook."

Perhaps it would be easier to forget the whole thing and drop the notion of heroes and the activity of hero worship altogether. Yet too much, I fear, would be lost in doing so. When heroes go out, quacks tend to come in. Heroes also happen to represent the culture at its highest reaches. "Only he who has given his heart to some great man," Nietzsche says, "receives the first consecration of culture." An age of skepticism is hardest on heroes. Everyone recalls the famous remark of Mme Cornuel that no man is a hero to his valet. Yet a country without heroes may well turn out to be, spiritually, a country of valets. It was Carlyle who neatly countered Mme Cornuel's remark by saying, "The Valet does not know a Hero when he sees him! Alas, no: it requires a kind of *Hero* to do that."

William James, who along with his brother Henry happens to be a hero of mine, in his essay "The Importance of Individuals" recounted an unlettered carpenter saying in his hearing, "There is very little difference between one man and another; but what little there is, *is very important.*" I happen to agree. I also agree with James when he remarks that for "a community to get vibrating through and through with intensely active life, many geniuses coming together and in rapid succession are required." As examples James cited the "sudden bloom of a Greece, an early Rome, a Renaissance." Did he know that in late Victorian England, of which in a sense he was himself a part, history had offered another such time? Or is it the case that one's own time always feels as if it is not only bereft of heroes but populated almost exclusively by pygmies?

In our own day, there seem to me no true heroes of culture, George Balanchine being the last such figure. I think Mother Teresa heroic, at least from what I have read about her; and I think Aleksandr Solzhenitsyn a great literary-political hero: he took on the Soviet Union and emerged victorious. Naturally, I view all these people from a distance; more precisely, with the exception of Solzhenitsyn, whose books I read, all I know about them is what I read or see on television, which is probably not enough. It may well be required that for someone to retain heroic status, we not know too much about him. Writing to his sister-in-law about meeting Professor and Mrs. Josiah Royce in France, Henry James noted: "I shall never, in future, embrace any man's philosophy till I have seen him—and above all till I have seen his wife."

Tell me whom you admire and I shall tell you who you are. Schopenhauer, for example, until well past fifty, kept a gilt statue of Buddha on his desk next to a bust of Immanuel Kant, while over his couch hung portraits of Goethe, Shakespeare, Descartes, Claudius, and (again) Kant. Montaigne doesn't use the word *hero,* but in a brief essay titled "Of the most outstanding men," drawing on all of history up to his time, he finds three men "outstanding above all the rest": Homer, Alexander the Great, and Epaminondas, the fourth-century-B.C. Theban general and leader known for his good character. And he cannot help mentioning Alcibiades: "For a man who was not a saint, but what they call a man of the world, of civil and common ways, of moderate eminence, [he lived] the richest life that I know to have been lived among the living, the one composed of the most rich and desirable qualities." Henry James's heroes included Balzac and Napoleon, whom Hegel once referred to as "that world-soul."

Napoleon is one of those figures whom one can admire without particularly liking. Sigmund Freud is another. Like Napoleon, he has, or at any rate his ideas have, become tyrannical. Goethe was easily the greatest man of letters in all of modern history, yet I wish he hadn't let Eckermann fawn and hang around quite so long, thus giving the lie to Hazlitt's notion that "no really great man ever thought himself so." Some heroes seem to me beyond such—or even any—criticism. Beethoven blew his nose in his hand, treated his nephew wretchedly, was clearly more than a little nuts, and yet remains Beethoven, which is more than sufficient. But then Beethoven was both a genius and a hero, and his heroism consists of his getting the most out of his genius under greatly arduous conditions.

Not all heroes are geniuses nor geniuses heroes. All things being equal—perhaps the emptiest phrase in the language, since they never are—I prefer my heroes not to be geniuses. To be a genius is to have too great a head start in life. I much prefer heroes whose accomplishments amount to genius. I admire, for example, those writers who persevere and finish a great thick work of literature: Gibbon, Proust, Joyce, and, though less in this line, Macaulay, whose natural garrulity would have made anything other than a thick work quite impossible. I find heroic, too, those who have endured through long stages of unjust neglect and kept working with a strong sense of their worth. Schopenhauer qualifies in this regard; he put a masterpiece into the world in his early thirties and had to wait until his late fifties for it to be recognized as such. So, too, does Barbara Pym, whose novels were suddenly found insufficiently sexy, noisy, blaguey, you name it, during a violent period in Anglo-American culture, but who stayed the course, eventually finding acceptance and her true readership.

Endurance is a form of heroism open to those of us who neither have genius nor live obviously dramatic lives. Samuel Johnson, who may have been a genius, is another hero of endurance, playing through poverty, poor health, and feckless patrons and winning in the end by dint of hard work and powerful intelligence. Henry James seems to me heroic for continuing to write in the only way he knew how—with the throttle of complexity all the way out—in the face of his need to make a living and the flagging interest of his contemporary readers and editors, and hewing always to "the jolly great truth that it is *art* alone that triumphs over fate," which in his case it most happily did. Both Samuel Johnson and Henry James were also heroes of integrity, another mode of heroism open to those of us without genius.

On the face of it, one cannot hope to know about all the unknown heroes, those persons who do their job and know whereof they speak. I thought of this category of hero when I read a one-line obituary about one Leonard Greenburg, professor of preventive medicine at Yeshiva University, who died at ninety-eight. Now ninety-eight is the age at which every professor of preventive medicine ought to peg out. How much more impressive Dr. Greenburg than the woman who heads my own university's health center and who recently had to retire, giving as her reason bad health. I am also partial to those who, despite natural disadvantages, hang in there. In Ronald Hayman's biography of Marcel Proust I read that when Proust completed his military training he was graded sixty-third out of a class of sixty-four. I think that the fellow who finished sixty-fourth, who was a worse soldier even than Marcel Proust, has to be granted heroic status of some sort. As the beer commercial has it, "Buy that man a Miller."

My own heroes are figures who love life without being taken in by it: David Hume instead of Rousseau, Montaigne instead of Voltaire, Oliver Wendell Holmes, Jr., instead of Emerson, Degas instead of van Gogh, Brahms instead of Wagner. Some among them are skeptical—"as we said of the Valet," writes Carlyle, "so of the Sceptic: He does not know a hero when he sees him!"—theirs is never a skepticism that sours them on the world. They have an air of reality about them. They are undazzled by the world while remaining charmed by it. They are able to keep the seemingly contradictory notions in their heads that life is both a game and a deadly serious business, a play full of laughter and heartbreak.

As I grow older, I find that I am simultaneously less trustful of heroes and increasingly in need of them. To worship false heroes is quite as foolish as worshiping false gods, and in hero worship as in other activities there is no fool like a less-than-young fool. I take some small satisfaction that such hero worshiping as I have gone in for has never entailed subscribing to a hero's doctrine as part of the deal. One carries enough luggage through life without having to lug around another person's ideas. On the other hand, true heroes remind me of life's possibilities—of how difficulties can be overcome, of how often perseverance pays off, of how without integrity self-disgust becomes one's regular companion, of how lovely life can be when fear is conquered, of how gallantry is the highest form of elegance.

Had I at any time in my life been a true hero—had I won the big game, or survived the jungles of Vietnam, or gone into the burning building to save the infant—I wonder if I might regard myself differently than I do now. At a minimum, I would have had the self-assurance of knowing that, under pressure, I had come through. As things are now, I only hope that, should the occasion for heroism arise, I *might* come through. A vast difference between the two—knowing and hoping. Contemplating heroic lives, lives distinguished by physical or psychological courage, and sometimes both, helps to fortify one's own soul and to inspire one to be a little better than, deep down, one worries one is. One of the many fine things about having been a hero, I should think, is that one doesn't have to think about heroism. Never having been called upon to prove one's mettle gives one a lot to think about late at night, and particularly between gin rummy games, spades double, twenty-five points a box, Hollywood-Oklahoma, cut and deal, Winston.

Merely Anecdotal

I am moderately confident that I am not yet in my dotage, though for decades now I have been in what might be called my anecdotage. Not only the love of anecdote but the urge, almost never successfully resisted, to tell one's own anecdotes marks the condition I think of as one's anecdotage. The older one grows, of course, the more anecdotes one accumulates, the keener the impulse to recount them again and again—and yes, I fear, yet again. But in this line, if in few others, I believe I was precocious. I grew up in a strong anecdotal tradition; much value was placed on being able to tell a story with panache. Frequently, when I was a boy and something interesting or amusing was happening to me, I would begin formulating the language in which I would recount the experience to my friends even as I was going through it. Looking back at this now, I should have realized that this marked me, for better *and* worse, as a writer, to the somewhat-removed-from-life manner born.

As an early anecdotalist, I was fortunate to have a fairly large reservoir of boyish experience from which to draw. Mine was a big-city boyhood; it took place in Chicago, at a time when the city of the big shoulders had already developed a serious slouch but had not yet become, as so many modern cities now have, slightly menacing. My young friends and I roamed the city as if it were some lush new planet—sweets hanging from every tree, new and interesting forms of life turning up everywhere—that we felt we were the first to discover. As adolescents, we felt we possessed the city, and we picked the cityscape clean of all that it could yield in experience, with a special interest—there were no Eagle Scouts among us—in illicit experience. And then, quite as good, perhaps even a bit better, we took such experience as we found and touched it up and retold it again in anecdote. Not kiss and tell but live and tell was our motto. As a writing man, this has of course remained my motto to this day.

Not long after writing these first two paragraphs, I made a person-to-person call to London. My friendly MCI operator, while tapping in the London number, asked me if the party on the other end would be speaking English. It seemed to me an odd question to ask. "Rather better English than my own," I answered. I told my English friend about it straightaway. He found it amusing, and I suppose it is, faintly. But what is the point of it? That telephone operators nowadays know almost nothing about the world? That England's position in the world has been so greatly weakened that adults now walk the earth who do not know what language the English speak? Or is it that people, such as this telephone operator, get so locked into routine that they sometimes ask perfectly silly questions? I told it to two other people during the course of the day. I am writing about it now. Why do I feel the need to retell it? Is it, finally, a true anecdote?

Since I clearly have anecdote fever, perhaps I ought to attempt to define my germs. Samuel Johnson first defined an anecdote as "something yet unpublished; secret history." Later he enlarged his definition to include: "a biographical incident; a minute passage of private life." Isaac D'Israeli, in his *Disserta-*

tion on Anecdotes, called them "minute notices of human nature and of human learning." *The Oxford English Dictionary* is helpful in defining an anecdote as "the narrative of a detached incident, or of a single event, told as being in itself interesting or striking." Elizabeth Longford, who edited *The Oxford Book of Royal Anecdotes,* holds that all anecdotes "must make some attempt at punch." All these definitions are aided immensely by the reminder of Edmund Fuller, who edited the *Thesaurus of Anecdotes,* that "anecdotes are stories with points."

The anecdote has not had an altogether good press. While anecdotes can be one of the sweeter tricks up the sleeves of good talkers, they can as easily be the ultimate ammunition of bores, and often are. A Mrs. Warne-Cornish, when cornered by a bore telling a lengthy anecdote, was known to grasp him by the arm, lead him to a desk, and tell him, "It's so good, you must write it down." Eugen Weber has remarked that "a history of boredom would have much to tell," and much of it, it may well be, would be told in interminable anecdotes by men too confident of their charm. Even the best anecdotes ought not be too long, and anecdotes told about oneself ought perhaps be briefest of all.

"The evidence," social scientists have been known to say, "is purely anecdotal," which is meant as a put-down and a signal for dismissal, denoting something unscientific, unscholarly, trivial. But those among us who hold the anecdote in greater regard might be interested to learn, as I did not long ago from Robert Conquest, that defenders of the Soviet Union, even in its darkest days, used to dismiss the testimony of such writers as Boris Pasternak, Nadezhda Mandelstam, and Aleksandr Solzhenitsyn as "merely anecdotal," and thus not to be taken seriously. The "anecdotal" was posed against the "documentary," which meant the statistics and accounts given out by the Soviet government. On the same occasion, Robert Conquest said that his Russian friends in the Soviet Union could understand why their fellow Russians wished to lie about the conditions of life there—they, after all, faced serious deprivation and even death for telling the truth—but could never understand why so many writers in the West wished to lie about the Soviet Union. But then this, too, I suppose, is an anecdote.

"I have an answer, I have an answer," cried the yeshiva boy, running through the streets of his village. "Does anybody have a question?" I sometimes feel like a grown-up version of that boy, who, in my case, is crying out, "I have an anecdote, I have an anecdote. Does anybody have a conversation into which I might fit it?" E. M. Forster said that every writer has essentially one story to tell. But every man who fancies himself even slightly more than charmless has more than one anecdote to tell. He may have a dozen or more, which, over a long life, he may tell forty or sixty or even a hundred times. Your true anecdotalist knows not of restraint; repetition, to him no deterrent, is viewed chiefly as an opportunity for further polishing. He will take advantage of any opening to insert into conversation one of his gems, as he thinks of them, with only the least invitation or excuse. Nothing for it, I fear, short of an anecdoctomy.

I wrote "every man" in the previous paragraph. My experience reveals men to be more frequent anecdotalists than women. I have known women who tell anecdotes exceedingly well, but I have never known a woman who tells them regularly. Doubtless in olden days, when in upper-class English and American homes women went off, leaving men to their cigars and port, they had much more interesting things to convey to one another out of male hearing than warmed-over anecdotes. Women do not seem to have the same interest as men do in a certain kind of embellishment, exaggeration, artistic lying—those talents required by the true anecdotalist. Clifton Fadiman, in his excellent anthology *The Little, Brown Book of Anecdotes*, laments that his collection is "sadly deficient in anecdotes about women," and he speculates that this can be accounted for perhaps because literature has until fairly recently been largely written by men. Much truth to that, but I suspect, too, that this paucity is owing to a sense of good breeding in many women that did not allow them to tell anecdotes or to serve as grist for them. On this point, Mr. Fadiman, in his introduction, quotes Edith Head saying of Grace Kelly, "Grace doesn't allow anecdotes to happen to her."

Some while ago I informed a friend that I am an early riser. Ah, he asked, as if warming his hands before a nonexistent fire, did I know the story about the Austrian playwright (whose name I had never heard and have since forgot)? It seems that he happened to see an accident and was called in to be a witness in a trial that was to begin at 9:30 A.M. The playwright, being a man about town, a midnight-supper man, had never awoken before noon in his adult life. He missed the trial not once but thrice, each time causing the proceedings to be delayed. Finally the judge, in anger, wrote to the playwright to inform him that should he again miss performing his duty as a witness, he would be held in contempt of court, from which serious penalties would follow. Altering his schedule, the playwright retired earlier than usual the night before the appointed court date, and, not without struggle, arose, prepared his toilet, and at 9:00 A.M. opened the door of his town house leading onto the street. When he noted the street athrong with people, he was astounded. "Amazing!" he muttered to himself. "So many people on the street at this hour. Who would have guessed that in this city there were so many witnesses?"

A nice little story, I think. Not least, I admired my friend's tact in placing it so adeptly into our conversation. Shortly thereafter he, my friend, died, and not long after that I met another friend of his, and we condoled with each other about how we should miss him. "He was a great storyteller," this man averred. "You must know that story of his about there being so many witnesses on the street." He then told me other of our now-deceased friend's stories, and I had to allow that I knew them, too, including one that involved a splendid imitation of Sir Isaiah Berlin. Plainly, we were talking about an established repertoire of successful anecdotes that a bachelor, as our dead friend was, used to help pay his social way when dining out. (Hence the meaning of the phrase, which I did not understand when many years ago I first heard it, "dining out on a story.") My dear friend's performance was superior; his bill was marked paid in full in our home and, my guess is, in every other where he was a guest.

All anecdotes ought to be interesting, and the better ones also qualify as amusing, in the loose sense of the word. Not all need be humorous, though increasingly they have become so. In the *Thesaurus of Anecdotes,* Edmund Fuller remarks: "Today the true anecdote is still the counterpart of the parable and fable. Time has tended to shorten it somewhat and, as an attribute of our temperament, we have made it often funny." My own taste runs to anecdotes that have a bittersweet twist. Isaac D'Israeli, in defense of anecdotes as a form that truth can take, says that "opinions are fallible, but not examples," which seems to me a very clever observation. Not many anecdotes give more pleasure than those that show opinion and action in serious conflict. Surely, I am not alone in having a taste for those anecdotes that highlight people caught in the web of their own pretensions: the liberal politician with his children enrolled in expensive private schools, the psychologist whose three marriages have not turned out well, the official prude met grinning on the steps of the bordello in Macao.

Good anecdotes often catch famous people out in weaknesses to which they wouldn't wish to own up; they demonstrate their ignorance or vanity or impossible self-importance, and they usually have a nice touch of comeuppance at the close. A friend not long ago told me an anecdote about the playwright Harold Pinter, who occasionally also writes less than impressive poems. Usually he makes copies of these poems and sends them to thirty or so friends, then sits patiently back to await their praise. According to the anecdote, he had apparently written such a poem about the famous English cricketer Len Hutton, which, in its entirety, read:

> I knew Len Hutton in his prime.
> Another time, another time.

Pinter, the anecdote goes, waited fully two weeks for a response, but none was forthcoming. Finally, able to wait no longer, Pinter called up one of the people to whom he had sent the poem. He claimed that he was concerned about its arrival, the mails being so unreliable, as everyone knows they now are. Did this man receive the poem? Pinter wanted to know. "Actually," the fellow said, "I received it ten days ago." What did he think of the poem? Pinter wondered. "Actually," the poor fellow said, "I haven't quite finished it."

A lovely little anecdote, I think, but it wouldn't be anywhere near so good if it didn't have a name attached to it, and it is all the better for having a recognizable name. If it were an anecdote about an unnamed poet or obscure playwright, it would, I suppose, be faintly amusing, but only faintly. Another example illustrates the same point. I was not long ago talking with a friend, who has been much closer to the working of government than I, about those congressmen and senators who have real power as opposed to those who are very good at gaining attention for themselves in the press and on television.

My friend then told me that he was once, at a dinner, seated next to a powerful but not especially well known congressman from Brooklyn named John Rooney, whom he asked about the performance in the Congress of John Lindsay, who had by then gone on to be mayor of New York. "I would describe John Lindsay's record in Congress," Rooney said, "as no hits, no runs, no errors. And the reason he made no errors," he added, "is that he never got near the ball." Good stuff, but, again, much less good if unconnected to an actual name.

Not all anecdotes need be, implicitly, put-downs, deflating and diminishing the pompous and the putatively great. Some anecdotes are stories of pluck in the face of misfortune or of acts of moral elegance. Many anecdotes about Winston Churchill seem to be of this kind, though many others have to do with accounts of his brilliant repartee. Displays of repartee and spontaneous wit themselves often make for mini-anecdotes. Anecdotes about Babe Ruth are mainly about his feats of eating and dancing between the sheets and about the comedy brought about by his candor. When once asked if he was interested in any one character in history—Lincoln, Washington, and Napoleon were mentioned—he said that he couldn't say, since he had never met any of those guys, which, when one comes to think about it, isn't so stupid. The rebarbative personality of W. C. Fields, who, as Kenneth Tynan once said, "played straight man to a malevolent universe," was powerfully productive of anecdote, most of which derived from his wicked tongue. "And how," Fields once said on camera to Mae West, "is my little brood mare?"

But then some people are more anecdotable than others. Outsized personalities—Bismarck, Sarah Bernhardt, Charlie Parker—tend to generate anecdotes almost as a condition of their being. Stick around one such person long enough, as James Boswell learned to his everlasting fame, and you will have anecdotes in more than sufficient supply, for the good reason that what such people say and do is so often amusing, odd, outrageous, penetrating, charming, foolish, vain, significant—all the things that make for good anecdotes.

Henry James was perhaps the most highly anecdotable among writers of the relatively recent past. Nearly everyone who met him brought away an anecdote or a scrap that, with a touch or two of artful embellishment, could be turned into one. Whether it was something witty or profound or absurd, James seemed to leave everyone who met him with a literary souvenir. One thinks of James saying, in response to Edith Wharton's telling him that the grand automobile they were sitting in was purchased in part from the royalties of her last novel, that he had bought a wheelbarrow with the royalties from his last novel and intended to have it painted with the royalties from his next.

Oddly, James did not himself tell many anecdotes, though he could be a severe critic of badly told ones. Ford Madox Ford, whose truth quotient wasn't always the highest, recounted a story of Henry James imitating Mr. William Rossetti telling, and telling badly, of witnessing Herbert Spencer propose marriage to George Eliot. After mimicking the absurdly stiff way in which the anecdote was told, James remarked: "Is that the way to tell *that* story?" Doubtless James did not himself tell many anecdotes because he used all such material for his own stories and novels. There is a moderately well known story about James abruptly leaving a London dinner party during someone's telling an anecdote that he thought might be useful to him—he left precisely at the point in the anecdote where he felt it would be best for him not to hear more, so that his imagination could fill in the rest. This is in part corroborated by his friend Violet Hunt recounting how she "used to suffer, as other people did who told him anything that might

amuse him, from the summarily truncated anecdote. He would
hold up a story as soon as he had got all he needed out of it;
extend a finger—'Thank you, I've got as much—all I want'—
and leave you with the point of your anecdote on your hands."

Can it be that great men and women do not tell anecdotes
because they recognize that their purpose is to furnish the
material for the anecdotes of others? Exceptions exist: Virgil
Thomson claimed that "Stravinsky is always shaping great
man stories about himself," though the job must have been
made easier owing to Stravinsky's having been very nearly a
great man in fact. Still, when Napoleon met Goethe and announced, *"Voilà un homme!"* it must have been a third party,
not Napoleon or Goethe, who told the story. The one striking
exception I can think of to the rule that the great do not usually
indulge in anecdote telling is Abraham Lincoln, who had a
genuine love for it. In Carl Sandburg's biography of Lincoln,
a Pittsfield, Illinois, woman named Susan Scanland says of
Lincoln, who was then still a lawyer: "The laziest man there
ever was, good for nothing except to tell stories." In the Illinois
state legislature, Lincoln, to make a point, would on occasion
say, "I beg leave to tell an anecdote," and then, usually quite
winningly, do so. A good many anecdotes have apparently
been falsely attributed to Lincoln. But Lincoln anecdotes, it
must be said, tend to be close to parables, usually, even when
amusing, carrying a moral freight heavier than most anecdotalists usually want to tote around or than most anecdotes can
bear.

Men of action don't tend to tell anecdotes, partly for reasons of temperament, partly because anecdotes are generally
considered small talk and hence beneath them, though I myself
consider a well-told anecdote a minor work of art and thus, if
small talk it be, then small talk carried to the highest power.
Perhaps, though, this is why those writers who have wished to

bill themselves as men of action—in our century they include André Malraux, Ernest Hemingway, and, at a much reduced level, Norman Mailer—have always seemed slightly unbelievable, if not actually comic, when doing so. In the second volume of his autobiography, Anthony Burgess remarks that at a certain point in his life, he "was too much preoccupied with living my own life to invent lives for others." Something to it. Those who truly do, needn't really tell; and when they do tell, they seem a bit diminished by doing so.

I remember, as a student at a party at the University of Chicago, hearing about a small and bespectacled American graduate student who asked a tall Nigerian student with an Oxford accent what it was like to hunt lion. The graduate student went on at great length, beseeching the Nigerian to tell him what it was like, standing there, while this magnificent beast, intent on your death, powerful paws pounding down on the dry African plain, the two of you alone under the boiling sun, the lion fifty, forty, thirty, twenty, now only ten yards away, ten yards between you and death—what, good God, he wanted to know, was it like? "Had you been there, Mr. Slotnik," replied the Nigerian, in splendidly enunciated English, "I daresay you'd have wet your pants."

I used to tell that anecdote fairly often, even though it wasn't quite mine to tell. I used also to tell an anecdote about a man named Severn Darden, who was a University of Chicago campus character some six or seven years before I arrived at the school. (Darden, along with Mike Nichols and Elaine May, was one of the leading figures in the Compass Players, the cabaret company that became known as Second City; he later had a number of tertiary roles in the movies, but was never allowed in the movies to do anything so winning as his own cabaret improvisations.) Darden dressed the part of a character; heavyset, he had one of the country's early unkempt beards and often went about wearing a cape. The cape had a significant role in the anecdote.

As the anecdote goes, Severn Darden was, in the cool of an autumn evening, strolling about the university's main quadrangle, reflecting on the vicissitudes of life as he languidly tossed rocks through the windows of the university's ersatz Gothic buildings. Two of the university's security policemen, an older and not a physically impressive duo, caught him in the act and, attempting to apprehend him, gave chase. Darden lit out—with his bulk, one imagines not very swiftly—for nearby Rockefeller Chapel. Up the nave of the immense chapel Darden ran, the elderly security cops not so much hotly as perhaps tepidly in pursuit; he hopped up on the altar, drew his cape back across his mouth and nose, and, in the voice of a broken-down Shakespearean actor, croaked out, "Sanctuary, sanctuary, sanctuary."

I have no idea whether or not this ever really happened. I never met Severn Darden and so never confirmed its truth. But I told it as if it were true. I told it exclusively to people who had not gone to the university. I told it because I thought it not only funny in itself—I still find it mildly amusing—but because it gave a good bit of color to life among the gray Gothic at the University of Chicago, which, as I realize now, needed it. So, too, did I need a bit of color in those days—as an undergraduate in that primarily graduate institution, my own position was akin to that of an intellectual tourist—and I think that in telling exotic anecdotes about the University of Chicago, I was hoping that some of the color I attempted to infuse into university life would rub off onto me. I am fairly sure that none did. I am not even sure that anyone believed such anecdotes or found them in the least interesting. But I felt the need to tell them nevertheless. Life, like the show, must go on, even if one is forced to half make it up.

Still, my telling these anecdotes marked a demotion in my emotional life. Before this I had been someone about whom anecdotes were told; or when I myself told an anecdote, I was usually somewhere attractively near the center of the action. Truth to tell, I did what I could to help this along. If I had some minor exploit to my credit, I added a touch of coloring to it in the telling where needed; I made sure word of it got around; and if the story came back to me even better than my own touch-ups had rendered it, well, I let it stand. Did I, as an adolescent, do somewhat outrageous things with a sense that the more outrageous they were, the more readily anecdotable they were likely to become? I believe I did. If, as I sensed long before I read it, all the world's a stage, I felt it best to begin as soon as possible designing my own part and contrived early to do so.

I regaled friends with accounts of slipping out of the house to join an all-night poker game, of being caught in flagrante delicto by suburban police in the backseat of a cream-colored-with-green-trim 1954 Chevy Bel Air, of going to two racetracks in the same day, of a wildly illicit friendship with an impressively devious teacher. I turned these events and incidents into anecdotes that, I like to think even now, nearly forty years later, were not without their small artful touches. I had the good sense not to build myself up too much in these stories, for the audience of my friends was a wary and highly critical one, and going too far could be punished. One boy who went to school with us was given, to go with his penchant for exaggeration, the nickname of Uncle Remus, after Joel Chandler Harris's teller of fairy-tale parables, which he was forced to carry through his school days, and it was no light load. In my own anecdotes, I always made sure to add many comic details, both for verisimilitude and for sheer entertainment. I wanted nothing more than to be thought to have a remarkable life, and the most efficient way of obtaining this reputation was, through the subtleties of storytelling, to create one for myself.

I could, of course, be quite deceived about the effect of my youthful performance. It may well be that, with my handful of stories, I was even then thought a bore, possibly a liar, maybe someone too eager to please. But I don't think so. I think my anecdotes, designed to seem neither self-aggrandizing nor hopelessly exaggerated, came off fairly well. When I embellished, invented details—"God is in the details," Mies van der Rohe is supposed to have said, but not in those of my youthful anecdotes, He wasn't—shaped, and polished my rough experience into anecdotes with which I hoped to enrapture my friends, I was, quite without realizing it, setting the trap for the man I would later become. I would henceforth become someone whose life seemed organized for the manufacture of fresh anecdotes. Ever after I would become one of those odd people who take their task on earth to be not to live life but to tell, or actually retell, it. Chekhov knew a thing or two about this strange condition, and into the mouth of the writer Trigorin, a character in *The Seagull*, he put these words:

Oh, it's a crazy sort of life! . . . Do you see that cloud? Looks remarkably like a grand piano, doesn't it? The moment I saw it, I thought, I mustn't forget to mention somewhere in my story that a cloud looking like a grand piano sailed across the sky. . . . I snap up every word, every sentence you or I utter, just for the sake of locking them away in my literary lumber room. . . . And so it goes on and on. I feel that I am devouring my own life.

A friend, a lawyer, recently told me that he is bored blue listening to other lawyers tell anecdotes about their cases. He is bored listening to himself retell stories about his own cases. "I'm ready to wipe the hard disk clean," he said. But then every occupation—law, medicine, politics—has its own ample fund of anecdotes. Alas, the people with the best source of anec-dotes—psychiatrists, psychoanalysts, and others in the head trades—are supposed to keep them to themselves. For the most part, I am sure that they do. Still, the motto of psychology, as W. H. Auden once remarked, ought to be "Have you heard this one?" One I had never heard before was told to me by a psychiatrist I scarcely knew, with whom I was talking about memory lapses. It concerned a patient of his, a female gynecol-ogist, who told him that she had lost the capacity to remember any of her patients' names and could only call these names up through recognition of their private parts. Fantastico!—to put it very mildly.

In lines of work where temperament is given relatively free rein—in opera, music, the theater—where egoism runs ram-pant and adulation is handed out in triple scoops, the incidence of memorable anecdote is especially high. It will come as no surprise that there are books of anecdotes devoted to all these occupations just as there are books of anecdotes about royalty and about writers (two other ego-heavy occupations). There is as yet, so far as I know, no *Oxford Book of Plumbing Anecdotes*, though doubtless the material for such a book is there in abun-dance.

I am glad that books of anecdotes exist, without particularly wishing to read through any of them. They are rather like collections of jokes—too much of a good thing—and even when one comes to them with what one supposed was a serious appetite for anecdote, one discovers oneself fairly quickly sated. Used too patently in journalism—"In Klamath Falls, Oregon, last week a man sued his left leg"—as I thought they were in the news magazines before I stopped reading them, anecdotes seem dopey at best, a ridiculous falsity at worst. To succeed an anecdote requires an air of spontaneity, even if that air is slightly fraudulent.

"Of conversation as I love it," wrote Evelyn Waugh in *The*

Loved One, "with anecdote occurring spontaneously and aptly, jokes growing and taking shape, fantasy—they [Americans] know nothing." A hard man, Evelyn Waugh, and not least hard on us Yanks. But I suppose he has to be forgiven for supplying, through his own life, a rich fund of anecdotes. Most of these had to do with his uttering some deliciously witty, or devastatingly outrageous, remark, such as the following: when, as a captain in the British army during World War II, he came out of his foxhole during a German aerial bombardment in Yugoslavia, he was supposed to have looked up at the sky and declared, "Like all things German, this is vastly overdone."

"Remarks aren't literature," Gertrude Stein once said to Ernest Hemingway. But remarks, intrinsically clever and well enough placed, can in themselves constitute anecdotes. Almost every Samuel Goldwynism seems a self-contained anecdote: "I am willing to admit I may not always be right," he once told one of his subalterns, "but I am never wrong," and, the odd thing is, I believe I know what he meant. When Bruno Walter went to visit Gustav Mahler at his new country house, Walter looked up, enchanted, at the nearby mountains. "Don't trouble yourself," Mahler said, "I've already composed all that." That may seem only an amusing remark, but I think it qualifies as an anecdote because it contains, in such brief compass, so much information: about the parties involved, about rivalry among artists, about artistic creation.

I myself like to quote the remarks of people I have known who are now dead, when the remarks themselves seem to have the kind of point that qualifies as anecdotal, for they serve the double purpose of amusing the listener and bringing these people, however briefly, back to life. "The least expensive way to acquire a book," Arnaldo Momigliano once said to me apropos of books given to one by their authors, "remains to buy it," by which he meant that if you bought a book, at least you didn't have to read it. At a meeting at which I sat next to the greatly Teutonic conductor of opera Kurt Herbert Adler, he leaned next to me and whispered something, of which I could only make out the word "lozenges." I handed him a pack of Life Savers I happened to have on me, which he turned down politely with the reply, "I zed Los Angeles." I once had some editorial business with the economic historian Alexander Gerschenkron. I told him that I would shortly be sending him galley proofs of an essay he had written. "I shouldn't worry about it," he said coolly. "I'll probably be dead by the time you have them." And he was. This, I believe, constitutes an anecdote.

One of the problems with remarks as anecdotes is that of misattribution. Clifton Fadiman is surely correct when he says that a great many mots and joky incidents either never happened or were "fathered on notables." He cites in this regard many of the splendid put-down retorts attributed to Dorothy Parker, Oscar Levant, and Groucho Marx. Along with misattribution must be placed misappropriation. Someone once reported to me that a man we both knew had said that the three most overrated things in life were home cooking, marital sex, and Princeton, which I thought very funny. When I repeated it to someone else, he said, "Oh, I heard that one years ago, only then it was Harvard."

It may be that misattribution, misappropriation, near-total expropriation are in the very nature of the anecdotal enterprise. One does what one can with the material at hand. A reviewer of Kingsley Amis's *Memoirs* noted that "one gets the distinct impression that many of these anecdotes have been carefully squirreled away for decades awaiting this opportunity for airing." In his book Amis all but concedes the point, practically embraces it, when he writes that his "attention and emphasis tend to go to those people and those characteristics of theirs that are suitable to an anecdotal or at least a narrative approach, as in a novel."

Clifton Fadiman calls anecdotes "the thistledown for biography," which they most certainly are. Parson Weems's famous biography of George Washington, after all, carries the lengthy title of *The Life of George Washington with Curious Anecdotes, Equally Honorable to Himself and Exemplary to His Young Countrymen.* But anecdotes into the bargain can also supply the seed, planted in the right soil, out of which the flower of art can grow. I was at a small dinner party recently when, after dessert, the host, a fine talker, was stirred by something one of his guests had said to mention that this reminded him of a story. He began: "Sernoff, who was then head of the KGB in London, met with the head man at Scotland Yard, whom he asked, 'How many Jews are there in England?' " I felt I was listening to Somerset Maugham; I was transported; this was no doubt a true story, but it was also art.

Not long after, I had lunch with someone with whom I had gone to high school, who reported to me that a friend of his who went to our school—but who was not someone I had known well—reported to him that, more than thirty years after high school, he had had a brief love affair with a girl (now woman) about whom we all fantasized in those adolescent days. She was a girl who was not only beautiful but notably kind. He, this fellow, had not had a markedly successful life, and this seemed to be a great high point in it. Being told the story, I felt a bit like Henry James at that London dinner he so swiftly departed. I wanted to leave before I heard more, for in this anecdote resided a lovely short story, but to have done so—we were in a restaurant—would have been to have stuck my lunch companion with the check, which would, I fear, only have resulted in an anecdote about my cheapness.

Perhaps the best anecdote in history is the story of Antony

and Cleopatra. It has everything: high stakes, big names, sex.
All that is missing is humor. But then no anecdote can have
everything. As any student of anecdotes instinctively knows,
that is one of the fine things about them. If anecdotes are a form
of knowledge—about the zaniness of human behavior, about
the shocking stupidity as well as the startling intelligence of
people, about our irrationality, our unpredictability, our hopeless comicality—then it is a form of knowledge that is cumula-
tive and yet without end. If anecdotes teach anything at all, it
is probably that it is best never to think we know the last word
about any human heart, not even our own.

Which reminds me of the time . . .

Time on My Hands, Me in My Arms

As we grow old, our sense of the value of time becomes vivid. Nothing else indeed, seems of any consequence.

—*William Hazlitt*

The other night, while I was struggling to stay awake late in the second, longish act of a less than superior performance of Handel's *Semele* and my mind was floating off and wandering where it wished, two things occurred to me: first, I wasn't going to make it through the third act; and, second, evenings may not be the best time for concerts, at least not for those of us who arise early in the morning. What might be a good time for a concert? I asked myself. Ten in the morning, I decided. But then listening to serious music fairly late into the night is only one item that, in my view, is badly placed in time. Others occurred to me. Undergraduate education is probably best begun at the age of forty, when one is a bit wiser about the world and so can better test the wisdom of both books and teachers. Along with serious education, sexual vigor is probably wasted on the young. People would be better off coming into their greatest sexual strength in middle age, when they begin to know what they are doing. While I was at it, it also occurred to me that it might be useful to place death somewhere other than at the end of a person's life, so that he or she wouldn't have to spend so damn much time thinking about it.

To fill in the time between thoughts about death—the "ugly Customer," Hazlitt called it—one can think about time itself. Some of us already do, and I, increasingly as I sense my own time running out, am among them. A vast amount, in both a philosophical and a poetical way, has been said on the subject, though not much that I have seen helps. Like everyone else, I know that time flies, often going about in a winged chariot; that it is probably a sound idea not to delay picking up any rosebuds that fall within reach before the curtain drops; that some among us leave footprints in its sands; that procrastination is its thief; that it is equivalent to money; that it is the great healer; that it is the avenger, the devourer of everything, the reaper, the refreshing river; you name it, friend, time is it. So what else, you might say, is new?

Can it be that to think about time is the greatest waste of time of all? If so, I have wasted more than my share in this way. I cannot remember when time wasn't on my mind. When I was very young, I thought longingly of how good life would be when, with the passage of time, I grew older, a condition I earnestly wished to see come about. I was something like Philip Larkin, who had his first doubts about heaven upon hearing that there one would become a child again, when what he, Larkin, longed for was the prospect of adult life and feared being deprived of its perks, among them "money, keys, wallet, letters, books, long-playing records, drinks, the opposite sex, and other solaces of adulthood," and above all not having to deal any longer with children.

Time had a different feel when I was young. It felt, to begin with, much longer. Summers especially seemed lavish in their lengthiness. I can recall endless sunny summer days, when I was ten or eleven, playing a variant of baseball called line-ball on our gravelly school playground, with breaks for nickel-a-bottle grape soda drawn from an ice-laden metal case at Miller's School Store, days that seemed longer than entire fiscal quarters do now. Drives on vacations with my parents to visit relatives in Canada stretched out longer than reaching Mecca must have seemed to Sir Richard Burton. Events one looked forward to—the end of school term not least among them—took what felt like millennia to arrive. Now the minutes and often the hours move quite as slowly as then. It is, alas, only the months, years, even decades that rush by.

Sorry to strike so downbeat a note so early, but the difference between time now and time when I was young is the prospect of death. Not that I was ever ignorant of death, but I was rather better at keeping thoughts of it at bay. I still don't have the attention span to brood about it for very long, but it does keep bobbing up in my stream of consciousness, like some rusty, jagged tin can that blights the otherwise fairly clear waters of my thought. By the time one reaches forty, unless one is a very great fool, one realizes that one is no longer playing with anything like a fully loaded shot-clock, to take a trope from the National Basketball Association. By fifty, despite all the cheerful talk about expanded life spans, it is better to assume that one is already playing in overtime.

I don't think myself a dark character, but I have always assumed that I could be taken out of the game at any time through death by heart attack, cancer, plane crash, car accident, falling object, choking on food, murder, or any other more or less painful, ignominious, or tragicomic mode of departure. In whatever manner the ugly Customer arrives, I hope that, upon greeting him, I shall have the strength to be ticked off by his appearance—and ticked, as the kids say, to the max. But when he shows up I don't think I shall be surprised. I have been expecting him for years.

Much in the way I live is based on I won't say a bargain— he doesn't make deals—but an attempt to stall off the ugly Customer. I quit smoking when I did, some sixteen years ago, chiefly because I would have thought myself silly, really quite embarrassed, to have to leave life seven or eight years earlier than scheduled because of the small but real pleasures of the weed. I restrain the glutton in myself for much the same reason. I try to work efficiently so that I can get the most out of myself, in good part because I should feel an idiot on my deathbed knowing that, in this regard as doubtless in many another, I had blown it by wasting time.

T. S. Eliot, himself obsessed by time, noted:

> Time present and time past
> Are both perhaps present in time future,
> And time future contained in time past.
> If all time is eternally present
> All time is unredeemable.

I am betting otherwise. I am living as if I can redeem time; or, perhaps more precisely, redeem myself in the time left to me by pressing for more time and hoping to make the most of what portion of this abstract but clearly precious commodity remains to me.

Some people appear to live with very little consciousness of time, and a part of me admires them, as one tends to admire those who can do a great many of the things one cannot oneself do. They do not feel themselves chased, hounded, under a strong obligation to keep glancing up at the clock. Other people pretend to ignore time: dressing younger than their years, indulging (sorry for this language of moral disapproval, but I cannot control myself) in the fantasy that time hasn't really touched them, never permitting time to enter into their calculations or even into the assumptions behind their lives. Many of both sorts of people live by the principle of free fall, do not plan beyond next week, don't even wear a watch. They should only live and be well, as the Jews used to say of the Tsar, but not too close to me.

I, very differently, factor time into everything I do. Any day that I sleep past 6:00 A.M. I consider very near a lost day. Want to set me on the road to flip city? Change my time zone, steal my watch, keep the exact hour from me. I should crack, crumble, tell you the combination of the safe containing the diamonds, reveal where the secret weapons are hidden, anything you want to know—if only you will let me know what time it is. I am one of those people who think digital clocks a swell invention, because I like to know to the minute what time it is when I awake at night. The lit-up digital clock—now here is real progress, at least for those among us who are sufficiently compulsive, and to be compulsive, I have generally found, is sufficient unto itself.

This sense of being haunted by time was not something I grew up with. I don't believe I owned my first wristwatch until I went off to college. Before then time was not something that seemed to press upon me; light and dark was all I needed to know. This first watch was a round-faced Bulova, which showed its innards through its crystal, and was given to me by my father. Watches have become a great status symbol in our day. *Town & Country, Vanity Fair, Esquire,* and other of the high-glitz magazines must be able to pay the rent and the printer with the advertisements they run for watches. Rolex watches are high on the list of stealables—if there can be "collectibles," why not stealables—being easily fenced. Truman Capote, I seem to recall, used to buy wafer-thin watches for his friends. He would doubtless have been appalled by the coarseness of my rectangular Seiko, but I can live with such criticism. I don't look to my wrist for my status, for one thing; and, for another, I am already on a tight enough schedule not to worry about owning a watch that loses a minute or so every few years, especially since I feel I myself lose hours, days, whole weeks in indolence, serious sloth, and diversions cunningly self-devised.

Just who set up this schedule for me is far from clear. But once I had determined, however roughly, what it was I wanted to do in life, the schedule went quietly, inexorably into effect. "To produce some little exemplary works of art is my narrow and lowly dream," wrote Henry James, another man on a schedule, to his friend Grace Norton. My own dream, to be sure, was a good bit lower and narrower than Henry James's, but I did know that I wanted to get a good deal of writing done, and I didn't want to be one of those writers who are always complaining about how painful writing is in defense of their own small output. But before I could put my own schedule into effect I had first to learn how to write and then to discover what it was I wished to write. Perhaps it was because it took me so long to get these little prerequisites out of the way—I was nearly forty when they were—that the feeling of the clock always running, of time ticking away, of the gun about to go off continues to haunt me.

By a schedule I do not mean anything all that specific: 11:00–11:10 A.M., author free, that sort of thing. Instead I have in mind the sense that certain things ought to be done by certain ages, that if time is truly money, as the adage has it, then it ought not to be wasted, damn it. If you think of yourself as a writer, then by thirty you ought to have published a book, which, by the way, I hadn't. You have the summer off from teaching, you ought to have something to show for it by autumn: essays, stories, pages of a new book. Thinking or reading is not good enough. (Whenever I come across a politician or business executive who, when written up in the press, mentions that one of his hobbies is reading, I invariably mutter, so, too, is one of my hobbies reading—and another is breathing.) If you are on a schedule, it's not good enough, either, simply to enjoy yourself. Not that enjoyment is disallowed, or breaks, or even holidays precluded. But the schedule must be met. No pain, no gain; no work, you're a jerk.

I had a friend, an intelligent and very learned man, who gave no hint of having been in the least troubled by time. He was a university teacher, who taught well but scarcely bothered to publish. After his retirement from teaching, the one mild pressure in his life, meeting with his classes, was removed. He rose, read the daily press with a mordant eye, watched one of the morning television talk shows with his second cup of coffee, drew a bit, read some, taught himself (slowly) the rudiments of Chinese, wrote comic letters, looked up French words, considered etymologies of English ones, gave delight to his friends, took pleasure in his food and drink, and thus lived out his days until a benevolent (or so it seems in retrospect) heart attack took him out of what seemed a not very taxing game. It seems rather pointless to say of him "May he rest in peace," since, as near as I can determine, he pretty much lived in peace. I'm not sure he owned a watch. Not a man, clearly, on a schedule.

Did he, I have often wondered, have any doubts? Had he got the most out of himself? In suppressing ambition, did he not also kill a certain kind of joy—that very genuine joy connected with achievement? He left no children. His friends, those who have not already died, grow old. His memory will fairly soon be extinguished. He was too clever a man not to have thought about all this. He lived, if not all that intensely, still almost entirely in the *now*. He met all his obligations, not least among them giving pleasure to his friends, though apparently he never felt that he owed any obligations to the future. Was he more or less intelligent than I in eschewing the notion of a schedule?

I wish I had the answer to that question, but even if my friend was right and I am wrong, it is too late for me to change. When it comes to time, I am in the condition of a miser whose money is in gold dust in a large sack that has a hole he cannot find. I do not mean to say that I am incapable of leisure—of enjoying the hills of Tuscany, the seacoast of Maine; of languishing, drink in hand, in lengthy whimsical talk with friends—for I am not, but I do view myself as entitled to such delights only if I produce in sufficient measure to have earned it. What after all is the point of being compulsive if you don't feel yourself compelled, and most of the time? In saying this I suppose I resemble the writer La Harpe, of whom Chamfort said that he "hid his vices behind his faults." But the plain fact is that there isn't much I can do about my condition with respect to time. Do older, well-to-do Jewish women drive Japanese cars? Do surrealists use dental floss? Does the Institute for Advanced Study at Princeton have an office pool for the Super Bowl? All of these things go against nature. Asking me to ease up would go against mine.

If anything, I feel time pressing down harder, more insistently than ever. Among the things I feel lost to me is what I believe is nowadays called turnaround time. The city magazine in my town—like so many magazines devoted to consumer interests it informs readers of the ten best places to get creole gum balls, the eight best used phylactery shops in town, and the five most efficient hospitals to go to for a double lobotomy—not long ago ran a piece about people who made radical career changes when well into middle age. There was the scientist who became a sculptor, the secretary who became a journalist, the small businessman who became a chef, the lawyer who became a filmmaker, the nurse who became a lawyer, the chiropodist who became a commodities trader . . . you get the drift. True, the chef has a wife who is a professor at a prominent business school, but let us not get caught up in details. The piece is titled "Awakenings," and its point is that life is infinitely expandable, filled with practically endless possibilities, and that there is time enough—for everything. Do you believe this? If you do, I know where there is some chiropractic equipment that I could arrange to get you cheap.

I don't believe it, not for a single valuable moment. The clock is running, Reuben, and if you don't believe it you are making a serious mistake. In the National Football League they sometimes speak of a man dropping a pass because "he heard footsteps," by which they mean that he heard the heavy tread of a bruising defensive player about to crunch him once he caught the pass. I do not hear footsteps but the tickings, the endless tickings, of a clock in my head. I am running what, in the same league, they call a two-minute drill, playing against the clock. I have no urge to mount a motorcycle and head for the coast, to sail the Atlantic alone with the woman I love and a complete set of the Great Books in our cabin. I am too old to change careers—even if I wanted to, which I don't—too old to have a midlife crisis, though I must confess that, even at midlife, which must have passed some while back, I never felt the need for one. I am too old even to change my hairstyle—and consider myself fortunate to have enough hair left at my age to be able to reject the possibility.

Now in my late fifties, I realize that I am not chronologically old; nor do I feel spiritually old. But the determining factor here is that I happen to view my life not as malleable material, to be shaped and reshaped as often as the mood or the time-spirit takes me, but as a work of art—possibly, I grant you, a botched one—that I have been putting together for more than half a century and am not about to abandon now. I have it in mind to end my days reading Tacitus and contemplating the astonishing vagaries of human nature, and not running in the old codgers' marathon and dancing the boogaloo that same evening at Gay Nineties Night at the home for the especially fit elderly.

I realize that I am unlikely to make anything like serious philosophical penetration into the mysteries of time, and it would be silly to waste much of my time (or yours) in attempting to do so. Not even Saint Augustine felt himself at ease in these turbulent intellectual waters. "What is time?" he asks in *The Confessions.* "I know what it is if no one asks me what it is; but if I want to explain it to someone who has asked me, I find that I do not know." It was Saint Augustine who claimed that his soul was "on fire to solve this very complicated enigma," and confessed that, on this subject, it was "a bad state indeed to be in, not even to know what it is that I do not know!" In Book XI of *The Confessions,* Saint Augustine makes many an elegant formulation and cuts many a fine distinction, yet finally concludes that the impressions that things leave in the mind form the measure of time—that time, essentially, is in one's mind. This does not seem very satisfactory, except for the inconvenient fact that it also seems true.

It seems true because it accounts for the duality of time—its strict measurability on the one hand, and on the other its highly variable measure in our minds, so that there are hours that feel like days and days that, in retrospect, feel like an hour. It is the intrinsic irrationality of time within the extrinsically most strict system of rationality that gives time its (almost) endless fascination. The invention that is needed to take account of this duality, obviously, is a clock that measures both real and psychological time. Details would need to be worked out, of course, but it seems to me that such a clock would measure how long certain dull lectures and dreary dinner parties *really* are.

The psychological measure of time would be extremely important if one knew precisely how much of it one had left. A common fantasy, surely, is that of being told that one has, say, six months to live. How, if one could get around and function normally, would one spend the time? The trick, I should think, would be to find ways of doing the things that one enjoys most, which almost always make time pass all too quickly, but under conditions in which time passes very slowly. I, for example, would eat chocolate-covered orange peels, which seems to take no time at all, but only at laundromats, where time hangs so heavily.

That is no example, you say, that is an absurdity. But then, I would rejoin, so often is time, with its mixture of the real and the unreal. Consider age. Someone once said that, early in life, a woman decides whether she will live as if she is either eighteen or eighty, and then, having decided, sticks with her decision throughout her life. Something to it. I lock in friends at certain ages, and then am astonished to learn that they have become—who'd have thunk it—senior bloody citizens. The lives of certain writers have been built upon the assumption that they will always be at ages they have long since passed. The novelist Norman Mailer's entire career, with its attraction to violence and let-'er-rip, leaping-off-the-high-dive sex, assumes a man in his late thirties, early forties, tops, not the white-haired, potbellied little grandpa Mailer has become. John Updike has always seemed the too-sensitive sixteen-year-old, Philip Roth the unpleasant wise guy at nineteen, John Irving about fourteen. Best, probably, for a writer to allow a bit of slack in his style to accommodate the distinct possibility of arthritis and collecting Social Security.

Much of this aspect of time has to do with how one regards oneself. One of the hallmarks of our time is that people want to seem as youthful as possible for as long as possible. Some occupations encourage this, some discourage it. What man who as a boy was interested in sports is not taken aback when he first hears an athlete ten or so years younger than he described as "a wily veteran" or "over the hill"? Careers in sports are much under the tyranny of time. Academic careers permit one to remain as young, even childish, as one wishes, almost up to the grave. Professors who went to graduate school in the 1960s or early 1970s, though now themselves in their forties or fifties, dress largely as their students do. They wear jeans, tote backpacks, don't think much about haircuts. Many of them, for all I know, may wish to be buried in denim, a Sony Walkman plugged into their ears (extremely long-playing batteries, I trust, included). "There is," writes Milan Kundera in his novel *Immortality,* "a certain part of all of us that lives outside time. Perhaps we become aware of our age only at exceptional moments and most of the time we are ageless." I suspect that this is probably true for most people, though I know it isn't true for me.

As for me, I have begun to conclude that I have the gift of perpetual middle age. I at any rate think it a gift. I hope it is as perpetual as such things are permitted to be, and I know that I am now middle-aged chronologically as well as spiritually. I rather like being middle-aged. I feel in this regard like Henry James, who wrote to a friend: "I like growing old: fifty-six!—but I don't like growing *older.* I quite love my present age and the compensations, simplifications, freedom, independences, memories, advantages of it. But I don't keep it long enough—it passes too quickly." Just so. How to slow things down, that seems to me the question. Living all one's life in laundromats or listening to commencement addresses delivered by the

prime minister of Sweden—a little time stopper I once under-
went—doesn't seem to me quite the solution.

One of the habits of the middle-aged (and above) that I have
had for a number of years now is, when the newspaper arrives,
going first to the obituaries. Ezra Pound said that literature is
news that stays news; the same is true about death, which also
stays news; and I have long found the obituaries the most
interesting and important item in the papers. Each morning I
turn to them looking for—what? In part for notification of the
death of the famous, the death of enemies, the element of
surprise that someone whom one thought long dead was until
the day before still alive, the shock of youthful death through
AIDS. All these items the obituary columns supply.

I also like to read the obituaries for a sense of averages and
hence of probabilities. I prefer it when there are six or seven
deaths of persons in their nineties: a lawyer who worked at
NATO, an Italian archaeologist, a monsignor, an ex-judge, a
woman who danced for Diaghilev. One hopes—against
hope—that these are all people who were able to slip off the
earth without first raising the yellow flag of senility. I cannot
remember her last name, but a few years ago I was much
touched by the brief obituary notice of a woman whose first
name was Lily, a lepidopterist who had discovered and named
a butterfly and who died—perhaps here the euphemisms
"passed away" and "expired" for once apply—at one hundred
years old. Lovely Lily, may you rest in a gentle place where
perhaps a butterfly will sense your originality and rename you.

Quite as often the obituary pages contain news of men and
women my age and younger who have been taken out of the
game by cancer and heart attack. Then one's own heartbeat
feels a bit irregular, one's respiration a touch jumpy, one begins
to worry about that minuscule lump just below the wrist.
"Identification," the boys in the head trades call it, but the

more precise phrase is "fear of death." My late friend Erich Heller used to say that he was not afraid of death; it was only dying that had him worried. Hazlitt, who after a hard life filled with disappointment pegged out at fifty-two, thought that "in reflecting on death generally, we mix up the idea of life with it, and thus make it the ghastly monster that it is." As always with Hazlitt, nicely said.

Hazlitt felt that the fear of death was tied to the loss of religious belief; he thought that a life of action and danger modified the fear of death; and he knew from personal experience that "sedentary and studious men are the most apprehensive" about death, and he cites Dr. Johnson here as a case in point. As for himself, Hazlitt said that he would rather hang around until he saw "some prospect of good to mankind, such as my life began with" (a reference to the French Revolution); left "some sterling work behind me"; and "have some friendly hand consign me to the grave." Well, before his life was over Hazlitt had achieved one out of three of his wishes. In baseball as in life, .333 ain't bad.

Hazlitt wrote "On the Fear of Death," the essay in which these observations appear, in his early forties. As young as that, he began to feel the dreamy quality of life. This, too, may be owing to the sedentary and studious life, but for some while life for me as well has seemed shadowy, a dream, a luscious sleep from which I don't quite wish to be wakened but from which I await a terrifying alarm to signal that it is over and that the warm bed must be evacuated to make room for the next dreamer. The imprecision of memory has added greatly to this dreamy feeling. The older I become, the less strong my memory for time, except for the years of my boy- and young manhood, which become more and more vivid to me. But I now frequently find myself misplacing four-, five-, even six-year clumps of my life. "Didn't we go to Greece seven or so years ago?" I ask. It turns out to have been thirteen years ago. "Weren't you a student in my class four years ago?" It turns out to have been eight. Have I met that man before? Did I once give a lecture in Ohio? When was it that I owned an olive-drab suit? Lost, all of it, in that wash of time which the poet all too rightly referred to as its "dark backward and abysm."

Two of the greatest problems time provides (neither of which I have a solution for) are how to slow it down and how to make it seem less the stuff of dreams. One of the reasons I keep a journal is to prevent, in howsoever small a way, life from seeming a dream; by recording what has happened to me, no matter how trivial, I feel that I have somehow made it real. Written out, it has been salvaged, plucked from the Heraclitean river, or so at least I have come to believe. This is a fine prescription for graphomania, I grant you, and of course writing in a journal takes time, which is another problem.

Eating and sleeping also take time—and how I admire those fortunate people who need only four or five hours of sleep each night!—and so does everything else, including getting one's watch fixed. The odd thing about my own life is that it would seem to be nicely set up to save time. I rise early—usually at 4:45 in the morning. I do not travel to work on buses or subways or fight freeway traffic in my car. I have taken a pledge never to jog. I do not golf, I read no detective fiction. From all appearances my life seems a lean, mean, time-saving machine.

Yet I notice that the least disruption often shoots my day. If, say, I have to go downtown for an appointment with a dentist or an accountant or to meet a friend for lunch, poof! wham! it's gone. Lunches with friends, which I much enjoy, are especially effective at killing afternoons. Yet other people seem to spend three hours getting to and from work, are able to shop around during the day, go to great numbers of meetings, have leisurely lunches, carry on love affairs, and still find time to do the *New York Times* crossword puzzle.

Or is it only that the clock always seems to be running slower in the other fellow's pocket? Are we not all under the tyranny of time? Aldous Huxley, in a newspaper column written in the 1930s, claimed that industrialization, with railroads, factories, and machines at its center, is what has placed us under this tyranny. "For a modern American or Englishman," he wrote, "waiting is a psychological torture." It was not always and everywhere thus, according to Huxley, and not to him alone. Even the concept of the week, a unit of seven days, with a Sabbath day at its end, is perhaps fewer than two thousand years old. The claim made by those who wish to return to simpler times—not to set back but to throw away the clock—is that in attending so fastidiously to seconds and minutes, while locked into these man-made, entirely artificial distinctions of time, we forgo the great sweeps, the grandeur of time presented by the course of the moon and stars, the changing of the seasons, the larger rhythms of life itself.

Not so long ago it used to be said that they ordered these things better in the Orient, where people were not so time-bound as we in the West. Ah, the mysterious East, where waiting is not a concept, but a way of life. Russians, too, are said to be untouched by time, or at any rate never to feel their style crimped by the need for punctuality. Invite a Russian to lunch, he might show up for dessert and coffee at that evening's dinner. Blacks, among themselves, joke about CPT, or colored people's time. But for those white-eyes among us, as the Indians in old Western movies used to refer to cowboys, cavalry troops, and settlers, the clock keeps running, the sand continues to dribble down, the timekeeper's pistol is poised in the air. For us time has become an obstacle that we try to overcome by living at even greater speed—in the hope, I suppose, of lapping ourselves in the race of life. I do not mock this; I am in the race myself.

As one of the country's leading solipsists, I am pleased to learn that I am not alone in this feeling that time seems out of control, whirring by, regardless of all attempts to make the best of it. A psychologist named John P. Robinson, who directs something called the "Americans' Use of Time Project" at the University of Maryland, reports that Americans today generally feel more harried, even during a period when free time in American life has actually increased. Professor Robinson defines free time as time when people do not have to attend to work, family, errands and chores, or such personal needs as eating, sleeping, and grooming. Married women with children are said to feel this harried condition more acutely than other groups, but almost everyone feels rushed, frenzied, and finally defeated in his or her efforts to make the best use of time. "We are at a point," Professor Robinson is quoted in the *New York Times* as saying, "when the value of time to most Americans is reaching parity with the value of money."

We speak of killing time, but in fact time is killing us. Even leisure has become time-haunted, tinged with anxiety, as people struggle to sneak in time for a run, sail, swim, walk, ski, workout, couple of sets of tennis, nine holes of golf. Don't forget all the paintings one hasn't seen, books one hasn't read, music one hasn't heard, not to mention those one wants to find time to see, read, and hear at least once again before the big sleep. Let us not speak of the countries one has not yet seen, mountains not climbed, rivers never crossed. Once more around the Louvre, this time perhaps not so lightly. "Hurry up please it's time," announces the barman in *The Waste Land.* "Hurry up please it's time."

"Slow down," some anonymous genius once declared, "you're in a hurry." What splendid advice! Of course, life has its own way of slowing us down. As Chamfort noted: "The intensity of absolute pleasures, as metaphysicists say, diminishes with time. Yet time apparently increases relative pleasures; and I suspect that this is the artifice by which nature has been able to bind men to life." Not for everyone, apparently. Yeats claimed that "one never tires of life, and at the last must die of thirst with the cup at one's lips." But then Yeats must have known that a life beyond his own days, in posterity, was guaranteed him through his magnificent poetry. Great art, heroic or evil action on a large enough scale—these are among the things that will put one beyond time, that will make one immortal.

It would calm one down a good deal, I should think, to give up all dreams of immortality. Yet nearly everyone must believe that he has some claim on posterity and hence some long shot at immortality. "Posterity will know as little of me as I shall know of posterity," said W. S. Gilbert (of the team of Gilbert and Sullivan), wrongly. Even Heraclitus, the philosopher of flux, who was known as the "weeping philosopher," presumably because he felt that everything in the world changed, dissolved, or vanished, even he in the midst of the demon flux, belied his own theory, and his name has lived long enough for me to bandy it around today.

One lives out one's days, hoping and dreaming against the shockingly bad odds that something that one or one's children will do might cause one's name to live on, making one immortal: by committing an act of great kindness or courage, by being the recipient of immense good luck, by producing an imperishable book, painting, or musical composition. To be immortal, to live out of the touch of time—is that too much to ask? If only I could be assured of it, I could relax, knock off early, put my feet up on the desk, have a couple of chocolate-covered orange peels, look at my watch, and smile. No hurry at all. But until then there are deadlines, real and imagined, to meet; miles to go before I sleep; and the hope that the knock at the door isn't the ugly Customer but only the guy from Federal Express.

Toys in My Attic

On the campus where I teach, there is a landmark, a large rock on which fraternity and sorority members paint their Greek letters, the political-minded announce their slogans, and the whimsical occasionally indite their usually unobscene graffiti. The other day walking past it, I noticed that some less-than-advanced student of Latin had written: "Veni, vidi, vici." Instantly, my mind rejoined, "Veni, vidi, vici / Your mother looks like Nietzsche." Why does my mind do this? Where do such items come from? What sort of thing is this for a man in his fifties to be thinking? Ought I to seek, as they say, professional help?

Early on a spring morning in South Bend, Indiana, sitting alone in a quiet room overlooking a swimming pool, I notice two ducks alight on the water. "A pair of ducks," I think, "a pair of dukes, a pair of docs, a pair of dice, a paradise, a pair of Dekes, a pair of dorks, a paradox." I could go on, and that morning, for a bit longer, I did. In the newspaper I glanced at soon thereafter, someone was referred to as the "heir apparent" to some job I cannot now recall; but the phrase suggested to me another, which my pun-spewing mind put in the form of a riddle: "What do you call a toupee? You call it, obviously, 'hair apparent.'" A friend remarked that her eyes itch. "Eyesitch Bashevis Singer," I blurted out, since I happened to have been recently reading his novels. In the fullness of time, I was forgiven.

How long has this been going on? asks a fine old torch song sung, in my youth, by June Christy (the Misty Miss Christy, old guys may recall). How long has my mind been subject to such nuttiness? Only as long as I can remember, though the condition seems to be becoming worse as I grow older. Who put these toys in my attic? Can they ever be cleaned out, so that I can turn my thoughts to more serious matters? Is language therapy indicated?

Or is it not my mind but the silliness of words themselves that provokes me to such zaniness? Surely I am not the only one who has noted it. "I went over to Dover," Henry James wrote to a friend, then he added: "What a language we have, 'over to Dover'—it would have made Flaubert an even greater maniac than his own did." Is the English language inherently zany? Why is it so often the case, at least for me, that one word powerfully suggests another, often in some comic fashion? I hear the word *adhering* and I invariably think of the phrase *add herring,* and I don't even like herring. I hear the word *intuit* and I feel I ought to put more *in to it.* I see the name Immanuel Kant and my mind turns it into Immanuel Won't. When I hear the word *paradigm* all I can think of is the phrase from the Depression, "Brother, can you spare a dime?" I am like the little boy mentioned by F. L. Lucas in his swell book *Style* who remarked that *death* does not seem a very good word for what it describes, and when asked what word might be better, promptly replied, "Hig."

Have I been working with language too intensely for too long, like a man left out in the sun without a hat, who is consequently a bit touched? Are we talking here about a mild case of James Joyce fever? Truth to tell, I have been wandering about in (I won't say reading) Joyce's *Finnegans Wake* and, strange to report, finding whole passages not only comprehensible but charming. This in itself is, as anyone who has taken up this book, a work seventeen years in its highly involuted making, a bit disturbing. What is disturbing is that I have come to think I know what it is that Joyce had in mind writing this just about unreadable book. But, here, do please try a passage on your own:

What then agentlike brought about that tragoady thundersday this municipal sin business? Our cubehouse still rocks as earwitness to the thunder of his arafatas but we hear also through successive ages that shebby choruysh of unkalified muzzlenimissilehims that would blackguardise the whitestone ever hurtleturtled out of heaven. Stay us wherefore in our search for tighteousness, O Sustainer, what time we rise and when we take up to toothmick and before we lump down upown our leatherbed and in the night and at the fading of the stars!

What I believe the old boy, Mr. James Choice himself, had in mind was to demonstrate the comic instability of language, the way almost every word in English resembles some other word, if not in English then in another language, so that, if one is sensitive enough to language, its soundings and resoundings, one is lucky to be able to communicate at all. Setting aside the problem that language provides in meaning and precision, consider for a moment its hidden traps. The falling into unconscious puns, the double entendres, the boners, the howlers, the lavish prospects for lapses, the unconscious sexual metaphors, the horrendous comic possibilities awaiting anyone writing and speaking English—all these things make it apparent that the language is not altogether, as the folks down at computer city say, user-friendly.

In this list I haven't even mentioned irony, the disease that sets in among writers at a certain point of sophistication, and from which, once begun, return is impossible. "One is taught to refrain from irony," says Max Beerbohm in *Zuleika Dobson*, "because mankind does tend to take it literally." And in a radio broadcast, Max once remarked, "I wish, Ladies and Gentlemen, I could cure myself of the habit of speaking ironically. I should so like to express myself in a straightforward manner." You don't suppose he meant that last sentence, do you?

Please do suppose that I entirely do mean it when I speak of the comic instability of language. I do not have in mind here anything so fancy as tony deconstructionist notions about language being mystifying, illogical, hopelessly political, and therefore itself, somehow, discredited (to be replaced by what—seashells, perhaps?—has never been even murkily suggested). Nor do I have in mind the struggle to make words mean precisely what one wants them to mean, over which Flaubert daily racked his brain (cracked his crane?). Poor Flaubert, whose letters to Louise Colet, his mistress, are filled with such groaning complaints about his endless wrestle with language: "Last week I spent *five days writing one page*, and I dropped everything else for it. . . ." "Do you know how many pages I have written this week? One, and I cannot even say a good one." The poor man had with words what must now be called a real "Flaubertian" problem. (There goes language, making a fool of one again.)

Flaubert's difficulty was in straining after an idea that might not have been achievable. "Oh!" he complained. "If only I wrote the way I know one has to write, I'd write so well." What he had in mind was a style in which every *mot* was absolutely *juste*. (Le Mot, I not long ago learned, is what many of his friends call the novelist Ward Just, and I like them and him straightaway for this little joke.) Here is what Flaubert had in mind:

I envision a style: a style that would be beautiful, that someone will invent some day, ten years or ten centuries from now, one that would be rhythmic as verse, precise as the language of the sciences, undulant, deep-voiced as a cello, tipped with flame: a style that would pierce your idea like a dagger, and on which your thought would sail easily ahead over a smooth surface, like a skiff before a good tail wind.

What a lovely passage! "I believe he's got it," as Professor Henry Higgins might say. "By God he's got it!" But of course Flaubert, being Flaubert, would not have found this or anything else ever good enough. The writer's—or at least certain writers'—road to hell is paved with the desire for stylistic perfection.

Imagine the state Flaubert would have been in if he had had to oversee translations of his ever so meticulously constructed works. It would have taken him onto the stage above madness. Isaac Bashevis Singer, who achieved fame as a writer in English and not in the Yiddish in which he grew up and wrote to the end of his life, noted of translation that "the 'other' language in which the author's work must be rendered does not tolerate obscurity, puns, and linguistic tinsel." It is, of course, possible to enjoy the splendidly spare English translations of Singer's own stories and novels and still love the literary tinsel that he felt these translations must eschew. (The English writer Richard Church once noted that the sound of the word *eschew* was responsible for his deciding to become a writer, so fascinated was he by it when, as a child, he heard it for the first time. My own reaction to the word is rather different. When I hear someone say "eschew," I have to suppress saying "Gesundheit!")

Some often-translated writers have not let foreign languages stand in the way of their love of linguistic tinsel. Often these are writers who have command of not one or two but several languages. It may well be, it occurs to me, that one of the tests of command of a foreign language is to be able to recognize puns in it and, at a still higher level of command, to make puns in that language. Vladimir Nabokov is a case in point. (Is a man living in a rough neighborhood who carries a knife someone who has a point in case? Just thought I'd ask.) In the second volume of his biography of Nabokov, Brian Boyd tells of Nabokov's friend Alfred Appel reporting to him, during the wilder days of the sixties, that a nun in one of his classes at Northwestern University complained that a young couple near her in class was always spooning. Nabokov mockingly reprimanded his friend for missing a lovely opportunity. "You should have said, 'Sister, be grateful that they were not forking.' "

One good pun tends to provoke another, often less good pun. With Nabokov's pun in mind, is it not possible to say of Brillat-Savarin, the great chef and writer on gastronomy, that he was a forking genius? Yes, it's certainly possible, though probably not a good idea. Yet those who take pleasure in making puns are perpetually crouched to leap—couched to sleep?—always ready to fire away. Using puns in captions has long been considered an opportunity for a bit of fun, and journalists wait to get in their shot at it. Some seem rigged, such as the caption I once read beneath a photograph of trainers with stopwatches during an early-morning workout at Aqueduct: "These are the souls who time men's tries." Which doesn't lay a glove on the journalist who had the chance to write a caption for a photograph of the late Aristotle Onassis looking at the home of Buster Keaton, which Onassis was thinking of buying. Under this photograph the lucky fellow was able to write: "Aristotle contemplating the home of Buster." Did yet another journalist caption a photograph of Mikhail Gorbachev, with a Kurdish child in his arms, "Kurd-carrying Communist," or did I make this up because I want it to be so?

You know you have the disease bad when you have puns ready-made and hope for situations to arise in which you can call them into play. There is a very good young writer on philosophical subjects named Josiah Lee Auspitz. If ever I were to know him well enough, I should like to compliment him on something he has written and go on to ask him if he wrote it at home or at the home of relatives on his father's side—that is to say, under different Auspitzes.

"T'ain't funny, McGee," as the wise Molly McGee used to say on their old radio show when reining in her husband at those times that his humor threatened to veer out of comic control. But then punning is famously a low art. One has to have a taste for whimsy to go in for it; and it is no surprise that those two most whimsical of English writers, Charles Lamb and Lewis Carroll, both went in for it in rather a large way: Lamb, always the good host, used to complain about his "nocturnal alias knock-eternal visitors." But then the distinctly unwhimsical Winston Churchill appreciated a good pun, and in his essay on Herbert Henry Asquith he recommends an elaborate pun off the words *wait* and *see* and *weight* and *sea* that he allows may be apocryphal but "deserves to survive."

Groucho Marx suffered this same weakness, which he turned to a strength as a comedian, and once wrote to his brother Gummo that he and T. S. Eliot had three things in common: "(1) an affection for good cigars; and (2) cats; and (3) a weakness for making puns—a weakness I have tried to overcome. T. S., on the other hand, is an unashamed—even proud punster. For example, there's his Gus, the Theater Cat, whose 'real name was Asparagus.' "

Groucho's sense of the comic instability of language was at the heart of much of his humor and hence of his charm. He was able to spin off the fragility of words like no other comedian of his time or of ours. I cannot recall specific examples of his doing this, so regular a feature of his performance was it. But if one was talking with him, one did well to watch one's vocabulary. Say "disgruntled" around him and he was likely to ask you if you ever felt "gruntled." Mention that you were "nonplussed," he would likely ask when last you were "plussed"; he might even go a step further and ask if you ever read Marcel Plussed. He would wish things untrammeled, trammeled; things impeccable, pecced; things invincible, vinced. If you mentioned that you thought something feasible, he would doubtless ask how precisely does one feas it. Tell him he was frivolous, and he would beg leave to frivol on. When Groucho was on a roll, which was most of the time, it was probably safest not to speak around him at all.

Groucho could also be death on odd names. W. C. Fields, too, thought, as he might have put it, nomenclatural exotica riotously funny, and he became something of a connoisseur (a kind of sewer) of odd names and used them in his movies whenever possible, the odder the better. That someone happens to be named Velveeta Hickenlooper or Montague Fortinbras really lit up old Fields, a man who always had plenty of alcohol in his lamp in any case. (And couldn't Groucho have done fine things with a phrase such as a "lamp in any case"?) I do not share this appetite, though I sometimes indulge in it myself. I once owned a Volvo that had something called a Manual Choke; whenever I noted it written on the dashboard, I would say to myself, "Manual Choke, wasn't he one of those Cuban pitchers on the old Washington Senators?" To Shakespeare's question about what's in a name, I say, usually, a hell of a lot. What if Shakespeare's own name, for example, were Lou Peltz? Quite hopeless. Under the name Lou Peltz he couldn't have turned out a haiku.

But one doesn't really have to fall back upon names to find amusement in language. Neologisms supply enough comedy on their own. The cant phrase *work ethic* has always seemed to me to suggest its opposite, which would be *loaf ethic*. One can readily imagine coaches using the phrase: "We like his loaf ethic, the way he seems to be able to kick back and do absolutely nothing for weeks at a time." To stay with sports, there is much talk these days in games about "momentum," but if there is momentum why not, as a matching item, "nomentum," when teams seem to lose their energy, slow down, fall apart? Teams with "nomo" would require plenty of players with a strong loaf ethic. Pleasing to know that I am not alone in finding so many of the neologisms of our day a bit goofy. Here is Richard Wilbur's take on the uncharming and not very useful "role model":

> When Jack came tumbling down the hill,
> The record shows that sister Jill
> "Came tumbling after." Was he her
> Roll Model, then, as I infer?

I have also taken much pleasure of late in the word *judgmental,* which is almost always used pejoratively, implying as it does that making judgments about anything is very bad form. I happen to have a friend who is a judge, and it delights me to be able to say to him, "Oh, Dick, don't be so judgmental," when the man has no other choice. To revert to names again, I am sure that there must, somewhere, be a man or woman on some bench, federal or local, named Judge Mendel. As Henry James says, "What a language we have."

Along with freshly minted neologisms, another prominent incursion upon the language of late has been the disappearance of the hyphen. I rather miss the darling fellow, so much that I have agreed to become Chairman of the National Committee to Rescue the Hyphen. Who stole it? you may wonder. Copy editors seem chiefly to blame. It evidently caused everybody too much trouble getting the little bugger right, so the decision was made to eliminate it in all but a minority of cases. The consequence is that one now comes across such strange-looking words as *multiethnic, neoisolationist, rechoreograph, postpleistocene, antiodorous, prowoman, daylong, weeklong, monthlong,* solong oolong howlong ya gonna be gone. Please make checks payable to the Com-mit-tee to Res-cue the Hy-phen.

Typographical errors have become another playground for the vagaries of language. Everyone knows how common they have become in recent years. Rare is the book that nowadays contains none. If you ever wish to depress a writer, tell him about all the typos you have found in his book. If you wish to make an enemy of him, tell him his book is "bristling" with typos; be sure not to forget that word *bristling.* Isaac Bashevis Singer has said, "An author doesn't die of typhus, but of typos." (The pun works better with a Yiddish accent.) Many have speculated upon why typos show up so much more frequently now than in earlier days. Some people have blamed it on computer typesetting; others on the belief that the kind of people who used to devote themselves to careful proofreading are simply not around.

For the present, typos, like love in the George Gershwin song, are here to stay. May as well get what enjoyment one can from them. I was not long ago told by an editor of the *Times Literary Supplement* that in a review I wrote of a book about White Anglo-Saxon Protestant culture in America, my phrase "the way of the WASP" came out on galleys as "the way of the Wisp," which is rather charming. The same week the word *Freudian* came out *Fraudian,* which is rather telling. Twice the last line in Vladimir Nabokov's novel *Bend Sinister,* "A perfect night for mothing," was changed by proofreaders to "A perfect night for nothing." The situation is not so different with *discrete,* with a single *e* between the *r* and the *t;* use it and some proofreader is almost certain to change it to *discreet.* Be discreet; forget about *discrete.*

Then there are those words that one cannot be sure are typographical errors. "Only connect" famously begins the epigraph to E. M. Forster's *Howard's End*. Edward Shils, who knew Forster at King's College, Cambridge, once told me a story about persuading Forster to send some pages of a diary he had been keeping to the magazine *Encounter*, which was about to publish an anniversary issue, but in the end Forster sent the pages to *Harper's*, where he was able to get the larger fee. "Do you suppose," Shils said, recounting the story, "that what he really meant was 'only collect'?"

And let us not forget those typos of the mind and tongue—"mindos" and "lipos" they ought perhaps to be called. Richard Sheridan had the genius to give them, through a character he invented for *The Rivals*, the name of malapropisms. "As headstrong as an *allegory* on the banks of the Nile," says the blithely confident Mrs. Malaprop. The English journalist Jilly Cooper reports that her charwoman, learning that a house the Coopers had bought was reputed to be haunted, said: "You'll have to get the vicar to circumcise it." Samuel Goldwyn made of such slips almost a specialty. "In two words," he once reportedly said, "im possible." On another occasion, he told an employee, "If I want your opinion, I'll give it to you." I'm sure he did, too.

Foreign-born English speakers often—and understandably—fall into these lapses. "Gingée Rogée," a Frenchman who taught at the University of Chicago used to pronounce the Hollywood actress's name. Did I actually hear a woman describe another woman as "no longer a sprung chicken," or did I make it up? Probably not, for the foreign-born are especially good at muddling clichés. "You don't want to take the baby out of the bathwater." Or: "When they made her, they really broke the gold." I like to invent these on my own. "I am eating these strawberries," I recently announced, "like I'm going out of style." I have also been heard to mutter: "In for a penny, in for a pounding," and "You live and you yearn."

"Mother," a little boy is supposed to have announced upon returning home from school, "do I have a cliché on my face?" "A cliché?" his mother asks. "You know," the boy replies, "a worn-out expression." Except in the realm of ideas, I have come rather to prize clichés, provided they be old enough. Of Lytton Strachey, Max Beerbohm wrote, "He is not afraid of clichés," and he meant it as a compliment—a sign, I suppose, of self-confidence in a truly accomplished writer. Even H. W. Fowler allowed that there were clichés and clichés, and some were not only better than others but indispensable:

> To take one or two examples from the many hundreds of words and phrases that it is now fashionable to brand as clichés, writers would be needlessly handicapped if they were never allowed to say that something was a *foregone conclusion,* or *Hobson's choice* or a *white elephant,* or that someone was *feathering his nest* or *had his tongue in his cheek* or *a bee in his bonnet.* What is new is not necessarily better than what is old; the original felicity that has made a phrase a cliché may not be beyond recapture.

I seem to have spent much of my life avoiding clichés, only now to confess a secret, small but steady pleasure in certain of them. Hoist, you might say, on my own foulard.

I also enjoy using slightly I won't say archaic but nicely out-of-it words. *Crosspatch, fussbudget, pernickety, zealot*—it's words such as these that I enjoy unfurling when the occasion permits. I have a preternatural regard for the word *trousers* and go with it every time over *pants* and the all-too-slick *slacks.* I say *alas* so often and with such earnestness that I don't believe it qualifies as affectation. I like, too, old clichés whose meanings I don't quite understand and don't always try to discover. I am grateful for the occasion that allows me to say that someone or other left "hell-bent for leather" or that something or other was done to "a fare-thee-well." I wish there were more opportunities for me to use the phrase *shiver my timbers,* but then I guess you can't have everything.

Having always had a strong taste for metaphors, I have done a fairly brisk business in them in my own writing, and I admire them greatly when they are cleanly struck off in the work of other writers. But they do provide delicious food for unconscious comedy. Mixed metaphors are rarely in short supply. Literary critics can be depended upon to talk about "fictional voices that have grown teeth and are ready to bite into the heart of the artistic enterprise." (Get that metaphor to an orthodontist.) Near misses are always interesting to contemplate, too, such as John Updike's "I awake in light, feeling as if my soul had a slight sore throat." (Get that metaphor to an eye, ear, nose, and throat theologian.)

The miscast metaphors that give me most pleasure are the unconscious and perfectly, delightfully inappropriate ones. "A good metaphor," said Aristotle, "implies an intuitive perception of the similarity in dissimilars." A comically bad metaphor has a mildly grotesque inappropriateness, often implying the failure of the perception of dissimilars in similarity. "A broken toe," such a metaphor might run, "is a real pain in the neck." Sex, being a subject strewn with slang, is one in which these unconscious metaphors show up to most hilarious effect. Using metaphor in the realm of sex is, to speak metaphorically, like walking in a poison-ivy-covered cow field filled with land mines—danger lurks wherever one steps. I shall always prize the student who wrote that "Madame Bovary's problem was that she couldn't make love in the concrete." So, too, the man who announced that "it is time for some straight talk about the gay liberation movement." And, again, the journalist who wrote that "urbanology is a virgin field pregnant with possibilities."

For many years now editors have played off the comic

richness of language in the titles they have given articles and reviews in their magazines. Sometimes these are plays on words ("When Putsch Comes to Shove"), sometimes reversals of words ("Britannia Waves the Rules"), sometimes sheer whimsy ("Yes, We Have No Cézannas"). Nearly thirty years ago, I tried my hand at this sort of thing when I was a subeditor on a small political magazine, but I was sent from the principal editor's office in disgrace when I tried to title a review of a crybaby autobiography "The Days of Whine and Neurosis." A pity, really, for after all this time I still like it.

I am very glad that English is the language I grew up in, if only because I don't think I would have had a chance to learn it as an outsider. I am altogether too literal-minded to have been able to accept with serenity its vast number of inconsistencies. Why, any foreigner must wonder, does one drive on a parkway and park in a driveway? A slim chance and a fat chance—how can these be the same? What is a homeless community? What has egg to do with eggplant? Drink up, call up, dummy up, slow down, drink it down, play it down, be bored stiff, blue, out of one's gourd, big deal, no deal, do a deal— yumpin' yimminy, *bon Dieu, oy gevalt,* forget about it!

And what would a foreigner make of the new all-purpose American adjective *fun?* The word sometimes even had its problems as a noun. The late Vernon Young, an Englishman, film critic, and immitigable highbrow, once asked me what I supposed it was Americans had in mind when, upon parting from him, they sometimes instructed him to "have fun." But what would he have made of such more recent locutions as a "fun person," a "fun time," the "fun part"? I once left a restaurant, which attempted to duplicate the food and what its owners misconstrued to be the feel of the 1950s, in the company of a woman who is often rather stringent in her opinions about food and language. "We must never go here again," she said.

"I fear this is a restaurant for fun couples." Sorry but there are not enough italics and quotation marks to signify the completeness of the contempt with which she used that last phrase.

But as an American I am not always clear on what words mean, so fast is the language moving, so wild are some of its inventions. What does it mean, for example, to call something "freezer-fresh"? ("Don't get fresh," mothers used to say to children of my generation who looked as if they might attempt to sass them. And whatever happened to the word *sass*? We still have the activity but no longer the word.) Cars are no longer "used" but "preowned"—with an extra charge, doubtless, if they throw in the hyphen. Slums and now even ghettos are gone, leaving people who used to live in them gamboling in the "inner city." "Terminal living" apparently means you are just about dead.

Sometimes I ask myself how this mania for language, which has been my making and threatens sometimes to become my undoing, came about, both in myself and in others who share in it. Why am I such a sucker for sentences that have a kick in their tail, such as this by Kingsley Amis, who in his *Memoirs* writes that "one does rather go through life constantly suffering from unpreparedness for how awful things are going to be, starting with human nature." I have a weakness for happy linguistic inventions. Chips Channon's "antipatico" seems to me quite as helpful as the "simpatico" from which it derives. Donald Tovey's referring to detective and spy stories as "illiterature" is a helpful addition to the language, as is "neodoxy," which means obedience to the new. I like Kitty Muggeridge's description of the television johnny David Frost as someone who has "risen without trace." I am also respectful about precision in connection with the unknowable. When Maurice Richardson describes a Hungarian drink as tasting "like hornet's piss," it strikes me that he has chosen well, for, though I haven't kitchen-tested any of this, the urine of a hornet sounds, somehow, much bitterer than that of a wasp or a bee.

"The limits of my language," said Wittgenstein, "are the limits of my world." That seems a true, an almost commonplace statement, but neurophysiologists, in their recent researches, are beginning to make it seem rather shaky, claiming that language can only be explained at the neural level. It is now thought that different parts of language—proper and common nouns, regular and irregular verbs, and so forth—are processed in different areas of the brain. The latest view is, according to an article in the *New York Times*, that "language and perhaps all cognition are governed by some as-yet-undiscovered mechanism that binds different brain areas together in time, not place." This is all much more complicated than I can hope to grasp, but it does begin to explain to me the linguistic oddities bequeathed to many victims of strokes. I had a dentist who, suffering a stroke on a photographic safari in Africa, lost his memory for all proper nouns and his powers of consecution, or of following anything consecutively. After his stroke, H. L. Mencken lost his ability to read and write and could only speak haltingly, the right words refusing to come to him. Different bitter jokes for different ghastly strokes.

But does the brain perhaps play tricks on others of us who have had no stroke by giving us a larger drawer than most for frivolity in the ample cabinet of language? Why is it that some of us are more alert to the capriciousness of language than others? Possibly the problem could have to do with nothing so elegantly scientific as studies of the brain but instead with an ingrained whimsicality of nature. Such, I have little doubt, is my own nature. I have long believed, for example, that I would be very good—too good—at writing advertising copy, and I am glad that I was never given a chance to try, lest it turn out

to be so. I also have secretly believed that I might have been
a decent lyricist, for whom the meaning and weight of words
mean less than their playfulness and rhyme.

Not long ago a friend who holds an option on the F. Scott
Fitzgerald story "The Diamond as Big as the Ritz" asked me
if I would like to try my hand at turning it into a musical by
writing what I believe is called "the book" and lyrics for it.
This is not one of Fitzgerald's great stories, I think, but it is
one of his great titles. As a musical, this title could go a long
way. Somehow I saw, in my mind's greedy little eye, people
talking about having seen *Diamond*—yes, *Diamond,* that is of
course how they would refer to it—in London, where the cast
was much better than in New York. Everyone would see
Diamond, and I would see gold, much gold, pile up around me.
My friend asked me to think about it.

I tried not to but couldn't help doing so. Suddenly free
moments—in the shower, walking the street, before falling off
to sleep at night—seemed all to be given over to my writing
song lyrics in my head. Good to be able to report that the
world will be spared having to hear such half-composed, not
quite half-witty classics as "He's Got That Midas Touch,"
"Champagne Is the Only Pain That Glorious Life Need Ever
Contain," and the really quite unforgettable "Still Priapic Over
You," with its delightful opening line: "No matter what the
topic, I'm always quite priapic, darling, priapic over you."
Diamond—I fear that, for the present, you'll have to miss it, at
least in my version.

Not only does the world not need my song lyrics, but
neither do I, for I already have a plenitude of other people's
bopping around in my brain: you go to my head, and I think
I'm going out of my head, when we are dancing and you are
dangerously near me, cheek to cheek, with sand in my shoes
in Havana, in a small hotel, on a horse with no name, as time

goes by, nice work if you can get it, s'wonderful, alone again, naturally, or is it (in the words of the all-too-mortal Temptations) just my imagination, so let's call the whole thing off.

As lines from songs both lovely and junky regularly pop into my head quite without being called up—and let us not speak of commercials: "The heartbeat of America, that's today's Chevrolet"—so, quite as insistently, do punch lines from jokes: "This could lead to dancing," I want to say to a student who says something quite foolish in class. "What! And leave show business?" I think, when someone suggests that I give up some boring task or other. "Mark it down, Morris," I say to myself, when I know I am apt to forget some small item, "mark it down." "And about my humility," I mutter within when someone offers me a few kind words of praise, "about my humility, not a word?"

In danger of being flooded by language, I need every so often to find a life preserver, and I look for it in stately language, in which solid words stay moored to sound thought. Whenever I am addressed by the title of Doctor, I always want to—and sometimes do—say, "Please read two chapters of Henry James and get right into bed." But, in fact, when I am myself suffering from the linguistic equivalent of seasickness, I tend to take my own advice and read a writer whose language does not bob around: Samuel Johnson, or George Eliot, or Santayana, or Winston Churchill. A few pages from any of these or from a few other writers and I am ready to return to the battle.

The English poet and essayist Alice Meynell, in a brief essay on dialects, writes of the dialects of Venetians or Genoese of another day: "We may believe that it is a simple thing to die in so simple and so narrow a language, one so comfortable, neighborly, tolerant, and compassionate; so confidential; so incapable, ignorant, unappalling; inapt to wing any wearied thought upon difficult flight or to spur it upon hard travelling." Dying in a simple language, which had never occurred to me before I came across it in Mrs. Meynell, is a charming and devoutly to be desired condition.

But what if, as seems more likely, my physicians and nurses speak the standard psychobabblified, jargon-ridden, watery lingo of the day? What if my physician tells me that I am a "special person," my nurse mentions that she has a few thoughts she wishes "to share" with me, and the various technicians monitoring my passage into the next world speak to one another of being "conflicted in their career choice"? Perhaps now is the time to go back to that living will I not long ago signed. Where in it I give instructions to pull the plug—and what a happy phrase that is!—I ought to add that another set of plugs be immediately placed in my ears, preferably ones connected to a machine playing Schubert sonatinas and blocking out the blight of sappy language that most distinctly is not the last sound I wish to hear. When mustering-out time arrives, I do hope no special persons are around—and no bloody caring ones, either—and all will keep their conflictions to themselves, so that I shall be left alone with the few people I love and the music of Schubert, in repose, lying there, like a bunny easterized upon a table, as the poet didn't quite say.

Whaddya Drivin'?

"Ep," said my old friend Willy Stein, as he accompanied me to my gray, then-one-year-old 1973 Volvo at the close of a summer night on which we had met with two other fellows to play in a moderately high-stakes gin-rummy game, "Ep," he said, pointing to my car, "you got air in this shit-box?" I did in fact have air conditioning— "factory air," as they say on the used-car lot—in the Volvo, but the remark, I had to confess, took the air out of me. I was rather fond of this Volvo. Willy himself drove a new, long white Cadillac Sedan De Ville, and had begun driving Cadillacs soon after he had dropped out of college and gone into his father's business. One of the other players, a commodities-market guy, had arrived in a tan Mercedes sedan; and the fourth member of our party drove a sleek black Lincoln. Willy's remark suggested that the Volvo might have belonged to one of my kids, or was a car of the kind that one bought used for a plain and undemanding wife in whom one was clearly no longer much interested. I drove the Volvo home that night with the air conditioning all the way up, listening to the *Eroica* Symphony on FM radio, speeding down the expressway, getting as much pleasure out of it as I could. But, after Willy's remark, I have to confess that I never quite felt the same about it.

I have for all my adult days—with lapses I shall get to presently—been committed to modesty in automobiles. I grew up in a home where the family car was for much of my boyhood a Buick or an Oldsmobile, never top of the line, with a deviation for a Hudson (a Hudson Hornet, to give the machine its hopeless sobriquet) in the early fifties and, at one point, a few Cadillacs leased in the name of my father's business. My father's interest in cars was so negligible that I can remember his once being asked, by a parking-lot attendant, what color his car was and his not being able to come up with the answer. Although I admired that almost Olympian unconcern about details, I myself have only been able to pretend to such indifference.

While maintaining, lo, these many years, an impressively pristine ignorance about what causes cars to run, I have always been very attentive to what you might call their social ramifications. I can account for my own commitment to modest cars only through snobbery; I should have said simple snobbery, except that in my case what is entailed is reverse snobbery, which is a bit more complicated but in the end comes to the same thing. Since a handsome car is perhaps the most obvious sign of having done well in the world—a sign, moreover, available to a great many people, too many if the truth be known—the reverse snob looks elsewhere for his status. To drive the fine car, in this scheme, becomes rather infra dig. Your reverse snob goes instead for the dull, in some cases even the drab, car, and is thus able secretly to look down upon the fellow in the grander car.

I recall once being in the garage of a building of costly condominium apartments in Hyde Park near the University of Chicago. The building was lived in chiefly by senior professors at the university, many of them professors of law and medicine and of other subjects that made impressive consulting fees available to them. The quality of the cars in that garage—lots of older Volkswagens, Volvos, run-down Saabs, Dodges, an occasional Ford station wagon—was quite out of proportion to the expensiveness of the apartments above. I asked the man I was with about this obvious discrepancy. "Academic motors," he said, with a worldly shrug, "what do you expect?" Something to it, I'm afraid.

Cars have been important to me for as long as I can remember. When I was five years old, our family took an apartment on Sheridan Road in Chicago. Sheridan Road, now as then, is a four-lane thoroughfare, with a regular stream of traffic whirring by at almost all times. Ours was a small apartment in a deep courtyard building, and my bedroom window faced the street. I can recall kneeling at the window after being sent to bed, watching the cars go by and doing an automotive version of counting sheep, telling myself that I would go back to bed when, say, twenty Packards, or twenty-five DeSotos, or thirty Plymouths had gone by. Knowledge of cars was the first knowledge I was able to organize, preceding baseball statistics, which was the second. I was able to recognize different makes by their varying grills and hood ornaments and, in some cases, by their differing body shapes. I was aided in my comprehension by World War II, during which new cars were not manufactured, and so, for once, knowledge had stood perfectly still to allow a little boy to store it away. I remember being extremely pleased that I had something close to mastery over a field of knowledge, however small and insignificant the field might be. Here was something I knew, and knew cold. I am not sure that I have ever since known anything else quite so well.

My family always had a car, and many of our vacations—most of them to Canada, where my father was born and still had relatives—were made by car. Expressways were not yet in business; and, though passing through small towns and cities was mildly interesting, for the most part I remember those nine-hundred-mile drives to Montreal and the Laurentian mountains as mildly boring. During the war years, we would sometimes pick up hitchhiking servicemen, as soldiers and sailors were then called, and at night we would often stay in private homes that had tourist rooms to let. There was an atmosphere of trust in the country then that is unfortunately now long gone. Think, for example, of the old traveling sales-man jokes. Impossible today. What farmer—or anyone else— would let a stranger into his home? Besides, the salesman him-self is probably flying these days and staying at Holiday Inns, and would probably be quite as wary of the farmer as the farmer would be of him.

Cars became immensely—make that intensely—interesting when I arrived at early adolescence. I was an adolescent under the *ancien régime*—before, that is, organized play, psychologi-cal understanding, and the birth-control pill came into exis-tence. In exchange for these—how shall I call them—little conveniences, we were allowed to drive cars young and were given a fair measure of freedom by parents who, never having heard of such words as *nurturing,* did not cloyingly hover over us. A pretty fair exchange, or so I have come to believe. In Chicago, when I was growing up there, a kid could get a driver's license at fifteen. (There used to be stories about farm kids driving when they were twelve or thirteen.) A driver's license was the great document of one's youth. It set one free from the confines of one's village, as neighborhoods in Chicago then seemed, and provided a passport to the larger world of the enticing and not yet menacing city. In those days in Chicago, when one obtained a driver's license, one was told immediately to place a five-dollar bill between it and the window in one's wallet. The purpose of this finsky was to have it at the ready, so that any cop who might stop one for any of a hundred little traffic violations could take it and pay himself off if he chose. A driver's license, more than anything else, marked one's passage into early adulthood.

Another little convenience we missed was the high school course called Driver's Education. Our fathers generally taught us how to drive, or perhaps a friend did; a few kids took lessons at driving schools. My father attempted to teach me one day in the bulky Hudson, which had a manual transmission and a most delicate clutch. It was no go, in every sense of the word, for as I let out the clutch, the odious Hudson lurched forward and the motor sputtered, fluttered, and died. My father's patience, for reasons unknown to me, was on empty that day, so after six or seven such lurches, we agreed to try it another day. As it turned out, we never had to do so.

A week or so later, I was in the car of an older friend, who wanted to visit his girlfriend on the sly, and thus didn't want his car, which was distinctive—it was the current year's two-tone green Chevy, hardtop convertible, with automatic transmission—seen parked in front of her house. He asked me if I would mind driving it around for a couple of hours and picking him up a few blocks away. I said I would be glad to. What he didn't ask me was whether I knew how to drive. I learned that afternoon, teaching myself, driving around quiet residential streets.

Not long after that my father took me to get my license. It was a rainy weekday morning. A man with the fine figure of a Chicago political hack—pallid, paunchy, ready to doze—after waiting half an hour or so for the rain to subside, said, "Hell, the kid looks like he can drive," and promptly issued me my license without an examination. My father, in thanks, gave him a little something extra for his lunch along with the fee for the license. The driver's license in my wallet, the five-dollar bill betwixt it and the plastic window containing it, I felt like crying out "I am free!" in imitation of some stagy plantation slave in *Gone with the Wind*—"Lordy be, I am free!" And, the fact is, I was free, or at least freer than I had hitherto been to roam the city and sample its hidden delights.

Although I have never had a car accident (touch wood), I do not consider myself a particularly good driver. I was from the beginning, and grow even more toward the end, a bit dreamy behind the wheel. I like to have the radio or, in more recent years, tape deck going, usually playing classical music, and sometimes I listen to a baseball game. The scene passes, my mind floats on clouds of fantasy, calling up phrases or formulating sentences for essays or stories I am writing or planning to write, imagining lives I shall never live. Even as a boy, I was never greatly enamored of speed—it wasn't my idea of a good time, and anyway I always found other ways of showing off—and never drag raced or played the horrific game called "Chicken," in which two cars came at each other head-on until one or the other chickened out and turned away from a certain collision.

Once, during a summer when I was a college student, while driving back in the early morning after visiting a girlfriend who was a camp counselor in Michigan, despite deluging myself with coffee and Pepsi-Cola, and pouring cold water over my wrists at gas stations, I fell asleep at the wheel on the Outer Drive in Chicago in my mother's car, a red-and-black Plymouth Belvedere with pushbutton automatic drive. I awoke to find myself driving into oncoming morning-rush-hour traffic, which certainly got my attention. When I managed to get back on the right side of the median, I thought there was something wrong with the steering wheel, so violently was it shaking. It turned out that it was my hands that were shaking. Later I discovered that all four tires were de-

stroyed by the hop over the median. Naturally, I lied to my
parents about what might have caused such damage, mumbling
some nonsense about young vandals being much on the prowl
in the part of Michigan I had visited. They didn't for a moment
believe me, but in their kindness neither did they press me.
Another small item for which I owe them.

My friend Robert Ginsburg drove splendidly. As others
can swear or paint or play the cello, he drove—with great
authority. Had I ever planned bank robberies or perfect crimes
requiring a getaway car, Robert would have been my driver.
There was a steadiness about his driving and a smoothness.
Gunning the engine lightly, he would zip without hesitation
through a narrow opening in an alley, or smoothly slide into
what seemed an impossibly small parking space, or run nearly
a full block in reverse without—hey, no sweat—showing the
least strain. Behind the wheel he could, as they say about
superior infielders in baseball, really pick it. In college one
summer he had a date with an attractive young woman named
Karen Black, who later went on to become a Hollywood actress. How did it go? I remember asking him. Did she say
anything interesting? " 'You drive well,' she told me," he replied. I have remembered it all these years because the line still
sounds like something written by Hemingway for *Road &
Track.*

Robert tooled around in a gunmetal-gray 1950 Chevy coupe
with standard transmission and plaid seat covers that had a lot
of green running through them. I must have clocked forty or
so thousand miles with him in that car, and I cannot recall the
least breakdown, not even a flat tire. It wasn't Robert's own
car—it was a family car—but he had fairly frequent use of it.
I saw a great deal of the world from the window and backseat
of that car when I was between the ages of fifteen and eighteen.
If I had that car in my possession today, I would bronze it, the

way people used to bronze their children's baby shoes, and tell people it is a piece of contemporary sculpture.

Part of the lore of my adolescence had kids owning their own beat-up old cars, or jalopies as they were then called—a word for which *Webster's* says the origin is uncertain—or "beaters" as they are called today. I did not own my own car in high school or in college. The first car I owned was a more-than-ten-year-old green Ford, which, just before my discharge from the army, I bought for two hundred dollars to transport me from Little Rock, Arkansas, to Fort Sill, Oklahoma, and thence to Chicago. It got the job done, and I sold it soon after. The only time since then that I have not owned a car is when I lived, in the early 1960s, in New York. Even then owning a car in New York was more burdensome than pleasurable, at least if one lived on short financial rations. But I felt the want of a car. I grew up in a car city, where the only reason for not owning a car was that you couldn't afford one. Without a car I felt like a cowboy without a horse, a sailor dry-docked—less complete, less happy, less free. "In America," a Havoline Motor Oil commercial begins, "your car is not just something you own. It's part of your life." It's only a commercial, I know, and even rather a loathsome one, but I fear that, in my case at least, there's something to it.

As a Midwesterner, I am sometimes surprised at the number of "muh fella Amuricans," as Lyndon Johnson used to say, middle-class ones, I run into who do not drive. Driving seems to be one of those activities best learned when young and, usually, not easily learned when older. For a long spell, women did not drive, though this changed not long after World War II. I remember being proud of my mother, who first began driving in her forties and who turned out to be a very good driver. A number of men I know who don't drive are now in their seventies and eighties, and were the sons of poor immigrants who did not have the money for so grand a luxury as a car. When these men came into adulthood, they faced the Depression and so couldn't afford a car themselves. They have learned to make do with taxis, wives who drive, friends who chauffeur them around, or mass transit. Perhaps the most notable case in recent modern literature of a nondriver is that of Edmund Wilson. "The Bunny," as Karl Shapiro refers to him, always adding that somehow deflationary definite article, found nothing at all odd about stepping into a cab in Manhattan and instructing the shocked driver to take him to Martha's Vineyard. It was owing to such habits that Wilson's father made sure that he never came into his inheritance until his, the Bunny's, mother was dead.

American car culture par excellence, in my experience, is to be found in the South. In the South, not only was every man expected to know a great deal about cars, but he was expected to know how to fix his own cars. Since the Southern climate is gentler on cars, people tended to keep them longer and thus needed to repair them more often. I can recall, in the probably vain attempt to pass myself off as a regular guy, listening to Southerners talk to me about overhead cams, torque, mag wheels, and Holley four-barrel carburetors, while I tried to keep the franchise-doughnut glaze out of my eyes and to pretend I knew what the hell they were talking about. I once asked a fellow I worked with in Little Rock if he knew how to replace some kind of bearing in a Chevy, which I then drove. He seemed to think I might have to lift the engine. "How do you do that?" I inquired. "No big deal," he said. "You just get a rope and pulleys, fix 'em to two strong tree branches, and crank her up." I nodded my head, as if to suggest that I should have realized how easy it was. Had I been fool enough to attempt it, I should by now, I have no doubt, have been dead for nearly thirty years.

Living in the South, I drove a number of not very sleek used cars. One of them was the Chevy called a Corvair, which gave Ralph Nader his start when he wrote a book about it entitled *Unsafe at Any Speed.* Quite as memorable, though, was an old Cadillac someone sold me that, roughly six weeks after purchase, refused to go in reverse. I seem, as a result, to have done quite a bit of driving around various blocks with it. But the real adventure was buying cars, new or used, in the South, where, apparently, they had never heard of car-salesman jokes. Once I attempted to buy a used Volkswagen bus at a place called—you are going to have to believe me on this—Cliff Packer's Auto Ranch, whose salesmen wore Levi's checkered shirts, and ten-gallon hats, generally nicely set off with a toothpick in the left corner of the mouth. (I didn't buy the bus because they weren't interested in selling it for cash; the low price was predicated on the profit to be made on financing charges.) At a Mercury agency where I bought something called a Comet, the salesmen wore maroon blazers and carried red canes; they, too, added that elegant, confidence-building touch of the rakishly placed toothpick.

But even under the best of conditions, I have always found buying cars sheer hell. Too much is at stake. I am not talking about money here. I am talking about self-respect. (Let us not speak of self-esteem, which departs as soon as you hit the door of even the grandest car dealer.) A no-nonsense, leave-a-fellow-his-dignity car salesman is, in my experience, rarer than a Hasid in a red Porsche convertible. A serious drama is going on when one is buying a car, much of it, to avail myself of a feminist term, purely masculinist. I have myself come to think of the activity of dealing with car salesmen as dancing with wolves.

First, while you know that you are never going to win in this transaction, you hope at least to come out of it with your fillings still in your mouth. You hope, that is, to make a deal of a kind that, at least, won't cause your salesman and his fellow highwaymen to laugh about your naiveté together over scotch and steaks when they meet at the end of the evening. Then, if you can bring this off, you have to hope that your deal is not too much worse than that of any friends who might have bought a similar car. Learning that someone has purchased roughly the same car you have for, say, three thousand dollars less can put tinted glass around your spirit for the life of the car.

Part of the problem is that car salesmen are so damnably confident in their underestimation of your intelligence. The last car I bought before the one I now drive was sold to me by a man with a strange language tic. After every statement of mine, either of fact or inquiry, he said either "Hey, no problem" or "Right." I chose him among salesmen on the floor, you should know, out of sheer prejudice; as a Jewish-surnamed American, he was my co-religionist, and I thought, naively, that he would give me the *emess,* or no-nonsense lowdown. Wrong again. At the end of our introductory colloquy, he allowed that he wasn't interested in what he called "the numbers"—to us cognoscenti, the price—but "in finding you a car you are really comfortable with." "Ah, Mr. Pearlman," I announced. "I am the son of a salesman. Please to cut the crap forthwith. Don't worry about my feeling comfortable. It's the numbers we want to concentrate on. They mean everything." What did he reply to this, I had thought air-clearing, remark? What he said was, "Right, no problem." I, for my part, said to myself, "Hey, you gotta love 'em."

To make buying a car a touch more complicated, I note that nowadays every so often women have begun to sell cars. Generally these are rather good-looking women, which can put a clangorous sexual note into the proceedings. I bought my last car from a woman, an impressive woman, as it turned out, a European, who made me feel very little of the standard edginess leading on to full Sturm und Drang, car buyer's division. However, in the middle of our fairly simple negotiations, she received a telephone call from which I could not help but overhear that she was due in divorce court the next day. When I queried her politely about this, she said yes, it was true, then added, "My husband ran off with my best friend." All the way home I thought, what an odd way to put it! I should have thought that your best friend might have run off with your husband. Why did I find this odd? Maybe it's the general paranoia that buying a car induces in a man of normal nervous organization.

Still, despite all these difficulties, I think it likely that in the field of car buying, I have a good shot at realizing my ambition—perhaps my only perfectly realized ambition, even though a negative one—of never owning a station wagon. As I sink into general physical decay, it's looking better every day. I am told that as they age, station wagons tend to rattle. But it's the suburbanity of these vehicles that appalls, the sense one has that once any of its doors is opened, two large dogs, six children, and a vast quantity of gardening equipment will pour out. I knew a man, a bachelor and a sedulous chaser of women, who, because he drove a station wagon, which he needed for his business, always had a difficult time convincing the women he perpetually pursued that he was indeed single. Seeing him in that car, I wouldn't believe him myself. The only argument for a station wagon is that of utility. Which has always made the silliest car on the road, in my opinion, a Mercedes station wagon—a piece of comically misplaced luxury, like a diamond-studded lawn mower or a mink briefcase.

Another kind of car I should not want to own, though I have never been in danger here, is a limousine, especially a

stretch limousine. If I had the money, I think I should prefer
to hire a lighting director than a chauffeur. The picture of a
number of stretch limos parked outside a club, as I have seen
them parked outside the elegant F Street Club in Washington,
is an unpleasant reminder of plutocracy. In Washington, certain government jobs have the added status of having a car and
driver go with them. ("Never take a job with a car and driver,"
Malcolm Muggeridge told the journalist Paul Johnson. "When
you lose it, that's what you'll miss most.") Now that there are
so many livery services, and airports are practically clogged
with stretch limos, every man can be a plutocrat for an hour
or two. Not every man can be the actor Kevin Costner, however, who not long ago in a movie made love in a stretch limo,
which ought to add nicely to the ample stock of car-connected
sex fantasies in American life. (Which reminds me that mine
is also the drive-in movie generation, and I shouldn't be at all
surprised to learn that many of my contemporaries, when first
married, may have required a steering wheel and gearshift
installed in their marital beds to make easier the transition to
normal conjugal sex.) I recently did a bit of work in a nearby
city for a firm that "sent a car" for me; a few days later I was
driven home in another. Both were stretch limos, very handsomely appointed, and immensely comfortable too. Unlike
Kevin Costner, I used the time spent in them reading the
letters of the dour Henry Adams—a case, no doubt, of letting
the punishment fit the crime.

It won't do to call Henry Adams himself a car enthusiast,
since there was nothing he was enthusiastic about except
spreading gloom, yet he was an early user of cars. In 1901, he
reports "automobilising" from Paris to Chantilly ". . . all the
way hanging on to my hair and ears." The following year he
writes to his brother Brooks: "If I were just a trifle richer, I

should set up an automobile stable, which is now the only amusement worth cultivating." In 1904, he bought an eighteen-horsepower Mercedes, driven, of course, by a chauffeur. He used cars to travel about France for his researches for his book about the great Gothic churches. In 1908, Adams wrote to his friend Elizabeth Cameron that "my only solid comfort is to have got rid of my automobile," though, as Henry James reported, Adams had "a surviving capacity to be very well taken care of." Not altogether what we should today call "a fun person," Henry Adams.

One cannot say the same for Edith Wharton, who unequivocally adored cars. In one of her ample Panhards, she would swoop down upon Henry James in Rye, stow him alongside her in the backseat, while her husband Teddy sat next to the chauffeur in the front, and roar through the Sussex countryside. My "angel of devastation," James used to call her. Mrs. Wharton, it will be recalled, wrote *A Motor Flight Through France*—and how splendid the word *Flight* is in that title! The book opens as if a firm foot had pressed down on a beautifully crisp accelerator:

> The motor-car has restored the romance of travel.
> Freeing us from all the compulsions and contacts of the railway, the bondage to fixed hours and the beaten track, the approach to each town through the area of ugliness and desolation created by the railway itself, it has given us back the wonder, the adventure and novelty which enlivened the way of our posting grandparents. Above all these recovered pleasures must be ranked the delight of taking a town unawares, stealing on it by back ways and unchronicled paths, and surprising in it some intimate aspect of past time, some silhouette hidden for half a century or more by the ugly mask of railway embankments and the iron bulk of a huge station. Then the villages that we missed and yearned for from the windows of the train—the unseen villages have been given back to us!—and nowhere could the

importance of the recovery have been more delightfully exemplified than on a May afternoon in the Pas-de-Calais, as we climbed the long ascent beyond Boulogne on the road to Arras.

How fortunate that Mrs. Wharton, with her fine spirit of adventure, never lived to drive the San Diego Freeway during evening rush hour!

The car I most want to own is no longer available to me. It was a lush cream-colored Packard convertible owned by a Dr. Henning Melville Swenson, the father of a high school friend. But then I remember, too, a black Cadillac convertible with red leather interior owned by a man named Pete Libby, a widower who when married used to live in our neighborhood and who was later said to have often gone out with the singer Patti Page. The night I saw him in this car, driving down Rush Street with an extremely blond person in the front seat, it looked like nothing so much as a gondola and he like the Duke of Corona. Then there was another Cadillac convertible I fancied, this one of a rich peach color, owned by Sugar Ray Robinson, the greatest boxer of my lifetime, who had a suit and a hat made in the same color. The photograph of man and car appeared a thousand years ago in *Life* magazine.

My fantasy taste seems to run to these largish American cars. When on holiday, and thus in a state of moral relaxation, I tend to rent approximations of them. In recent years, when out of town, I have found myself renting lengthy luxury cars, Cadillac Sevilles and an aircraft-carrier-size machine called a Lincoln Town Car. I was driving the latter when waiting for a large, heavyset man in a soft golf hat, a man I judged to be at the country-club stage of culture, to leave a parking space in a lot outside a restaurant in Maine. He was himself driving a Cadillac Fleetwood of a length that seemed to go on just beyond forever, and, as he pulled out of the space, he noted my

Lincoln and gave me a smile of approval. "Soul brother," I read that smile to say.

Ethnic tastes in cars is an unexamined but not uninteresting question. Someone told me that American Greeks who have a bit of money prefer Lincolns. Jews used to stay away from Fords and other cars in the Ford line because of the founder's anti-Semitism, though there may not be very many Jewish car buyers around nowadays with historical memory of that fact. Uneducated blacks once went in for big used Cadillacs, which they called pigs, because of the vast amount of fuel they used. There is an old joke about a black man who, out for a test drive in a new Cadillac, asks the salesman if the car doesn't make him look too Jewish. Generalizations are regularly drawn from cars to owners. Owners of Chrysler products—including Dodges and Plymouths—according to a survey of pizza deliverymen in Detroit, are said to be poor tippers. Physicians used to be instructed by the American Medical Association that it was unseemly to drive a car flashier than a Buick, lest they appear to be hauling in too many shekels, though that day is long past. I am myself always drawing conclusions about people from the cars they drive, estimating from this single datum their financial worth, their aspirations, their general philosophy. I make no claims for the quality of these conclusions, so highly subjective are they—I take solace, you should know, when I discover people driving Rolls-Royces who are homely—but I go on making them nevertheless.

In *The Bookmaker's Daughter* by Shirley Abbott, I discovered someone else making similar judgments. Miss Abbott is of my generation, and she knows whereof she speaks; she knows her wheels. In the town in which she grew up, Hot Springs, Arkansas, in the forties, she tells us that "the smart money . . . drove inconspicuous old Packards" and "women's automobiles showed what kind of men they had." When her father hadn't the money to take her mother out in the Depression year of 1933, he was at least able to take her for a spin in his red Pontiac coupe, and, while in that car, life was splendid enough. She remembers, and reminds me, that the door of a Buick of a certain era, when closed, "went *hershunk*, decisively, like the door of an Electrolux refrigerator." That is exactly how they sounded. How I wish that I could arrange with my publisher to make my own books, when closed, go *hershunk*.

I haven't actually owned any cars whose doors go *hershunk* either. For someone who has had a lifelong interest in them, I have taken delivery, to use that car dealer's odd locution, on chiefly rather boring cars. One of these was not so much boring as goofy. It was the car called the Pacer, whose body design resembled a turtle with impressive posture. The vast amount of window space it provided must have been what attracted me to it. I bought it during the time when houseplants were the rage; perhaps I thought I was acquiring a portable greenhouse designed by the late Buckminster Fuller. Earlier, before owning my aforementioned Volvo, I owned a hot car, a 1969 forest-green Pontiac GTO—*varoom, varoom*—that made me feel, while I was driving it, like the Green Hornet. After it and the Volvo and the Pacer, I went, automotively speaking, straight and very square. I bought two Chevys in a row, both Malibu Classiques, and then two Oldsmobiles, Cutlass Cieras.

Need I say that there was nothing remotely Malibuish, Classiquish, Cutlassian, or Cieran about any of these cars. But then, perhaps, on the principle that Humphrey Bogart enunciated in *The Maltese Falcon* of "the cheaper the gunsel, the gaudier the patter," the plainer the American car, the fancier the name given to it. Chevrolet currently has a model that it calls a Celebrity Eurosport. I have never noticed anyone remotely like a celebrity or a European sport driving it. Nor have I ever seen anyone in the least capricious driving the same company's Caprice. But then neither have I ever seen a true swinger drive an old Dodge Swinger, or a white hunter drive a Safari, a fisherman a Barracuda, a poet a Stanza, a musician a Sonata, but such are among the sobriquets of many cars of recent years. Buick, I note, has a new model that it calls Supercharged Ultra. This seems to me a brilliant ploy to sweep the boards, quite as good in its way as the term *pro-life*, a term that doesn't leave the other side much, which, I guess, is the point.

None of the cars I have owned has ever been, to use another car dealer's locution (this one to refer to accessories), "fully loaded." I am not sure quite what "fully loaded" means today; perhaps it includes a microwave oven, a rotating spice rack, a Jacuzzi footbath in the back. Nothing in this realm can surprise. Surely no contemporary car can be considered even half-loaded that doesn't have a car phone. I was once at a meeting with the songwriter Marvin Hamlisch, who noted that, high-tech though our society would seem to be, he had a very difficult time in Los Angeles getting a second line for his car phone. I hoped he was kidding, but have to report that he wasn't.

A car that is fully loaded nowadays must include, too, what are known as vanity license plates, or those plates that spell out your name or a brief wiseguyism or a sexual innuendo. Models of concision, these vanity plates: who would have thought people could demonstrate their witlessness in so few letters? Or sometimes their pretentiousness. I occasionally pass a Cadillac that has a license plate reading L'OPERA; more recently I found myself driving behind a recreational vehicle with a plate reading GOETHE. If a vanity plate, why not a philosophical or political bumper sticker? "Subvert the Paradigm" is a bumper sticker I not long ago noted that reminded me that I have not yet read Thomas Kuhn's book on revolution in science. "Stop Unnecessary Circumcision" was one sticker among many I saw on an old Volvo driven by a furry fellow in a ponytail. How pleasant, I thought, not to have to contemplate lunch with the car's owner.

In a novel by Maurice Baring I read that "St. James said that everything in the world is vanity except a carriage." I don't know which St. James this might have been, but the guy may have been on to something. I am currently driving a four-door 1993 BMW 525i. I like it exceedingly. I shall desist from writing a testimonial for it here, but I shall say that this car made me realize that, shallow fellow that I am, I sometimes forget that a small number of material things have the power to make me happy. Not for long, of course; no one is meant to be happy for long, but briefly, fleetingly, yet recurrently. This car seems to have this power. Large minds are free to think otherwise, to think that the entire matter of cars is a bit of American male craziness, and that anyone who looks to a car for pleasure is a damn fool. "I refute them thus," I imagine Dr. Johnson saying in response to such people, slipping in behind the steering wheel of my car, tires squealing as he peels away from the curb and speeds off into the distance.

Hair Piece

Plutarch, writing about Alcibiades, easily the most interesting if certainly not the most upright of fifth-century-B.C. Athenians, tells us everything about his adventures and quite a lot about his manner. The manner, there is reason to believe, was in good part the man. He was strikingly handsome; Plutarch, usually measured in his prose, goes so far as to speak of his "physical perfection." He writes: "As for Alcibiades' physical beauty, we need say no more than that it flowered at each season of his growth in turn, and lent him an extraordinary grace and charm, alike as a boy, a youth, and a man." So naturally elegant was he that even his physical defects came to seem attractive. "Even his lisp is said to have suited his voice well and to have made his talk persuasive and full of charm," notes Plutarch. Clearly, we are talking here about a nice-lookin' fella.

We are also talking about a fairly vain fella. Plutarch fills us in on the way Alcibiades wore his robes and on his disdain for the flute, which he refused to play because he felt that the instrument distorted the features of anyone who played it. He also makes plain that, owing to Alcibiades' radiant physical appearance, Socrates felt—wrongly, as we now know—that the young man must have natural virtue and sweetness of disposition. (No philosopher, you might say, like an old philosopher.) Plutarch tells us how many were the young Alcibiades' pursuers as well as the mature Alcibiades' admirers. But about the man's hair—its color, its texture, its length—not a word. Hirsutically, Plutarch has nothing to tell, except that when Alcibiades went to live among the Spartans, he wore "his hair untrimmed."

But what was Alcibiades' hair like when trimmed? Did he comb it forward or brush it back or over to the side? Was it curly or straight, wavy or lank, thick or fine? Black or blond or red or a shade of brown? Did he part it in the middle, or on one side, or not at all? Did his hairline recede as he grew older? (He died in his middle forties.) Did his hair turn gray? Did he carry a comb? Did he go in for oils, pomades, or other hairdressings, or did he leave his hair dry? Which did he prefer, Alcibiades, the wet or the dry look? If this man, noted for the excesses of his private life, was worried that playing a flute distorted his features, he couldn't have been unconcerned about the look of his hair. What a shame that we don't know how he dealt with the hair question! History, once again, leaves the significant facts blank.

Some writers are more hair-minded than others. Proust tells us little more of his M. Swann's hair than that it was red. Stendhal reports that Julien Sorel's hair is dark auburn in color, "growing down over his forehead [which] made it seem low, and gave him, in moments of anger, a rather forbidding, ill-natured air." Henry James could be—no doubt preferred to be—vague on the subject, never telling us the precise color of the Princess Casamassima's hair. Although James Joyce tells us everything else about Leopold Bloom—that he's five feet nine inches and 165 pounds, among other things—I'm not sure that he tells us anything about Bloom's hair.

I happen to be reading V. S. Pritchett's memoirs at the moment, and he is, so to say, a very hairy writer. In Pritchett's memoirs as well as in his stories men appear with forelocks and cowlicks and "waving mats of long thick white hair [with] a yellow streak in it" and "carefully barbered streaks over the long egg-like head." Pritchett remarks on his and his brother's youthful hair being "carefully greased by a hair oil we have invented: a mixture of olive oil and eau de Cologne, so that we smell like two young scented salads." Can it be that Pritchett, as a writer, is so attentive to other men's hair because his own, from the photographs I have seen, appears largely to have deserted him?

I would be inclined to think so, except that I am myself similarly attentive to this aspect of male plumage and always have been, without Pritchett's near baldness. My hair, like the nation at large, has been in a bit of a recession. Measured in hairline inches, I should say that, in my fifties, I have thus far along been allowed to keep roughly four-fifths of my hair, with a hairline that begins to resemble the southern portion of the continent of Africa, growing a bit thinnish around Mozambique. I shouldn't give, say, an index finger to have my lost hair restored to me, though I am generally pleased to have retained what hair I have.

I have been—how to say it?—hairdo observant all my days. When I was young I was even what I have seen described, in either *Esquire* or *Gentlemen's Quarterly*, as "hairdo intensive." In the earliest photograph of myself that I have seen, I have blondish hair combed into a large curl running the length of my head. Later my hair darkened and became not so much curly as wavy, but wavy understood in the context of stormy weather; unruly is probably the more precise word. Even today, in the somewhat impoverished condition of my scalp, if I fail to get regular haircuts, some impertinent and quite irrelevant wave appears atop my head, ready to crash against no known shore.

As a child I suffered no barber trauma. At least I can recall no tears at a barbershop. I do remember for a long spell in boyhood having to sit upon a board that raised me high enough for the barber to cut my hair, and I remember feeling that I had reached an important stage of maturity—perhaps at age seven or eight—when the board was no longer required. A boy's haircut was fifty cents when I was growing up, and then it shot up to seventy-five cents and then to a dollar. Once I began going to the barbershop on my own, my mother gave me an extra quarter and instructed me to tip the barber, unless he happened to be the owner of the shop, for it was thought undignified for the owner to accept tips. (My haircuts now cost twelve dollars, and I tip my barber three dollars.) The two rivaling barbershops of my boyhood were Levitan's and Ross's. I preferred Ross's, where the best barber was a tall, uncharacteristically (for a barber) reticent man named Dudley.

Dudley seems to me a fine name for a barber. So does the name Pete. I used to go to a barbershop called Pete's, where the owner, a very likable Austrian, cut my hair. I used sometimes to go in for my haircuts early in the day, at 9:30 or 10:00 A.M., in an attempt to avoid the rush; and more than once Pete, authoritatively flapping the sheet with which he covered his customers, asked, "Through for the day, Professor?" When he did this I wanted to but never did say, "Yes, Pete, except for my work on perfecting the hydrogen bomb, which is nearing completion and is there in my briefcase." A friend who also went to Pete's told me—when Pete had sold the shop to live nearer his son, an osteopath in Portland—that he had never had his hair cut by a barber whose name wasn't Pete. I told him to try the Yellow Pages. But he stayed with the new owner, an Italian named John.

My current barber, a West Virginian, is named Ralph, which strikes me as also a fine name for a barber. But then it may be that if you like your barber, as I do Ralph, whatever name he happens to carry will seem splendidly appropriate—just as, I have heard it said, the perfect title for any best-selling book is the title given to any book that happens to sell very well. The one barber in my past whose name I cannot remember was an elderly man in the basement of the old-fashioned barbershop at the Marion Hotel in Little Rock, Arkansas. He was frail and gentle, had rather fluffy white hair parted in the middle, and kept a portrait of Jesus next to his towels and barbering instruments and a pair of pajamas in the cabinet below his sink in case it snowed, which, in Little Rock, it almost never did. He had a memorably light and prettily rhythmic touch with the scissors.

I cannot say the same for Felix, a barber I went to in my young manhood. Felix used regularly to nick my neck and ears, and occasionally leave me with dried blood around and under my sideburns. He rarely gave me the same haircut twice. Like the man who said in defense of his continuing to go out with a notably unattractive woman that it wasn't the sex but the conversation afterward, so with Felix: it wasn't the haircuts but the laughter that went along with them that kept me coming back. An immigrant from Eastern Europe with a greenhorn's accent, Felix had my number; almost anything he said caused me to giggle. And much of what he said was what used to be called off-color—usually, let me add, way off, like chartreuse aquamarine or purplish magenta. I wouldn't say that Felix was lewd; he was the next two stages beyond lewd. No woman could pass his shop without Felix making an inappropriate comment. All his comments in this vein have left me, I am pleased to report, except for my memory of his once saying, as a woman who must have been in her nineties crept past his shop window, "Now dere, Epstein, is one built for speed."

Felix was also a super salesman, and I often used to leave his shop with conditioners, special shampoos, rubberized scalp massagers, tortoiseshell combs, and, on one notable occasion, condoms. Felix gave what I have elsewhere heard referred to, after the great power-tool company, as a Black & Decker haircut, and I finally left him when, one day, after catching the skin of my neck with his clippers, he caused me to take the name of the Lord in vain. I later discovered that, during this same haircut, he had badly, as I believe the term of art is, boxed off the hair at the back of my head, giving me a haircut that looked as if it had been acquired at the state prison at Joliet. I never returned.

I preferred smaller barbershops to larger, or what I sometimes think of as power, barbershops. Those were the shops where the atmosphere was generally a bit more Roman Empire (in decline) than I cared for. In such shops there were usually six or seven barber chairs, a manicurist (named—need I say?—Blanche), and at least one shoeshine man. I used to go to such a shop on lower Fifth Avenue in New York, and my mind retains the picture of many a businessman potentate having his hair cut while simultaneously taking a manicure and a shine, none of which distracted him from laying down the law on the forthcoming election or next Sunday's pro football game.

I enjoyed the spectacle provided by such shops—and I'm not sure many such still exist—but I couldn't quite partake in it. I have never had a manicure and think it safe to say that I shall go to my grave without having had one; somehow, I don't think there will be manicurists in the next world. I used to take shoeshines, but I no longer do, for getting one has become not only too expensive—two dollars and a one-dollar tip—but too fraught with social complications. In this realm as in many another we have come a long way from the time when the writer George Frazier could write a piece for *Esquire* titled "The World's Second Best Shoeshine." (This shine was available in those days at the thirteen-chair shoeshine parlor in the

Cleveland airport, where they used heat lamps on your shoes and a special blend of polish that didn't rub off on a clean handkerchief. The best shoeshine, as should always be the case with the best of anything, was, according to Frazier, in dispute, rivaling claimants being at the Waldorf, the Plaza, and a shop at the foot of Wall Street.) For some years now I have shined my own shoes and rather take pleasure in doing so.

But the great watershed moment in the history of men's hairdos, for me, came one day in Manhattan in the early 1960s when I passed a crowded barbershop on Lexington Avenue and through the window saw men in barber chairs getting their hair cut while wearing hair nets. I recall thinking that new heights of male vanity had been achieved. Arthur Koestler, I somewhere read, reported his anger when a rival for the affection of a beautiful woman told the woman that Koestler had slept in a hair net. A filthy lie, Koestler claimed; the truth, he allowed, was that he only bathed in a hair net. But now we had men sitting in plain public view in hair nets. A new age had arrived. Fantastico! The advent of male hairstyling was upon us.

Fancy male hairdos had existed in the past, beginning at least as early as the Persians, who cut off their hair and shaved the manes of their horses to lament the death in battle of a commander. In my own youth, there were ambitious pompadours, clean crew cuts, Chicagos (a flat crew-cut top with long greasy sides; in the city of Chicago, this hairdo was known as a Detroit), ducktails (to use the polite word), and a dramatic widow's peak with an added dippity-do effect at the front worn by the movie actor Tony Curtis, famous for the line, delivered in a movie to Debra Paget in the strongest possible New York accent, "Yonder lies da castle of my fadder the Caliph." If my own unruly hair could have supported a Tony Curtis, I, at the age of fifteen or sixteen, would have worn one proudly and looked, of course, perfectly ridiculous. Saved from this particular follicular folly, you might say, only by nature.

I wore my hair, as an adolescent, *en brosse*, with no part and no pomades. The great popular hair-taming potions of the day were products called Vitalis, Lucky Tiger, and Wildroot Cream Oil; the last claimed it would give any man who used it the fairly serious social problem of keeping all the girls away. I note that in French *cheveux en brosse* means "crew-cut hair," but in fact my hair, though cut short and brushed back, wouldn't support a true crew cut, at least not one that gave a spiky stand-up effect, for which straighter hair than mine was required. Crew cuts were worn by athletes—the derogatory word *jock* had not yet come into being. Boys who were more interested in the girl chase wore more ambitious hairdos.

Hollywood led in this realm as in many another. In the movies, a leading man's hair was often big-city black and lac-quered. The powerful movie hairdos were those of Clark Gable, Robert Taylor, Cary Grant, and Tyrone Power. Hum-phrey Bogart was an *en brosse* man, though closer observers than I inform me that he later wore a hairpiece, as did Bing Crosby. Gary Cooper's and James Cagney's hair seemed insig-nificant; so did Edward G. Robinson's and Jimmy Stewart's, though the latter took to wearing an unconvincing rug or toupee (pronounced among the cognoscenti as "toup"). Frank Sinatra was another big rug man and was said to have hired a woman, at a serious salary, to maintain his twenty-odd differ-ent hairpieces. John Wayne, too, wore a wig. In our own day, Burt Reynolds is of the wig party.

Clark Gable probably had the perfect movie-star hair. In a number of his movies, owing to this hair, he was given the name Blackie. Lots of people took on nicknames from their hair, the most common, of course, being the name Red, which is a tough nickname to maintain once one's hair turns white. Some kids took the name Sandy from the color of their hair. A towheaded fellow, five or six years older than I, from my high school named Whitey Pearson went on to play basketball at the University of Kentucky. The language is deficient in not having a word, the visual equivalent of onomatopoeia, for things that sound as they look. I have in mind here a frightening character who roamed the halls of my high school who had the impressively menacing name of Whitey Rasch. But the complications of race relations have put paid to the names Blackie and Whitey.

When I was in it, the military understood male vanity wonderfully well and, insofar as hair is a gymnasium for working out this vanity, made short work of it. One of the first events awaiting any military recruit is having his head shaved. The quickness of that first army haircut shocked. Three, perhaps four tracks across the scalp with a clipper—zip, zip, zip, zip—and one's individuality has suffered an immediate and powerful setback. That first military haircut was a great leveler, in a number of senses. All that careful coiffing was destroyed; all that empty vanity lay upon the floor. One felt so unsightly that one became almost automatically reconciled to the military life. With a haircut of this kind, where could one go anyway?

In the late 1950s and early 1960s, longish hair was not permitted in the army. I had a few sergeants, all of them black, who had mustaches. Nobody had a beard. I'm sure they weren't allowed. Today such restrictions would probably be subject to a civil liberties suit. I don't recall any bearded teachers at the University of Chicago when I was a student there, though there were a few with mustaches walking around. One of the most interesting mustaches, a small toothbrush job, belonged to the poet Elder Olson. The first man I knew with a beard was the literary critic Stanley Edgar Hyman. His was a brown beard, and it seemed right for him. Stanley was heavyish and had a good laugh and, when I saw him, wore three-piece brown suits, which rendered him a sepia and rather Jewish Santa Claus. In those days, the early 1960s, a beard was still a badge of bohemianism, an attention-getter, a conversation piece. People who invented personae for themselves wore beards—George Bernard Shaw, Monty Woolley, Ezra Pound—and if one had a beard, it was somehow felt that one ought to have a sufficiently interesting personality to go along with it.

Student upheaval during the late sixties and early seventies put an end to that. As California may be credited with the great cultural advance of allowing a right turn on a red light, so the late sixties and early seventies may be credited with making long hair and facial hair not only acceptable but, in some settings, practically *de rigueur.* Beards and mustaches are fairly popular among men, but they seem especially so among academic men. Beards were a phenomenon once common among graduate students, and, as some of these students grew older and became professors, they kept their beards. Where I teach, roughly half the professors sport beards, mustaches, or hairdos befitting the Spanish conquistadores that most of them despise.

What is the significance of this? Perhaps it is in part a way of keeping allegiance with the spirit of protest of one's youth; or perhaps it is a way of belatedly getting in on the protest one never registered while meekly studying for one's doctorate. Perhaps it is meant to show that, given one's passion for learning, shaving can only be a time-consuming distraction and is better done away with. Recall in this regard Albert Einstein's uncombed hair. Montaigne, in his essay "On Educating Children," writes about "how many have I known in my time made as stupid as beasts by an indiscreet hunger for knowledge! Carneades was turned so mad by it that he could not find time to tend to his hair or his nails." Perhaps life is simply made easier for them by not having to shave. (Most academic beards are not carefully trimmed.) Perhaps, again, they are there out of pure vanity, because the people who sport them think themselves damned good-looking in them—or at any rate better-looking than they would be without them. Perhaps some think beards and long hair make them look younger, though it is a discouraging fact that the hair on a man's face frequently turns gray before the hair on his head does.

My own sense is that the majority of men who grow beards tend only to add to their indistinctiveness. They become more Koren-ish—like those furry little figures in the cartoons of Edward Koren. (The combination of a woolly beard and a woolly head of hair reminds me of the child's game of men's faces that can be turned upside down and still show a face.) Some men experiment a good deal with different beards and mustaches. Facial hair is the poor man's version of cosmetic surgery, used to cover up a long lip, disguise a weak chin, camouflage bad skin. Beards taken on at midlife suggest discomfort with the way one has lived and looked in the first half of one's life. Too-frequent changes in the arrangement of a man's facial hair make him slightly suspect. One begins to feel about men who regularly experiment with different hairdos, beards, mustaches, and sideburns that they suffer a peculiar form of identity crisis—they don't know who they *aren't*.

The most recent trend in beardery seems to be the permanent one week's growth of facial hair. Show business once again set the precedent when an actor with the unpromising name of Don Johnson began wearing precisely such a scraggly beard on the television show *Miami Vice*. Yasser Arafat has long worn such a beard—and I call them, to myself, Arafats. How one sustains a permanent one week's growth of beard is not something I have been able to fathom. Long, unkempt hair and an Arafat can give a man what no advertising agency copywriter or designer has thus far thought to call "the homeless look," which, in a decadent society—who knows?—could become the rage.

George Balanchine, a very stylish and not notably hirsute man, once declared beards the very essence of stylelessness. His view was that the historical moment for beards had passed. They were authentic in his father's generation, but no longer. (Victorian men seem, somehow, appropriately hairy.) "All right," Balanchine said, "somebody wants to look like Christ, you know—the hair and all. But it's silly, it looks silly on people. It's all a fake."

And yet is it? I have known people, contemporaries, who have had beards for thirty years. (One of them once shaved the mustache portion of his beard and revealed that over the years he had developed a thin and disapproving upper lip; the mustache was returned instanter.) They will meet their maker in their beards. I should probably no longer recognize them on the street without their beards. Which reminds me of the joke, too elaborate to tell fully here, about the Hasid whom God does not allow in heaven because he fails to recognize him in an Armani suit and with his hair styled.

A beard, I feel, ought to be earned. Solzhenitsyn, in a Soviet labor camp, earned his beard and would seem quite unnatural without it. That he has an Amish look—a full beard with no mustache—seems even more appropriate. I have to strain to think of other earned beards. My own sense is that for a mustache to be earned, and not look fake, it probably ought to have been in place no later than 1947. Dean Acheson's Anglophiliac pencil mustache passed the test; so did Sidney Hook's small, dark, more Frenchified job. A mustache certainly ought not to have been grown after Robert Redford's mink-lipped appearance as the Sundance Kid in the movie *Butch Cassidy and the Sundance Kid,* which, because Redford looked so good in his, stirred many men to grow mustaches. Such a mustache, to work well, alas, requires the rest of Redford's face.

I once attempted a mustache, but a beard held no interest for me. I have never sported an Arafat, but years ago I used to prefer, if I had no social obligations, not to shave on weekends. No longer. Apart from occasional illness, I don't think I have failed to shave in nearly twenty years. I feel hygienically incomplete if I do not shave. A shave, like a haircut, has become something I look forward to, a positive pleasure. Now here, I do believe, is striking evidence of a quiet life.

I shave in the shower, afterward trimming my sideburns before the bathroom mirror. I use a safety razor. I regularly try new razors and new blades, though I secretly suspect that the companies who produce them do not provide improved products but instead merely lower the quality of the ones previously on the market. At various times I have contemplated using a straight razor, but have decided against doing so, lest the probable consequence, that of cutting my own throat, make my insurance company uneasy.

I have been shaved by a barber with such a razor four or five times in my life, enjoying every moment of it each time, from the hot towels upon my cheeks and jaws to the brushing on of lather to the rustling sound of the steel razor scraping against my skin. I do not tend to yearn for the good old days, but being shaved every day by a barber, as many men once were, must have been a fine and refreshing thing. At the conclusion of a good shave I feel, as Henry James remarked when, late in his fifties, he shaved off his beard, "*forty* and clean and light."

Henry James was, from fairly early in life, bald. But he qualifies, I believe, as importantly bald. Churchill was importantly bald. Edmund Wilson was, too. So were Montaigne and H. W. Fowler and Lenin, all of whom had well-trimmed goatees. Ralph Richardson was and John Gielgud remains not so much importantly as interestingly bald. In their own way, so were the novelist brothers Singer, I. B. and I. J., both of whom looked better bald than when, as young men, they had hair. (In his story "It May Never Happen," V. S. Pritchett describes "a stringy and dejected man, bald but not sufficiently so.") Robert Duvall, the actor, and Matt Williams, the third baseman of the San Francisco Giants, seem to me aggressively bald—bald men that you don't want to fool with. A. J. Liebling is not easily imagined with hair, nor is Socrates. Max Beerbohm, after he became bald, added a fine fluffy white mustache to his elegant get-up. Varieties of baldness are considerable, nearly up there with those of religious experience. I do not say bald is beautiful, but it can be manly and impressive.

The first historical figure whom we know to have suffered psychologically from his baldness was no less a personage than Julius Caesar. He was, according to Suetonius, a bit of a dandy, "always keeping his head carefully trimmed and shaved" and even removing his body hair. Caesar's enemies apparently mocked his baldness, treating it as a disfigurement, and Suetonius goes on to report that "of all the honors voted him by the Senate and People, none pleased him so much as the privilege of wearing a laurel wreath on all occasions—[and] he constantly took advantage of it." Caesar was also the first major figure in history to avail himself of the hairdo known as the "comb-over," or "cover-up," or "McGovern" (after the former senator and presidential candidate). In the vain—in both senses of the word—attempt to hide his baldness, Caesar used to comb the thin strands of hair that grew on the back of his neck forward. Napoleon, we know, was a comb-forward man; General Douglas MacArthur was a comb-over man, taking longish strands from the side of his head and pasting them across his scalp. From afternoons spent in athletic clubs, I have seen the intricate labors that go into such hairdos. The general anxieties of men who have chosen to wear them cannot, I think, be eased on windy days.

Few men take the loss of hair easily. For one thing, it is an early intimation of mortality, for as we come into the world nearly hairless, so do many of us depart it in something like the same condition. For another, baldness is viewed, in many quarters, as less than romantic. In the movies and theater, bald leading men are uncommon, though Yul Brynner, an exception, exhibited what most people would agree was virile baldness. Nowadays, too, many black athletes and white Olympic swimmers shave their heads. Yet, in television news, one never sees a bald anchorman. Without their hair and the careful coiffing expended upon it, Dan Rather, Tom Brokaw, and Peter Jennings, the major network anchormen, would have to sell neckties, which would be fine with me.

Wigs and rugs, toups and pieces are among the possibilities open to men greatly uncomfortable with their baldness. Hair plugs, a surgical implant procedure of some expense, is another. One can never predict what sort of men will avail themselves of such items. I know a podiatrist who is a hair-plugs man, a pharmacist who totes an ambitious widow's peak not of nature's making, the sweet father of a friend who dyed his hair shoe-polish black. "A permanent lifetime answer to baldness!" runs one advertisement seeking the shekels of the bald and balding. "Wake up to a full head of hair!" runs another. If the exclamation marks from such ads and the many thousands that have come before them could be used as hair, baldness would be at an end, for the growth of new hair has historically been one of the great fields of quackery. If anyone ever does discover a cure for baldness, his great-grandchildren and their grandchildren will be able to laugh from the pent-house balconies of apartments overlooking the world's most fashionable streets, so wealthy will he leave them. Customers will always be there.

Meanwhile, many men who lose their hair tend to go in for overcompensation. An unusually large number of men who wear ponytails, for example, seem to be balding. Pulling their hair back in a ponytail is a mistake, I believe, for it seems chiefly to emphasize their hair loss. Besides, few things are more dis-piriting than a gray ponytail. It suggests aging hippiedom, than which little is sadder: a flower child is one thing, a flower grandfather something else again. I have friends and acquaint-ances with mustaches and beards and comb-overs, but I don't, at the moment, know anyone who wears a ponytail. I do have a friend who tells me that, at his athletic club, he has encoun-tered men who own and wear false ponytails. What a piece of work is man!

Not long ago, listening to the excellent Vermeer Quartet, I noted on my program that it is composed of two beards (second violin and cello), one male permanent (first violin), and one longish hair-over-the-ears arrangement (viola). The two bearded musicians are balding, the second violinist from the front, the cellist in the back. The violist, when bowing, revealed a monk's cap of baldness, and he may also be a hair-plug man, a judgment I make based on the preternatural even-ness of the straight-across hairline situated midway back upon a high forehead. Longhair music has thus taken on a new meaning in our day. It is a cartoonist's delight.

I suppose the natural tendency is for each of us to consider others by the light of his own vanity. My own vanity, since becoming an adult, has directed me to appear as little obviously vain as possible. In my particular twist on masculine vanity, I seek a quiet, subdued, nicely understated elegance—and I am fairly confident that I don't quite bring it off. Pity. At the same time that vanity is the dealer in these hirsutical decisions, temperament, too, takes a hand. I would find it extremely difficult, soon after arising from sleep on a gray Chicago morning, with a vast quantity of obligations to fulfill, to look into the bathroom mirror and see staring back at me a gray Fu Manchu mustache, a thick set of snowburns (as I have heard white-haired sideburns called), and D'Artagnan-length hair waiting to be pulled back in a ponytail. No, with such accouterments festooned from my *punim*, I could not face the day. At the first glint of depression, I should doubtless shave it all off, and shave off the hair left on my head for good measure.

In these matters, one's own generation's ideal of masculinity also obviously plays an important role. One can either go with the flow or try to stop it. The first prospect renders a man ridiculous, the second hopeless. Yet another possibility is to take a seat on the sidelines, preferably in the shade, a glass of wine in one's hand, and not bark but laugh as the caravan passes. John Updike, writing in *The New Yorker*, after expressing the self-denigration that has become fairly standard with him, writes that "the impression has been growing upon me that I am surrounded by hostile haircuts," and he goes on to report that, in the wide range of male hairdos now current, "we're all butting for psychological space, and leading with our warheads." Something to it, perhaps. So many bizarre arrangements for male hair must have some meaning.

Peter the Great must have thought so in his time, for he, with his own hand, shaved off the beards of the boyars, which he thought a symbol of their backwardness. Montaigne, in his essay "On Ancient Customs," drew such a meaning from the dominant hairdos of his own day when he wrote: "Sidonius Appollinaris says that the ancient Gauls wore their hair long on the front of their heads and shaved close at the neck; that is precisely the hairstyle which has been brought back into fashion by the slack and womanish mode of our own century." We have here the hairdo view of history, which may be no goofier than many another put forward by postmodernist historians. (And who was it who said that the postmodernist always rings twice?)

True enough, our own century, or at any rate the last third of it, has seen some pretty wild do's. Blacks alone in this time have run through processed hair, the Afro, the drippy, the stack or muffin, cornrows, and dreadlocks, a hairstyle that is shared by black men and women and that is achieved by "dreading" one's hair. Some young blacks will tell you that a political statement is intended in many of these hairdos; others will say that it can all be chalked up to amusement. Certainly, the odious skinheads are making a statement, not to speak of a direct political identification, in shaving their heads as they do. Punk hairdos, among them high Mohawks, liberty spikes, and Day-Glo purple and orange dyes, are making a statement, too—one which I read to mean, "Look at me, Jack, test your own reaction, and get edgy."

But what does it mean that more working-class young men now seem to avail themselves of long hair than do young men of the middle class? Or that the two groups who seem to have the highest proportion of mustaches among them appear to be homosexuals and cops? Do you suppose that even to have a regular hairdo is to make a political statement, as Orwell—a high-pompadour and pencil-thin-mustache man—said that even to be apolitical is to be political, a formulation that, in my view, has more rhythm than truth?

Something rather unseemly there is about a man lavishing too much care upon his hair. In the end we are left with our prejudices, however implausible they might be. I prefer not to have waiters too much more fancily coiffed than I am. If I were a woman, I should prefer not to go out with a man who looks as if he has spent longer on his hair than I have. Worst of all is artificially induced naturalness. Carl Sandburg's rich mane of white hair is an instance of the artificial made to look natural. Sandburg must have felt that such hair was required of him in his persona as the "people's poet." Robert Frost, who almost specialized in put-downs of Sandburg (Sandburg was the only poet, said Frost, to gain in translation), once said of him that he was upstairs "trying to get the hair into his eyes."

"Behold my brother Esau is a hairy man and I am a smooth man," Jacob announces to his mother, stating a problem but drawing no conclusions. Perhaps he ought to have done. People have for centuries been judged by their hair. Redheads were thought to be hot-tempered. There is practically a sociology of blond women, not much of it very complimentary, except that they are believed to have more fun. A high forehead was said to have been a sure sign of intelligence. Many of us who have had high foreheads conferred upon us by hair loss have an instinctive distrust of a man with too low a hairline. Think about these things long enough and the traditional spelling of "*hare*brained" begins to feel as if it ought to be changed to "*hair*brained." My own last words on the subject, which I hope to repeat many a time more, are "Short on top, fairly close along the sides, and not too high over the ears."

Compose Yourself

As more and more of my illusions about myself continue to fall away—to name just a few among them: that I was a fine little athlete, not a bad dancer, a pretty serious lover, an elegant dresser, a nice-looking fella—the one that I can't shake is that I am a fast worker. This illusion is reinforced by various people telling me that I am very productive, though they usually stop short of using the term, vaguely insulting to writers of our day, "prolific." Odd, but somehow I don't feel in the least productive; I feel, in fact, rather slothful. I feel slothful, first, because I know how much of my working day is given over to empty diversions; and, second, owing to my illusion that I am a fast worker, I am always inclined to feel that I could—and should—be doing so much more.

It's far from clear that the world requires any more from me than I now provide. Some might prefer rather less. Philip Larkin, whose poetry I much admire, when reviewing a collection of my essays in the London *Times Literary Supplement* a number of years ago, remarked upon how queer it was that essays such as mine were written in the United States at all. He ended by saying that "the situation would seem to be one of supply rather than demand." Something to it, I fear. I fear, too, that one's writing resembles one's children, if only in the sense that, however much writing one does (or however many children one has), it seems all that one can possibly do (or have). And yet the nagging feeling persists that one should have done—should be doing—more.

The inky-fingered Balzac, whom no one is ever likely to have faulted for paucity of production, writing with debtors at his back and visions of glory before him, used to talk about smoking enchanted cigarettes, by which he meant conversation about books he wished to, but knew he never would, write. I have puffed upon a few of those cigarettes myself, going so far as actually to take publishers' advances for a biography of John Dos Passos and for a book on snobbery. (Returning a publisher's advance, which I had to do on both occasions, is not easy; one has to imagine setting a money-stuffed wallet with no identification in it back onto the street where one found it; not only does one feel bereft of the cash, but one feels that it will only fall into worse hands than one's own.) I have no great regret about not having written either of these books: I have discovered that I have too bulky an ego to devote years of my own life to writing a lengthy book about someone else's life; and, as for the snobbery book, well, I still puff on that enchanted cigarette from time to time, telling myself I may do it yet.

But the book I really regret not having written is the trilogy that I could have written on the job when, as a young man, I worked as a senior editor at a large midwestern publishing firm. True, I am not a novelist; true, even if I had been, when I worked there, in my late twenties and early thirties, I probably would not have had the material or the maturity to write a trilogy. But it was also true that, in nearly five years on this job, I had enough time to write three trilogies, a Finnish epic, and a study of net games in Patagonia. Viewed in retrospect, it was like being on some very generous grant, though not realizing it until afterwards.

On that job, for which I was quite well paid, there were long periods during which I was asked to do very little. A meeting might be called for Friday, and the Thursday before a secretary would appear to announce that the man who had called the meeting had to go out of town and wouldn't return until the following Wednesday. No further assignment was given; there was no backlog of work to catch up on. Five days lay before me, on each of which I put on a suit and tie, took a train into the city, and did nothing, *nada*, absolutely zilch. This happened fairly regularly. Much of this free time was spent in general grousing with fellow editors; some in audacious but quite useless philosophical speculation; a good bit more in office gossip. The years whirred by. I wrote twenty or thirty book reviews on the job and a few essays. But I have always regretted that I never did anything more substantial. A poet, the Russian proverb has it, always cheats his boss, which, I assume, means that his mind is on his poems when it should be on the job. Why should any other kind of writer do less?

From the beginning of my interest in becoming a writer, I found myself fascinated by the conditions under and methods by which famous writers worked. For a short while I was taken in by the false drama of the supposedly excruciating difficulty of writing. This drama was probably most economically set out by the excellent sportswriter Red Smith, who said, apropos of the difficulty he found in composition, that he merely sat at his typewriter until little drops of blood appeared on his forehead. It was not uncommon to find others comparing the act of writing to that ultimate act of creation, childbirth, drawing out an elaborate analogy between the stages of writing and those of pregnancy, from insemination (with an idea) through postpartum depression (after delivering a book). Thus the music critic and composer Cecil Gray, in his autobiography *Musical Chairs,* writes:

> Like everything I have written, words or music, or both, it was the outcome of a long period of gestation followed by a rapid parturition. The short score sketch of all three acts was completed in as many months, but the conception had been in my mind for ten years. (Oh, my elephantine pregnancies! How I envy and yet despise the quick, slick rabbit litters of the facile mediocrities!)

Speaking as (evidently) a rabbit-litter man, I have never had a baby, surprising as this news may be, but my view is that, not even nearly all things considered, if it is delivery we are talking about, I should much prefer delivering a piece of writing every time.

Another part of the drama of writing speaks to the deep loneliness of writers. Even my beloved Henry James could not resist sounding this note. "We work in the dark," are the words he put into the mouth of the novelist Dencombe in his story "The Middle Years," "—we do what we can—we give what we have. Our doubt is our passion and our passion is our task. The rest is the madness of art." Mencken, reacting to the general plaint of the loneliness of writers, suggested that any writer who felt overwhelmed by the loneliness of his task ought, as a cure, to spend a few days in a factory on an assembly line, where he would find plenty of opportunities to talk with his mates. If the drama of writers is even minimally true, why, one wonders, would anyone take up such a hard calling? I have myself always thought that it had something to do with the notion that writing, whatever its complications and difficulties, still beats working, though I could be wrong.

To continue with the *Iliad* of writers' woes, let us not forget the perpetual wrestle with language. Among the famous wrestlers, the great Hulk Hogan of modern literature, Gustave

Flaubert, reported regularly to his mistress Louise Colet on this endless tussle. "I spent *five days on one page* last week, and I gave up everything for it," he characteristically complains while at work on *Madame Bovary*. Joseph Conrad was another famous groaner about the excruciation of composition, likening himself to a criminal dragging "the ball and chain of one's selfhood to the end," but Conrad at least had the excuse that he was working in English, which was his third language. Valéry used to say that he never finished but only abandoned his poems. But with the great writers, in the end, pain dissolves into love, and even so incessant a complainer as Flaubert has to allow that, when it is going well, the world offers no keener pleasure than that provided by writing:

> . . . it is grand to write [he reports to Louise Colet], to cease to be *oneself*, and to move among creatures one is describing. Today, for instance, I have been a man and woman at the same time, lover and mistress together, riding in the forest on an autumn afternoon under the yellowing leaves; and I have been the horses, too, and the leaves, and the wind, and the words they spoke and the red sun that made them blink their eyes that swam with love. It may be out of pride or of reverence, from a foolish gush of excessive self-conceit or a vague but lofty religious sense, but when I reflect, after experiencing these joys, I feel tempted to offer up a prayer of thanksgiving to God, if only I knew he could hear me. But praise be His Name that I was not born a cotton merchant, a music hall artist, or a wit, etc.

Which brings me to a topic I approach with the apprehension that only serious superstition makes possible. I speak—fingers crossed, a string of garlic round my neck, and in supplication on my knees—of writer's block, that psychological condition that stanches a writer's flow of words. Baudelaire spoke of this condition of " '*stérilités des écrivains nerveux*' . . . that anguished suspension of all power of thought that comes to one in the midst of a very revel of production, like the slave with his *memento mori* at a feast." I have—touch wood, *kayn aynhoreh*, Lordy be—never undergone writer's block, but I have known people who have and have some inkling of what a horrendous psychological affliction it can be. Hard to know what causes this affliction that leaves writers stranded like ruptured ducks, and we are not talking here about *mallards imaginaires*. A psychiatrist named Edmund Bergler, in New York in the 1950s and 1960s, used to claim a high record of cure for writer's block. His modus operandi, I gather, was to inform writers that this block business was all a lot of nonsense, a sign of immaturity, and that they ought to knock it off and get the hell back to the typewriter. (Bergler was apparently a man who yelled in a German accent, which can be effective.)

My own guess is that a writer can be blocked because he is, in some fundamental way, unclear about what it is he wants to write; or he can be fearful, knowing that what he must write will expose him in a way that he senses could be ruinous to him, or at least to his sense of himself; or he may not have been able to recognize and work through some deep flaw in the composition before him; or, perhaps gravest danger of all, he is stung by tyrannous perfectionism, a perfectionism leading on to literary constipation. In his novel *To an Early Grave*, Wallace Markfield has a character, a minor critic named Holly Levine, who suffers from the latter variant of writer's block. "Certainly, Professor Gombitz's essays, gathered together for the first time, yield pleasure of a kind," Levine begins a book review. Then he alters the sentence to read: "An essay by Gombitz will clearly yield . . ." Then he decides that perhaps it is better formulated as "An essay by Gombitz will surely yield . . ." Which is supplanted by "Surely, essays such as these are bound to yield . . ." The possibilities being nearly endless, the review remains beginningless. The whole project is hopelessly blocked.

Out of fear of such blockage, every writer senses that he must manipulate things so that his flow of words not only begins but continues. The first trick is beginning. In a useful little essay, "A Writer's Discipline," Jacques Barzun, writing out of his own ample experience, states the problem and puts the point with precision: "There is only one way: to study one's needs and quirks, and circumvent one's tricks for escape." Barzun's excellent advice is to give in to those needs and quirks, but only as a reward against escape. "Suit thyself," he writes, "but pay for it, i.e., *work!*"

The needs and quirks, since I have quite a few of my own, especially interest me. I have always loved to read about the idiosyncrasies connected with the composition of other, chiefly famous, writers. Thornton Wilder must have had a similar interest, for he reports that "many writers have told me that they have built up mnemonic devices to start them off on each day's writing task. Hemingway once told me he sharpened twenty pencils; Willa Cather that she read a passage from the Bible—not from piety, she was quick to add, but to get in touch with fine prose. . . . My springboard has always been long walks."

My fascination with all this made me a natural reader—if "groupie" isn't the more precise word—of the interviews in the *Paris Review*. My interest was invariably most enlivened when the interviewer would get around to asking, What are some of your writing habits? Do you use a desk? Do you write on a machine? Here I always hoped for the most exotic responses. "I prefer to sumo-wrestle an alligator, eat two pounds of pastrami and a large, thinly sliced Bermuda onion on a baguette with strong horseradish, and listen to all six Brandenburg Concertos before getting down to work. For the actual writing, I like to wear my black velour FILA jogging suit, tie my hair into a short ponytail, slip into my Air-Faulkner writing shoes, and, hey, baby, like the Nike commercial says, 'Just do it!' " I hyperbolize but I do not entirely exaggerate. Here is how the then-young Truman Capote answered the same questions:

I am a completely horizontal author. I can't think unless I'm lying down, either in bed or stretched on a couch and with a cigarette and coffee handy. I've got to be puffing and sipping. As the afternoon wears on, I shift from coffee to mint tea to sherry to martinis. No, I don't use a typewriter. Not in the beginning. I write my first version in longhand (pencil). Then I do a complete revision, also in longhand.

If Capote was a horizontal author, Ernest Hemingway was a vertical one. He wrote standing up, usually in his bedroom in his house in Cuba, using the top of a bookcase, on which room was cleared, to quote the *Paris Review*, "for a typewriter, a wooden reading board, five or six pencils, and a chunk of copper ore to weight down papers when the wind blows in from the east windows." It gets better. Hemingway "stands in a pair of his oversized loafers on the worn skin of a Lesser Kudu—the typewriter and the reading board chest-high opposite him." He told his interviewer, George Plimpton, that he began in pencil, then shifted to his typewriter when his writing was going extremely well or when he wrote dialogue. Each day he kept count of the words he produced: "from 450, 575, 462, 1,250, back to 512, the higher figures on days Hemingway puts in extra work so he won't feel guilty spending the following day fishing on the Gulf Stream." Hemingway was a strange old man, as he himself might have put it, but, when it came to writing, no stranger than most.

Hemingway wrote in the mornings, as the majority of writers tend to do, though I seem to remember reading that John O'Hara used to do his writing only after the completion of the last movie on television—"The Late Show" as it was called before the advent of cable and twenty-four-hour television—ending his work only after sunrise. T. S. Eliot, whether writing prose or poetry, felt himself good for roughly three hours of work at a sitting. Evelyn Waugh, a more concentrated worker than most, thought two thousand words a good day's work and tended to write best in provincial hotels, generally finishing his earlier novels, revisions and all, in roughly six weeks. Georges Simenon seldom took more than eleven days to write his Maigret novels, and usually had a physical before beginning a new one, so intensely absorbed was he in the work before him. Thomas Mann, another morning worker, used to consider the production of a single good page sufficient unto any day, and most days he produced that page. A page a day, if you don't knock off for too many weekends, would give you approximately a book a year. Nothing to sneeze at.

Except by Anthony Trollope, who would doubtless have used up several boxes of Kleenex sneezing at what he would have considered such paltry production. Trollope, in his autobiography, recounts that he always kept a precise record of his literary production, and that it tended to average forty pages (at 250 words to the page) a week, sometimes falling as low as twenty pages but once having risen to 112 pages. Trollope, who may have been the most completely professional writer ever to have lived, took great pride in delivering all his manuscripts exactly on time and as close as possible to the agreed-upon length. He accomplished all this, what is more, while holding a full-time job with the English postal system. This achievement is a rebuke to every writer awaiting grants, inspiration, encouragement, or mother love. Trollope's view was that one ought to regard one's work as the normal condition of one's life. "I therefore venture to advise young men who look forward to authorship as the business of their lives, even when they propose that that authorship be of the highest class known, to avoid enthusiastic rushes with their pens, and to seat themselves at their desks day by day as though they were lawyers' clerks;—and so let them sit till their allotted tasks shall be accomplished."

Trollope tells of finishing his novel *Doctor Thorne* one day and beginning another, *The Bertrams*, the next. With a talent I have developed of improving upon already extraordinary stories, I artfully misremembered and retold this story so that Trollope had finished a novel in the middle of a morning's work and, rather than let the rest of his morning working session go to waste, took out a fresh piece of paper and began another novel that same morning. Not impossible, after all, for behind Trollope's impressive work habits was a strong conscience, a conscience quite properly fueled by fear of future remorse. "It was not on my conscience," he writes, "that I have ever scamped my work. My novels, whether good or bad, have been as good as I could make them." He then adds that had he put three months of idleness between these two novels, the second would probably not have been any better.

Conscience, remorse, heavy and even self-invented guilt— ah, now we are coming into my country—the country, to misappropriate Sarah Orne Jewett's famous title, of the pointed fingers. I am not sure I could function without fear of incurring guilt in letting down editors, publishers, and now even myself. I am a writer who writhes and therefore writes best under deadline (a phrase whose etymology derives from the Confederate prisoner-of-war camp at Andersonville; any prisoner who crossed the line drawn around the perimeter of the camp was to be shot on sight). As a writer, I am eager to please and anxious lest I disappoint; and here I am talking about pleasing and not disappointing readers and editors. But the critic toughest to get by is myself: not, let me make plain, only the critic of quality—though I hope he is on the job, too—but of quantity.

On any day that I do not turn out a reasonable number of words I feel poorly about myself. Let three or four such days go by and I am able to make myself quite miserable. Deep loathing sets in somewhere between five days and a week of less-than-decent work. Longer than this and it becomes extremely difficult for me to justify my existence. A decent day's work is somewhere between eight hundred and twelve hundred not entirely awkward, imprecise, or ignoble words. On those rare days when I have been able to write two thousand or so such words, I am so deliriously smug that I am really quite unfit to speak even to myself.

Because my own self-regard is at stake—and for so self-regarding a fellow, no stakes could be higher—it is important that I work well. And since I spend a fair amount of my waking life selecting and arranging words, I am intensely interested in anything that will make the job more efficient. Hence my interest in other people's ways of going about it. I am ever on the outlook for new methods, tricks, secrets to improve the flow of my own words onto the page. For years I thought there might be a magic fountain pen that would make me a better writer. I still think there may be stationery of a kind that will make my words, when written out upon it, stronger, clearer, longer-lived.

Is there some method of composition I have not yet tried that could make the difference? Lionel Trilling many years ago reported that the writer Robert Warshow "composed by a method which is unusual; he formed each sentence slowly in his mind, and, when it was satisfactory, wrote it down as irrevocable." Trilling thought it a method beyond his own practical comprehension. How astounded he would have been by the performance of Edward Gibbon, who, after remarking that, as his great history progressed, he found less reason to revise his prose and went on to state that "it has always been my practise to cast a long paragraph in a single mould, to try it by my ear, to deposit it in my memory; but to suspend the action of the pen, till I had given the last polish to my work." In other words—though why one should want words other than Gibbon's I am not sure—Gibbon formed entire paragraphs in his mind before writing them out, and he wrote, as everyone knows, wondrously intricate periodic sentences embedded in impressively lengthy, neatly pointed paragraphs.

My own mind runs only to remembering phrases, never more. I generally have no idea of what any sentence is going to look like until I write the damn thing out, and then I usually rework it a time or two. Because of this, I have never—not as a student, not now—been able to avail myself of outlines. Until I write that first sentence down, I can have no idea of what my second sentence is going to say or look like, let alone what my fifth paragraph will contain.

My method of composition, then, resembles on-the-job training, only at the verbal level. I have grown used to this loose, slightly riff-like method, which often brings with it pleasant surprises. "How can I tell what I think till I see what I say," E. M. Forster once remarked. I believe I may do him one better in not being sure what I write even while I am writing it.

Just because there is no order in my compositional life doesn't mean that I don't crave at least the appearance of order. I am extremely partial to having plenty of folders about, also lots of colored paper clips, and fine-leaded mechanical pencils. (I am quite nuts generally about office supplies.) But especially do I long for order, elegant order, in my manuscripts. "My Essay," wrote Gibbon, referring to his *L'Essai sur l'étude de la littérature*, "was finished in about six weeks, and as soon as a

fair copy had been transcribed by one of the French prisoners
at Petersfield I looked round for a critic and a judge of my first
performance." I have always loved the phrase "fair copy," and
seem to recall a photograph of the family of Count Tolstoy
writing out a "fair copy" of *War and Peace.* Fair copy—implying as it does a fine tidiness, a beautiful intelligibility of outward form to fit what one hopes is a genuine clarity of inward
thought—fair copy has long been the name of my desire.

Attempting to produce it without the aid of French prisoners or a large aristocratic Russian family has not proven easy
for me. But, somehow, without a reasonable tidiness in my
manuscripts, I generally feel a vague but quite real discomfort.
Freudians used to term this condition anality. ("Anality, my
ass," replies a character in an English novel when faced with
this charge.) My method of attempting to achieve this tidiness
was formerly a most complicated one. I wrote the paragraphs
of my first draft in longhand; then typed out each of these
paragraphs, usually making changes as I went; and, when this
second, typed draft seemed fairly decent, I would then retype
it, making still other, usually smaller changes, onto a final, or
what I thought of as a fair, copy. Truth to tell, I should have
preferred to make fair copies in a perfect handwriting, and
would have done so, but for the fact that my handwriting could
never produce anything considered anywhere near fair.

I took great pleasure in watching my typed fair-copy ver-
sions grow larger. But I also felt this fair copy, once created,
inviolable. Making changes upon it, which, given my penchant
for tidiness, would entail vast amounts of time in retyping, was
not something I looked forward to; I would, in fact, only agree
to do so in emergency situations: when I discovered something
on my fair copy that was simply wrong or when I felt I had
found something so pleasing to add that the additional pain of
retyping was less than the pleasure of having it in my manuscript.

And yet, unlike Peter De Vries, who once said that he liked everything about writing except the paperwork, I tend to like the paperwork above all. Writing, I hope it does not depress others to learn, has not only grown easier for me, but I find I enjoy it even more as I grow older. One of the nicest compliments I have ever had was that my writing seemed to show an obvious pleasure in the making; I took this to mean that the author (me) seemed to have a good time setting down the words. I fear it's true. Such cheerfulness about the act of writing, which is supposed to be so exasperating and hideously painful an activity, cannot do my small reputation much good, but there it is.

I remember, as a much younger man, walking down the street shaping sentences in my mind for a composition on which I was then at work, trying out and rejecting phrases and words, when it occurred to me that mine was a funny kind of life. I produced nothing but words about my observations and reformulated the words and observations of others who had written in the past. I also made up stories. For this I was paid, not handsomely but sufficiently. It's a living. Sometimes I have not been altogether certain whether it was also a life. But since I haven't another in mind, I ought, I decided then and there, to calm down and stay on the job, as Harry Truman once told the servants at the White House whom he found weeping upon learning of his decision not to run again for the presidency in 1952. Besides, by then I had been at it long enough to feel, with Montaigne, that "no pleasure for me has any savor without communication."

"The prospect of fame, wealth, and daily amusement encourage me to persist," wrote Gibbon somewhere in the middle of the composition of *The Decline and Fall of the Roman Empire*. When I first came across that sentence, I typed it out and taped it to the side of the black standard Royal typewriter I had used for some twenty years. I acquired that machine, which was probably already twenty-five years old, in trade for twenty-five dollars and a then-new Olivetti portable with an italic typeface that I couldn't abide. I adored—I use the word with forethought—that old machine. I liked the action of its keys, which I sometimes pounded as if I were playing the ending of one of the more dramatic of Beethoven's piano sonatas. I wrote everything but sonnets and suicide notes on it. I had it cleaned fairly regularly, frequently changed its ribbon— Dorothy Parker, a two-fingered typist, allowed that she knew so little about typewriters that she once bought a new one because she couldn't figure out how to change the ribbon on the one she had—and finally I wore it out. The key for the letter *d* refused to work. I hadn't been aware that over the years I had written so many words with the letter *d* in them. Damn.

This noble machine was replaced by a sleeker item, as it then seemed, a used IBM Correcting Selectric III. I am apparently someone who needs to be dragged into the future, even on small items. With the exception of indoor plumbing, I remain skeptical about most modern inventions. Gadgetry, in itself, does not much interest me. I was late to have a colored television set; and, though I now own a machine that plays compact discs instead of records, I continue to like the look and feel of my old albums. I am a sentimental, entirely passive, and in the end inevitably defeated Luddite. What sold me on the IBM was its correcting device, which, allowing one to dispense with Wite-Out for erasures, appealed to my instinct for tidiness. It gave—and continues to give—excellent service. On its beige metal side I have taped the motto, this one from Henry James, written after his disastrous adventure in writing for the London stage: "Produce again—produce; produce better than ever, and all will be well."

Perceptive readers will already have sensed that this essay is going to get around to its hero's arrival, round-shouldered and squint-eyed, before a computer. Some among them, who count upon me as a stalwart rearguard man and a permanent back number, may be a little disappointed to find me there. I do not seem to myself the very model of a computer man. For years I have made fun of computerese, both in my own mind and in the margins of the papers of students, for whom such language is not jargon at all but of the air they breathe. In place of such words as *user-friendly, hands-on,* and *interface,* I continue to say, at least to myself, *usure-friendly* (which you might call a genial loan shark), *pants-on,* and *in your face.*

Writing friends who have gone over to the computer worked at my conversion. All marveled to me about how using the word-processing portion of a computer improved both the quantity and quality of their writing. I listened to them, outwardly polite, inwardly haughty and disdainful. I think I should never have attempted to use a computer had not the university where I teach offered me the loan of a computer for nothing. I took a bite of the Apple (a Macintosh Plus, as it turns out) that many had promised would lead me into the new Garden of Eden, from where I am writing this essay.

I have, for more than a year now, been writing everything but my personal correspondence on a computer. I have not typed out and pasted to the side of this computer "Man rides machine." (Was it Emerson or some other hyperventilating nineteenth-century author who said that?) After what I am told was the standard two- or three-week terror of "losing" everything one has written and infuriation at one's own initial ineptitude, I came to grow enamored of the computer as a writing instrument. I shall not go on to report, à la the subtitle of *Dr. Strangelove,* how I learned to stop worrying and love my machine, but candor compels me to report that I have grown fond of the little bugger. Sometimes, at the end of a decent day's work, I have been known to rise from my desk, pat it gently in gratitude, and mutter, "Thanks, pal."

I am chiefly grateful to the computer for the splendid possibilities it presents for revision. Working with it, I find myself reworking things, I won't say endlessly and I won't say effortlessly, but with a freedom and ease that I never felt working on a typewriter. This seems to me an uncomplicated and clear gain. The computer also gives me a keen sense of false organization. On what is known as my primary screen—what a friend calls his "primary scream"—I have such handsome categories, or folders, as Essays and Pieces, Lectures and Letters, Snobbery (the butt from that not-yet smoked-out enchanted cigarette), and Stories and Tales (let it pass that I have never written a tale, and seem unlikely ever to do so). I find that I turn on my computer more readily than I used to go to my typewriter, and that I do so at different hours—in the late afternoon, for example—than formerly. I believe I spend more time word processing, if that is what I am doing here, than I used to spend writing.

Yet some of the pleasures are less. I used to enjoy watching my manuscripts grow larger, as their pages mounted up. I rather enjoyed the sound of the typewriter, with its sharp staccato as opposed to the muted clackety-clack of the computer keyboard. (Leroy Anderson, the composer, it may be recalled, wrote a composition titled *The Typewriter*, which was an orchestral arrangement that featured the sound of someone typing at high speed and which will one day be perfectly incomprehensible to people.) I prefer the noble look of an older typewriter to the portable-television-set appearance of a personal computer.

Then, too, the puritan in me sometimes thinks that writing is made *too* easy on the computer. I guess I believe that writing ought not to be too smoothly turned out. In ways I am not quite clear about, the computer, like statistics, doesn't care who uses it, and seems somehow to have made it possible for bad writers to write even worse. Alastair Forbes, writing in the London *Spectator*, refers to a recent biography of Anastasia as coming "from the ill-tuned, unmistakably American word-processor" of a writer who, though he may not be shameless, shall here be nameless. One rather knows what Mr. Forbes means. I cannot say exactly why, but a book ill written on a typewriter figures, somehow, to be a bit better than a book ill written on a word processor.

For one thing, the latter is likely to be longer, wordier, more garrulous generally—this owing to the ease with which words flow from the computer. As the television with its many carefully spaced commercials has decreased the national attention span, so has writing on a computer increased the national garrulity. I now often get four-, five-, even six-page single-spaced letters from people who once would have said all they had to say in a letter of a page or two. The great value of the computer lies in its editing and revising function. But the same machine also makes it so simple to add material; it is the great friend of second, third, and even fourth thoughts on any subject. Press a few keys, manipulate the cursor, clack in a few more sentences, then watch as the paragraphs nicely reshape themselves and the composition you are working on lengthens correspondingly. Imagine Balzac, Trollope, Dickens armed with computers! If Proust, who had a penchant for adding things to his already vast manuscript, had written *Remembrance of Things Past* on a computer, he would have had to retitle it "Remembrance of Things Past, Present, and Future, Including Many things Not Remembered at All."

In its editing function—the ease with which nearly endless revisions can be made—lies both the joy and the horror of writing on the computer. One of the most dismaying things about writing is the knowledge that nearly anything one writes can be cut fairly drastically—and then cut again. "You never cut anything out of a book you regret later," F. Scott Fitzgerald told Thomas Wolfe, who had a ferocious cut man—to use the word in a very different sense—in his corner in his editor Maxwell Perkins. The Gettysburg Address has 272 words; my guess is that an aggressive editor could pare it down to two hundred and not many people would notice. An editor in New York used to boast that he could cut the Lord's Prayer in half and improve it in doing so. The computer, of course, lures one to go the other way: not to cut but to add.

So seductive is the computer as a writing instrument that I find myself less and less ready to write without it. I still type my letters. I still write in my journal in longhand. I still travel with two fountain pens and a thick pad of graph paper, in the hope of adding to compositions I am currently working on. But I notice I now turn out less writing when traveling and away from my machine, so accustomed have I become to the ease it affords. (I think of my own laziness here with shame when I consider Aleksandr Solzhenitsyn, who wrote out his lengthy manuscripts in a minuscule handwriting, the better to hide them from the authorities and make them available in samizdat.) Dragged yet further into the future, I shall doubtless one day before long have to acquire a laptop computer. But I intend to defer it as long as possible. *Laptop* sounds awfully like *lapdog* to me. Not altogether clear here, either, who is the dog and who the master. There goes machine, it seems pretty clear to me, riding man again.

The fear in the heart of every writer is the arrival of the time when he must recognize that such magic as he has had has left him and he now writes not only differently but worse. A change in the methods with which a writer works is likely to turn the mind to this possibility. Henry James seemed to undergo no such worry when, in his late fifties, after suffering pain in his right wrist, he started to dictate his books to a series of typists. Some critics have contended that, with this new method of composing, James cut it too fine and began badly to garrulate. Others refer to his new period as Henry James's Major Phase. Who is correct remains in the flux of controversy.

What isn't in the flux of controversy is that the act of writing, even after one drains it of the often false drama some of its practitioners like to give it, retains a strong element of mystery. "Read 'em and weep," say poker players, confidently setting down what they are sure is a winning hand. But you can write 'em and weep, too, or write 'em and laugh, or write 'em and wonder, reverently, from where 'em derive. Whence derives that lilting phrase, that prettily precise formulation, that obliquely subtle observation, that perfectly paced paragraph? Are there more where those came from? Best, perhaps, to shut up and just keep writing.

Such Good Taste

Whenever I find myself in the West—in such states as New Mexico, Colorado, or California—I feel a distinct if ineffable sense of discomfort, no matter how glorious the day or how splendid the surrounding scenery. Only recently have I understood why this is so: the American West is about life lived outdoors, where, as it turns out, not one of my fantasies takes place—and in none of these fantasies, it ought to be added, am I wearing jeans. All this makes me distinctly an anti-Western kind of guy.

The place that makes me least comfortable is that indubitably most beautiful of American cities, San Francisco, where not only have I never come close to losing my heart but, on more than one occasion, I have been in serious danger of blowing my cool. It is the putative good taste of San Franciscans that gets to me; more precisely, it is the tyrannous, relentless, in-your-face insistence on good taste pervading the place that makes me want to end each meal I eat in that city with a resounding belch and a general attack on the importance of spectacular views and sun-dried tomatoes.

It's less the actual good taste of San Franciscans I mind than the pride in good taste everywhere on display in that city. Pride in one's good taste, someone ought to inform the head of San Francisco's Chamber of Commerce, is, prima facie, bad taste. The possession of good taste, like that of sexual prowess and other natural talents, is better demonstrated than discussed. If you've got it, you should feel under an obligation not to talk about it. But then if you truly have it, my guess is, it would never occur to you to talk about it. Not everyone in San Francisco does talk about it, but there is something in the general atmosphere one encounters there that suggests that San Franciscans, above all other Americans, truly know how to live. Since all this talk about good taste and the central part it plays in the good life seems to have spread to Berkeley and Palo Alto, and to the Bay Area generally, I have come to call it—until now only to myself—Bayarrhea, standing for tiresome babble about taste marked by the underlying assumption that one's own taste is superior to everyone else's.

Perhaps the problem here is that this confidence of San Franciscans in their good taste matches my confidence in my own rather better taste. My sense is that most of us do take a certain pride in having good taste. If we can't take pride in it in all realms, we feel we have the sense to know what in life it is important to have good taste about. All of us are a bit vulnerable on this score. La Rochefoucauld, taking his always-safe low view of humankind, wrote: "Our pride is more offended by attacks on our taste than on our opinions." I would take this a small step further. Most of us would rather be caught in an act of serious bad judgment than in one of singular bad taste. How else account for the fact that "He was a man of sound judgment with occasional lapses in taste" sounds, somehow, worse than "He was a man of impeccable taste with occasional lapses in judgment"? Bad judgment, unless it is habitual, seems a mistake of the moment; bad taste, an ingrained condition for which there is no known cure.

Taste is the choosing and discriminating sense. For taste to go into operation, a fairly complex society has to exist, one offering a vast buffet of aesthetic and utilitarian objects as well as social possibilities and points of view. Some even hold that humanity was happier, even morally better, before taste set in and became as important as it has in human transactions. Taste, in this view, desiccates, overrefines, smothers the instincts; it castrates the noble savage, sterilizes Aphrodite. In the novels of E. M. Forster, for example, a strong concern about good taste is a sure sign that one is a dry and dreary person, hopelessly out of touch with all the true wellsprings of life.

Yet there can scarcely be any overestimating the importance taste plays in some lives. I have known people who would have sooner been—and usually were—wrong about the Soviet Union than drive a car they thought vulgar. Politics is only politics, but for people of militant good taste, serving iceberg lettuce at a dinner party is, let us face it, a significant mistake. I hope I will be forgiven when I say that I can't take much more talk about lettuce. (Has the first upper-middle-class child named Arugula been born yet?) I could also live quite happily without ever again hearing the name Ralph Lauren. (When I see someone wearing clothes displaying his odious Polo designer logo or name, I exclaim to myself, as Art Carney used to do on the old *Honeymooners* television show, "Yo ho ho, Ralphy boy.") I could probably get by nicely, too, without seeing another advertisement for eight-thousand-dollar wristwatches. The same goes for Mont Blanc fountain pens, expensive, leaky little buggers that they are. Show me a man with a Rolex watch, a Mont Blanc in the (probably ink-stained) pocket of his Ralph Lauren shirt, and I'll show you a man besotted with, inundated by, led by the nose because of a concern for good taste—or, to speak more plainly, a concern for slavish and expensive conformity.

Another name for such items is *objets du goût. Objets du goût* include those things costing much more than they are worth, standing for much more than they ought, and bringing more extraneous pleasure than their owners deserve. The world seems very crowded just now with *objets du goût*— objects really intended to show that one has expensive and lovely taste, as opposed to objects of genuine art or utility, or those truly uniting elegance and utility. We now have in America entire towns that are essentially *objets du goût:* Mystic, Connecticut; Santa Fe, New Mexico; Aspen, Colorado. Thousands of kids walk the streets heavily mantled with names that are themselves little more than *objets du goût:* Kendall, Brooke, Scott, Ashley, Tiffany, Brittany, Page. One of the claims to fame of the philandering husband in Nora Ephron's novel *Heartburn* is that, as a boy, he went out with the first Jewish girl named Kimberly.

When confronted by such thick-fingered attempts at good taste in too-great profusion, I find I get a bit flippy, that condition of extreme agitation leading on to incipient madness. When the flippiness is upon me, my environment needs to be carefully controlled. At such times you would do well not to take me to a restaurant where the menu offers tuna tartar with seaweed, a terrine of goat cheese, beets, and pomegranates, and Armagnac ice cream mildly spiced with just a touch of tarragon, for my inclination, presented with such grub, is to want to slip out to the kitchen and prettily julienne the chef. Upper-middle-class shopping malls have a similarly darkening effect on me. Set me down in certain buildings on north Michigan Avenue in Chicago or on Rodeo Drive in Los Angeles and I find it is all I can do to keep from calling for the tumbril and the People's Razor, as the guillotine was known during the French Revolution; unbeknownst to my fellow consumers, amongst whom I walk, I become a perfect little Mme Defarge, minus the knitting, a virulent Communist long after every Red has pulled out of the Finland Station.

What is it about these little temples of good taste—be they

restaurants or tony shops—that gets me so worked up? It isn't
good old-fashioned class hatred. The social class of the people
frequenting such places is roughly my own: college-educated,
middle-class, still panting fairly heavily with aspiration. Not so
different from them, I am a card-carrying member of American
Express, a man of Visa (if not of vision). Even though my own
toy box is by now well enough stocked, I have not lost my
interest in acquisition. Do I not carry a costly Pelikan fountain
pen in the pockets of my too-numerous shirts? Do I not on
occasion wear shoes made in a boot-shaped country? Where do
I get off criticizing other people on this score? Really, I think
to myself, people driving in German cars shouldn't throw
phones.

I grew up in a home where the question of taste, good or
bad, was never discussed. My mother loved clothes, had a
dramatic flair in wearing them and a nice sense of what was
right for her. My father wished only to avoid outlandishness,
which he did, but otherwise was never bothered by questions
of taste. As a boy, I don't remember hearing the word "taste"
from either of my parents. The only object of clothing I was
ever criticized for wearing was a jacket I was much pleased to
own in high school that had the name "Kool-Vent Awnings"
written on the back. The reason I was so pleased to own it was
that, in those days in Chicago, this company sponsored a number of locally successful softball and basketball teams, and by
wearing it I hoped that I would be taken by strangers for a
more talented athlete than I was. My father took an immediate
dislike to that jacket, asking me why I wished to go around as
a walking advertisement for someone else's business. (The age
of designer logos, from Louis Vuitton to Nike, was still far in
the future.) Why not wear sandwich boards, he asked, and earn
a few bucks while I was at it?

For the rest—furniture, cars, and other appurtenances—

our family taste in no way exceeded or otherwise deviated from our social class. We had not advanced to that stage of culture where there was an interest in the antique; in all ways, the new was considered better than the old. An inherent social conservatism combined with a Depression-learned financial caution ruled in our family, so we never owned cars grander than we could afford, or belonged to country clubs, or did anything on a lavish, and hence particularly vulgar, scale. Because neither of my parents went to college, the level of sophistication where questions of taste begin to strike the nervous and, sometimes, comic note was never reached. Ours was not a family that, at dinner, sat around discussing the relative merits of Williams and Amherst; none of its members could have told you where, or even what, Williams and Amherst were. If you had mentioned William and Mary, we would have thought you were referring to the McDermotts, who lived upstairs. Actually, we never called it dinner; we called it supper.

None of this, be it understood, kept me from performing quite efficiently in school as a perfect snob of a kind. Mine was not a cruel snobbery—that is, I took no joy in putting people down or otherwise lording it over anyone. Mine was instead a more limited and entirely upward-looking snobbery. I simply wanted to be in what seemed to me the better circles of kids in the schools I attended. In practice this never proved to be a very serious problem, and I easily enough achieved what I desired. The exercise of taste, along with careful touches of salesmanship, had not a little to do with it.

Taste, in this context, meant never being too different, except perhaps to excel ever so slightly within the recognized pattern of conformity. This operated in the realms both of thought and appearance, and what one was required to conform to was not very difficult to figure out. In high school, good taste implied group taste, which in clothes for boys meant

Levi's or the khaki-colored trousers we then called wash pants, solid-colored (when possible, cashmere) sweaters worn over white T-shirts; letter sweaters (I had won a letter in tennis) or club jackets (my high school was divided into scores of social-athletic clubs) were also considered good form, as were the white Converse gym shoes known as Chuck Taylor All Stars.

Apart from the nerdish lack of style of the boys we used to call "science bores"—a rumpled look demonstrating a total disregard for clothes—one other style of dress was possible during my high school days, and this was a somewhat belated and more casual version of zoot-suitism. Bought on Halsted Street, near Maxwell Street, at a haberdashery called Smokey Joe's, these duds featured such nicely overstated items as electric-blue or rust-colored pants with outer stitching on the seams, rayon shirts with high Mr. B. (after the singer Billy Eckstine) collars, and boxcar loafers—thin suede belts and long key chains optional.

I should like to report that my innate good taste steered me entirely clear of such ridiculous clothes, but I remember once buying, not at Smokey Joe's but at a men's shop in the Loop, a then quite radically pink shirt with a collar pin and a slender black knit tie (known at the time, I believe, as a "slim Jim") with two pink stripes running horizontally near its bottom. I am further embarrassed by the recollection of going shopping with my mother, at the age of fifteen, at a store named Baskin's in Evanston for what was then described as "a one-button-roll suit," in powder-blue flannel, and my mother being told by the salesman that he thought such a suit distinctly a mistake for her son. The salesman was absolutely correct, of course, which didn't prevent me from hating him. Fortunately, I didn't get the suit.

I say fortunately because that one-button-roll, powder-blue suit would have been sufficient to keep me out of the fraternity

I was asked to join during my freshman year at the University of Illinois. (A friend, I was told, was blackballed by the fraternity of his choice at Michigan for wearing white sweat socks during rush week.) This fraternity was very clothes-conscious; its haberdasher of choice was Brooks Brothers; and deviations, which is to say lapses in taste, were not happily tolerated. Not long after moving in, I remember a particularly twerpy member coming round to check every new pledge's tie rack and feeling distinctly relieved for having had the good sense not to bring my slim Jim along.

The University of Illinois may have been in the Big Ten, but this fraternity's sartorial model was clearly Ivy League. (Or "Ivory League," as I have always thought it, after someone I know reported to me having been caught years ago as a graduate student at Princeton with a young woman in his boarding-house room. This was against the house rules and caused his landlady, an immigrant, to chastise him, saying she was greatly disappointed in him, having till now thought him "a nice boy, clean and cut from the Ivory League.") Ivy League snobbery in these matters was in itself bad enough—it was, after all, an imitation of English snobbery—but to encounter this at a reduced level in the Midwest was more than ridiculous; it was snobbery based on a snobbery itself based on a foreign snobbery, an imitation of an imitation. Pathetic, really.

I dropped out of the fraternity and soon departed the University of Illinois for the University of Chicago, where such snobbery as existed was exclusively of an intellectual kind. But my brief experience as a fraternity man taught me that I did not live comfortably under too strong a tyranny of taste. No doubt this experience has much to do with my edginess when I nowadays come up against little tyrants of taste in everyday life. All this might suggest a clear victory of good sense (mine) over social conformity (other people's). But I rather doubt that it does. I still buy a goodly portion of my clothes at Brooks Brothers (now owned by Marks and Spencer, the English discount kings), and now, nearly forty years later, I suspect I continue to look like a greatly aged boy, clean and cut from the Ivory League. Sadder still to report, some years ago I told a woman I know that I was once in a fraternity, and she responded by saying she thought she could guess which one it was. Damn if she didn't get it exactly right. Some marks, apparently, do not erase.

What makes taste so complex a phenomenon is that it is entwined, sometimes it seems inextricably, with style and fashion and social class and snobbery, and, at certain points, it even touches on morality. People for whom questions of taste loom very large in their own lives are likely to find a strong moral component in taste. I myself do not, except where taste lapses into snobbery of a kind meant to hurt others. But experience teaches—or at least ought to—that a person can have the most exquisite taste and still be a miserable creep, while another person can exist outside the realm of taste and be quite angelic. So many geniuses—Mozart, Beethoven, Balzac, Dostoyevsky, Dickens—were men of enormous bad taste, leading one to believe that genius is itself beyond taste, good or bad. It is the rest of us, those who are without genius, who are left to attend carefully to matters of taste.

Taste is a word that is subject to the most wiggly usage in the minds and mouths of some people and is used with impressive precision by others. To begin with, it is unclear whether we are to some extent born with taste or develop it as we go along in life. John Loring, the chief buyer for Tiffany's and hence one of the leading arbiters of contemporary taste, holds rather Rousseauesque views on the subject. He believes that "bad taste is the perversions of taste which people acquire," which implies that people are born with good taste. "Bad taste," adds Mr. Loring, "is received opinion." The more traditional view is that we acquire taste as we achieve culture, through education and self-cultivation.

Benjamin Jowett, in writing a recommendation for H. W. Fowler, who failed to receive a First at Oxford, noted: "He is quite a gentleman in manner and feeling and has good sense and good taste." By good taste I assume that Jowett didn't mean Fowler wore Calvin Klein underwear and the shoes of Salvatore Ferragamo. I assume he meant it was something that Fowler, through rigorous application, had acquired. Pressed, I should say that when Jowett praised Fowler's good taste, what he had in mind was his sense of suitability. Good sense and an understanding of what is suitable are certainly the qualities that Fowler would later reveal, to the highest power, in *Modern English Usage,* a book that is perhaps as much about taste as it is about correctness.

"The essence of taste is suitability," wrote Edith Wharton in "French Ways and Their Meanings." But how does one know what is suitable? We know, the answer is, in our bones. Here we get very near the matter of sensibility, one of the trickiest words in the language, which for me has been best formulated, if not quite defined, by Jacques Barzun, who writes:

Taste implies a judgment of some kind. Sensibility doesn't judge, it receives. Or it fails to. Sensibility equals the number and fineness of your nerve ends. It's the obverse of one's limitations.

Proust's friend the composer Reynaldo Hahn, in his book *On Singers and Singing,* defines taste as "a wide-ranging instinct, a sure and rapid perception of even the smallest matters, a particular sensitivity of the spirit which prompts us to reject spontaneously whatever would appear as a blemish in a given context, would alter or weaken a feeling, distort a meaning, accentuate an error, run counter to the purposes of art." That seems to me very good, except that it defines taste as the search for and elimination of flaws—which is to say, it defines it negatively. Hazlitt, in "Thoughts on Taste," went at things the other way round. He held that "genius is the power of producing excellence: taste is the power of perceiving the excellence thus produced in its several sorts and degrees, with all their force, refinement, distinctions, and connections." He felt that "fine taste consists in sympathy, not in antipathy; and the rejection of what is bad is only to be accounted a virtue when it implies a preference and attachment to what is better." Hazlitt believed that our true taste was revealed by our enthusiasms.

That one's taste is best revealed by one's enthusiasms seems very intelligent, too, except that I am not at all sure I can define my taste by my own enthusiasms. I not only have a fairly strong inconsistency, in my view a happy inconsistency, of taste—I am one of those people who can watch a professional football game in the afternoon and then go off to a chamber music concert in the evening—but in so many realms my taste is rather boringly conventional. In recent years, the four works of visual art that really caused the earth to shake under me have all been sculptural: Praxiteles' *Hermes with the Infant Dionysus*, which I saw at Olympia in Greece; the two very different *Davids*, Michelangelo's and Donatello's, both in Florence; and, finally and illogically, Sir George Gilbert Scott's Albert Memorial in London, which most people consider *the* monument to Victorian bad taste, but which blew me away. I prefer Degas and Matisse above all modern painters, Ralph Vaughan Williams and Darius Milhaud and Ravel (regretting that he wrote *Bolero*) above all modern composers. I tend to prefer the comic over the tragic, the light over the heavy, Montaigne and Pascal over Hegel and Nietzsche, the classical over the romantic, the Apollonian over the Dionysian.

Many of my tastes are generational, which is not very interesting, except that the generation isn't always mine. I seem to have fallen just the other, calmer side of the 1960s, that great divider of Americans, in taste as in much else. This often causes me to share tastes with people much older than I and sometimes to feel distant from people only slightly younger. I was recently with a man nearly thirty years older, who said that he could never consider sex a trivial act. I feel that way, too. I am deaf to all rock music after the Beatles and think that the songs of Gershwin, Cole Porter, Irving Berlin, Johnny Mercer, and other songwriters of that generation unlikely ever to be surpassed. I like to wear neckties. I like the very idea of Fred Astaire and of Duke Ellington. I like sophisticated women; and Myrna Loy is my notion of a dish, to use a word that probably gives me away. I am a sucker for what I take to be urbane and elegant. Much of my sense of what constitutes urbanity and elegance derives from the 1920s, a decade I wasn't alive to witness.

Nor does my taste always seem coherent. Take humor. I find Henny Youngman very funny. But I also love Max Beerbohm, who, among other knockout remarks, once, considering Freud, said: "They were a tense and peculiar family, the Oedipuses." W. C. Fields can also do the job for me. I am not above caving in at slapstick: a Buster Keaton walk into a wall, say, or an Oliver Hardy fall through a floor. But then I also think Henry James a very funny man. Men and women, I find, often show strong differences in taste in humor. Most women do not find W. C. Fields all that funny or H. L. Mencken, either; and I have yet to meet a woman who laughs at the comedian Rodney Dangerfield, which I do. Perhaps it is such dumpy men, which most men eventually become, whom women do not find funny. Then again a certain category of humor is about eschewing good taste, deliberately, which women of natural refinement are not easily able to do.

Examples of what I consider bad taste are not difficult to find. Not allowing men in prison to smoke strikes me as a piece of genuine bad taste, puritan division. Calling too much attention to oneself through one's clothes is another form of bad taste; Ben Hecht once called overdressing the only art we've developed in America. Marrying more than three times feels to me a display of bad judgment lapsing into bad taste owing to a man or woman simply not knowing when to call it quits. No shortage of bad taste in ideas. To continue to call oneself a Marxist in our day, after all the nightmares Marxism has caused in the world, seems to me in extremely poor taste. Some people have broader tastes than others, but to have a taste for everything—and I have met professors who never met ideas they didn't like—appears to me bad taste of a kind that renders one something close to an idiot.

In the article "Taste" in the old *Encyclopedia of the Social Sciences*—and I have a distinct taste for older over newer reference works—the art historian Meyer Schapiro remarks that "taste is identified with good taste, and good taste with the taste of the upper class." He goes on to claim that "good taste becomes the aesthetics of conduct, the aptitude for manners and politeness, the knowledge of formal practices, the arts and choices most favorable to the enjoyment of the conditions of upper-class life." Even as I copy that out, I sense its irrelevance. While once it was true, it is true no longer. Edith Wharton could acknowledge the philistinism of her parents, but she went on to allow that they were immensely well spoken, had a usefully settled code of conduct, and ate wonderfully well. An upper class of this kind simply no longer exists. We have the very rich, we have people at the summit of with-it-ry, we may even have power elites, but none of these suggest anything like the stability of taste that Edith Wharton and, before her, Henry James found in American life. Quite the reverse. Nowadays the richer, more powerful, more with-it one is, the more chaotic one's taste is likely to be. Such people made the fortunes of such dreadful painters as Jasper Johns, Andy Warhol, and Julian Schnabel. Apart from the knowledge that money talks—it makes, I fear, rather a squawking noise—they have no more confidence in their own views on taste than anyone else, maybe even a little less.

My own guess is that many of our clues about what constitutes good taste come from an upper class that no longer exists, if not from one that existed most elegantly in the imagination. American novelists of the 1920s and 1930s, not least among them such Irish-Americans as F. Scott Fitzgerald, John O'Hara, and, later, Mary McCarthy, wrote novels that spoke to a longing for upper-class standards of elegant good taste. It is because F. Scott Fitzgerald in particular was able to infuse so much style into his fantasies of upper-class good taste that so many kids named Scott and Nicole (never, alas, poor Zelda) walk the streets in our own day.

The combination of style and taste is not always so easily disentangled. Style tends to be free, taste restricted; style, by its very nature, independent; taste, by its nature, conventional. To have taste implies a strong sense of tradition; to have style is to think, act, feel rather like no one before you. (Much avant-garde style is intended to affront good taste.) Taste of a certain kind can be bought or, through training, acquired— Elsie de Wolfe claimed that the interior decorator's job was to introduce new money to old furniture; style appears to be something with which one is born. When from time to time people with style appear, they change taste, sometimes radically, more often ever so slightly. The late Audrey Hepburn, for example, made it possible for a woman to be skinny and still seem sexy.

At the same time that we admire style, we worry about

taste. Or at least some of us do. Meyer Schapiro writes that "good taste is essentially conservative, for while it is poor taste to be behind the time, it is still worse to be ahead [of the time]." I have never for a moment been in danger of being ahead of my time. When I was younger I felt a moderate urge to be at least abreast of my time, but less and less do I feel this as I grow older. Coco Chanel, savvy though she was about so much else, was, I believe, wrong when she said, *"La mode est toujours jolie."* I have seen too many past styles that, when they are done, are far from *jolie; hideuse* comes closer to describing them. To restrict myself to men's styles, consider the bell-bottom trousers of the 1960s, the long sideburns of the 1970s, the stone-washing and other perversions of denim of the 1980s. I am fairly confident that, before long, the oversized men's double-breasted suits of the 1990s will join this cavalcade of comic fashion, so that grandchildren will years from now laugh at photographs of you in your $1,000 Italian suit. ("Hey, Giorgio, you made the coat too long.")

I wish I were quite as impervious to fashion as that last paragraph suggests. Feeling happily well out of it, a touch old-fashioned by deliberation, a paid mocker of my own time, I nonetheless occasionally still feel myself gripped at the throat by the fashion of the day. I put on an old single-breasted raincoat I own, and it feels, somehow, skimpy. My blue blazer feels oddly narrow in the shoulders. The wool plaid shirt I have always fancied has a collar that nowadays seems too long. Why should I care? I am not in the permanent Easter parade. I am not in the skirt chase. I don't even yearn to be the sixth best-dressed man in the geology department. Yet, I find, I do care. I stop wearing my old raincoat. I buy a new, looser-fitting blue blazer. I have a tailor shorten the collar of my old shirt for roughly what the shirt originally cost new.

I seem to have slipped from taste to fashion. Quentin Bell,

in his little book on Ruskin, writes that "fashion is the grand motor force of taste." Certainly this is true to the extent that one of the few certain things about taste is that it changes. Chroniclers of taste have even charted a cycle through which taste in the modern age passes. "Indeed," writes Stephen Bayley, in a book titled *Taste: The Secret Meaning of Things*, "the cycle of taste—from modishness to disfavor and then to camp revival—is a familiar one upon which the spurious dynamics of the fashion industry depend." I feel rather sorry for people who have allowed themselves to become hostages to these changes—who become breathless in the race to stay ahead of their time. But perhaps I should save my pity, for the race probably makes them very happy, and another way of living may not, in any case, be available to them. In "Psychology of Fashion," Georg Simmel holds that there are "classes and individuals who demand constant change . . . [and who] find in fashion something that keeps pace with their own soul-movements."

Yet, I sometimes wonder, why does my own soul move so differently? Why am I not among the people who seem able to change styles, adopt new fashions, turn in their taste so regularly and so easily? Why is it that I myself prefer to remain in the outer purlieus of fashion, far from the chic and madding crowd, content to indulge in my own mildly out-of-it tastes? Is this owing to my temperament, upbringing, reason, propensity for moral judgment? I think perhaps it is because I have for a long while conceived of my life as a small work of art—a minor sculpture, perhaps, or a miniature portrait—while people who can change their tastes from week to week think of their lives as, perhaps, a television series or the nightly news. However ineptly I have shaped this work of art I strive to make of my life, I cannot suddenly recast it, switch to all black clothes, pierce an ear, go about in cowboy boots. I grow old,

I grow old, I shall wear my trousers with a one-and-a-half-inch cuff and a slight break at the ankle.

For all that taste changes, runs in cycles, is manipulated by designers and advertisers, and is often little more than a coefficient of social class, for all that it can be the agent of snobbery, an artificial way of separating people from one another, the product merely of the cultural environment in which one grew up—for all this, I believe that taste really exists. I believe, moreover, that there truly is such a thing as good taste whose roots lie in something much deeper and more mysterious than fashion. A friend who edits an intellectual magazine once returned a manuscript to an academic author, saying that he would be pleased to publish it if the author would remove the manuscript's heavily jargonized language. The author wrote back to say that he would be pleased to do so, since he assumed that the use of jargon was nothing more than a matter of taste. "Yes," said my friend, "it is a matter of taste: good taste versus bad taste." I agree completely. I agree, too, with Edith Wharton, who wrote of taste: "Divest the word of its prim and priggish implications, and see how it expresses the mysterious demand of the eye and mind for symmetry, harmony and order."

When good taste is removed, one feels the loss rather dramatically. A strong case in point is the changes that have taken place in recent years at *The New Yorker* magazine since the removal from the magazine's editorship of William Shawn. Much in the old *New Yorker,* under Shawn's editorship, was imperfect. I frequently disagreed with the magazine's politics, found some of its comedy only worked to tighten the lines in my natural frown, felt myself turn blue with boredom at many of its three- and four-part articles. But the one thing that could not be faulted during William Shawn's editorship was the magazine's inherent good taste.

Shawn did not permit four-letter words or other profanities in *The New Yorker,* my guess is, because he knew that such language was being used everywhere else and he knew that there was neither distinction nor courage in having them in his magazine. Perhaps for the same reason, he did not publish stories that described or talked about fornication, plain or fancy. And so when a John Cheever or a John Updike story appeared in a magazine other than *The New Yorker,* you could almost predict what it was about. You could rely on Shawn's regard for the integrity of words generally, so that under his editorship you would never find the word *intriguing* as if it were a synonym for *interesting* or *fascinating;* discover *presently* misused; or see so bloated a word as *prestigious* used at all.

Some might argue that Shawn did these things out of prudery or because he was a language crank. I don't think this was so. I think that William Shawn insisted on these points because of his intrinsic good taste. And nowhere did Shawn pass the test of good taste better, in my view, than in the unsigned obituaries he used to write on the deaths of longtime employees of the magazine. So perfect was his touch, avoiding sentimentality and overstatement, drawing out exactly the detail that revealed character and made plain the significance in these lives, that, in reading these obituaries, I used to feel a touch of something like envy for the person who had died for his having been so perfectly appreciated. These obituaries were matchless exercises in good taste.

When Shawn himself died, no one on *The New Yorker* could be found who could write anything like an obituary of the same quality for him, which, though sad in itself, suggests the loss of something serious. Much of the complaint one now hears about that magazine since Shawn was dismissed from its editorship, I believe, has to do with the loss of good taste that he brought to the magazine. Read the magazine today, with its unbuttoned and often sloppy language, its edge of political meanness, the childish obviousness of its attempts to outrage, and one comes to yearn for the quiet good taste that could once be counted on in a magazine one has been reading for decades. The result is as if a fine and reliable old friend, a little dull perhaps but always with beautiful manners, has, in his senility, discovered a novelty store and suddenly taken to pulling various obscene objects out of his pockets: rubber vomit, inflatable sex organs, plaster of paris dog droppings. None of it, shall we say, in the best of taste.

Good taste may not be as important as original thought, wit, or even charm, but life can seem more desperately competitive, haunted by snobbery, much less gracious without it. Under endemic bad taste, life takes on a decline-and-fall quality that is not easily shaken off; while being in the presence of unpretentious good taste allows one to feel—allows me at any rate to feel—both contented and calmly uplifted. Nicely muted but genuine good taste makes the world seem a pleasant place where you can relax and where you may even have a shot at becoming that apparently most difficult of all things to be— exactly what you are, your true self.

A Very Private Person

I am a very private person. My privacy means everything to me. If it didn't, I wouldn't say it—especially
in print, before several thousand people. True, several thousand people are not, in the modern day, all that many people,
certainly not when you consider the multitudes that watch
television. I was once on *The Phil Donahue Show,* where I had
the chance to announce to millions that I was a very private
person. I neglected to do so, though, and thus blew it, which
I much regret. I shall not blow it again. I am, let me repeat,
a very private person. It's important that you know this. Having established that, what would you like to hear about first:
my neuroses or, what some might say is the same thing, my sex
life? Or would you rather talk about how much money I
earned last year, which, as it turns out, was a very good year
for me?

With an unfailingly light touch, I parodize. Parodize now
lost, let me say straightaway that anyone so silly as to call
himself a private person, in public or even in private, almost
certainly isn't one. In the same way, I have often found that
people who think themselves sensitive are capable of much
greater cruelty than those who don't—their firm belief in their
own sensitivity allows them to get away with so much more.

But then brutality, I have heard it said, is often the other side of sentimentality, and so perhaps we should not be too stunned if we one day learn that the man who weekly places flowers on his wife's grave used to slap her around regularly when she was alive. Very private people—go figure 'em.

No one has ever looked me in the eye and told me directly that he or she is a very private person. Whenever I have noted it, it has been during an interview, either in the press or on television. I am a bit nutty on the subject of these very private persons because, of late, I have discovered that the form of the interview has become one that seems crude, even laughable, to me. Still, as they said about influenza during the 1919 epidemic, there's a lot of it—interviewing—going around. One can chew up a day watching television talk, which are essentially inter- view, shows: Phil, Oprah, Geraldo, and others less famous but no less odious. The interview may well be the form, the bloody leading genre, of our time. Famous writers have been known, when asked for a contribution to a magazine, to offer, instead of a piece of writing, an interview. Some writers have pub- lished entire books of their interviews. John Updike, reviewing Philip Roth's novel *Operation Shylock*, remarks that theorists might argue that "life isn't packaged in plots anymore, and why shouldn't a novel be a series of interviews, in this inter- view-mad age." We are all, you might say, private persons now.

I have been on both sides of the interview—as interviewer and interviewee—and, though I would rather be interviewed than interview, I find the entire proposition, from both sides, mildly but genuinely corrupting. This is not to say that the interview, as a form, hasn't a function; it has. At the same time, though, it is almost never quite what, ideally, it is supposed to be: a way of conveying information gathered by competent journalists who ask pertinent questions of interesting people on subjects of general curiosity. Usually the people aren't interesting, the questions aren't pertinent, and the journalists aren't competent. Taken all together, this tends to make most interviews a mite less than ideal.

I am going to give a talk in a middle-sized, Middle Western city next week, and earlier today I received a call requesting an interview by a reporter from the city's newspaper. The reporter, whose voice I have on my answering machine, seems young, earnest, and quite decent. I am not sure how I am going to get out of this interview, though I am going to try. I suppose I ought to be honored to have been asked to be interviewed, but, somehow, I am not. What, after all, can possibly be the point of such an interview? I have not even the standard commercial excuse of flogging a book, for I have no new book for sale just now. I don't have any ideas for sale just now, either. I hope the reporter doesn't want to do the interview to get my scintillating notions about the state of the world, for I seem also to be fresh out of such notions. Perhaps I ought to give the interview anyhow, just to show the people of his city what a sweetheart I am, and so witty, too. But I find I'd rather devote the hour or so needed for the interview to reading Cavafy or to watching a baseball game on television or to the highly refined luxury of not thinking—let alone talking—about myself.

I make myself sound as if the paparazzi are at my bedroom windows, a producer from *60 Minutes* is always on the phone, and a wry woman reporter from the *New York Times* wants to buy my lunch, on her expense account, at "21" in exchange for my answering just five questions that she promises to give to me well in advance of our meeting. None of this is even close to the truth. Virgil Thomson, a man I much admired for his good sense and prose style, once said that every time he had the notion that he was famous he only had to go out into the world to be disabused of it. I don't even have to leave my apartment to come to the same conclusion.

Still, I feel like the heavy drinker I heard about not long ago who suddenly stopped drinking at the age of fifty-five, declaring that he felt he had had "his share." About publicity, I feel that I, too, have had my share. I haven't had all that much publicity, but I really don't require any more. I like people who don't push it. I have great respect, for example, for Tom Lehrer and Julie London, two talented people who were able to do good work and quit when they were ahead and so never fell behind. I also respect people who are able to write one swell book and, never feeling the need to write another, close up shop. Why go on and on with it, sweaty, tongue hanging out, hounding after publicity, saying, as the bleak heroine of an Anita Brookner novel at one point does, "Look at me!"

"Methinks thou doth protest too much," I hear a voice cry out. "Is this really a serious problem for you, fella? How much publicity have you had, anyway?" By the standard of show business, not all that much. I have never been on the *Today* or the *Tonight* shows. I have never been the subject of an article in the *New York Times Magazine* or had my picture on the cover of *Time* or any other magazine. I haven't chatted with Larry King or Oprah. Such publicity as I have had has been fairly bush-league. I get called from time to time to go on radio talk shows that have some reasonable level of intellectual pretension. I have been asked to appear on *The MacNeil/Lehrer Report*. I once did, as I mentioned, appear on *The Donahue Show*—I believe it was in the same week that he had a show with Kareem Abdul-Jabbar and another with transsexuals; I'm certain you can't have forgotten it. I have been interviewed on a specific subject on a few occasions in the *New York Times*, and I have been interviewed in connection with books I have written in the *Chicago Tribune* and *Washington Post*. I once had a profile written about me for the *Chronicle of Higher Education*. I was interviewed at lunch at the Algonquin Hotel by a reporter from *Publishers Weekly*. *People*, in connection with a book I had written, did a quite dreary three-page spread on me.

All this has taken place over nearly two decades and is, I realize, peanuts to a really "very private person." But to me it has been a surfeit. At the end of each of these little publicity swims, I felt as if I had emerged from murky waters of my own polluting, seaweed in my mouth, something slightly slimy dangling from my ear.

Do understand that no one had to twist my arm for any of these minor media immersions. I do not want my brief affairs with the media to be likened, as were Edmund Wilson's flirtations with the Communist Party in the early 1930s, to a Boston virgin getting on a streetcar. (Boston virgins, it occurs to me, may by now be rarer than Boston streetcars.) Behind most of my publicity dips was a fine impure motive of one sort or another: the wish to sell a book, or push a line, or gently assuage my own itchy vanity. Every time out, moreover, I knew what I was doing, which was, very specifically, a deal: my opinions, views, and carefully rationed candor in exchange for public attention. What was in it for the journalists involved was copy, not very hot copy to be sure, but copy, which remains the only desideratum of the journalist. I, like many another fellow passing through town, was helping these various journalists to kill time (if they worked in electronic media) or to fill space (if they were print journalists).

"Killing Time and Filling Space" is the title I gave to a journal I kept nearly twenty years ago when I agreed to go on the road for my publisher at the time, E. P. Dutton, to sell a book I had written on the lugubrious subject of divorce. I haven't retained my itinerary of this publicity tour, but I recall that I was intensely scheduled: 11:00–11:10, author free—that sort of thing. I was sent to five cities—New York, Pittsburgh, Cleveland, Baltimore, Washington—in five days, beginning with two days in New York. Interviews had been arranged in these cities for television, radio, and newspapers. Divorce was a good media subject in those days. It was still a social problem—the statistics were, as one might say, merely alarming—not yet a wretched commonplace and hence a catastrophe of American life. Everyone could muster opinions about it, and chat-show hosts—the word *hosts* suggests to me hosts and parasites, but in these matters it isn't quite clear who is who—didn't have to read my book to be able to talk about it. It was all splendidly media-able. I was like Herbert von Karajan, who, when asked where he wanted to go by a Paris cabbie into whose cab he had just stepped, is said to have remarked, "It doesn't matter. They want me everywhere."

Bits and pieces of those five days on the road talking about myself and my book have stayed in my mind for nearly two decades. I was on insult radio shows in New York that seemed to float on a cloud of pure hostility, most of it directed at the host; I ran into a very angry psychiatric social worker, a fellow guest on an afternoon television program in Pittsburgh, who, in the green room before the show, informed me that, as a young girl, she had to watch her father, a furrier, gas minks in the Pocono Mountains; I met with a hungover disc jockey in flowered pants at 6:45 A.M. in Cleveland who announced me as a guest, said I was prepared to answer everyone's questions about divorce, and proceeded to play a recording of Helen Reddy singing "Two Against the World"; I was interviewed by a horny-handed journalist from New Jersey who asked me, in confidence, what I thought "these crazy broads nowadays want anyhow"; I was photographed by the *New York Times* while standing out in front of the St. Moritz Hotel, squinting into the sun, as people passing by shook their heads, expecting a celebrity but clearly not recognizing me; I recall lots of journalists' tics, among them reporters saying "Yeh, yeh, I know what you mean" to my every utterance and, even more distracting, their anticipating how I would finish my sentences and finishing them along with me; I had, in Baltimore, a quotation from Mohammed attributed to me, but I decided to let it pass; I was asked many a trivially personal question about my social life and at one point found myself on a sappy television panel that was discussing living alone. Most of all, I remember an extreme, an almost furious, boredom, bordering on self-loathing, with my own endlessly repeated answers to not very penetrating questions.

I recall, too, that as I began that week of self-promotion I was concerned about how well I had done on each show. I didn't want to be a disappointing—you should pardon the expression—"guest." As I left, I said thanks and shook hands with the producers and hosts of these various shows. I assumed that a genuine contact had been made, a human relationship, however fleeting, formed. As the week progressed, though, this assumption disappeared. I would finish my bit, then get up and leave—off to my next show or interview, where I would repeat the by-now-formulaic answers that I had been spouting all that day. No goodbyes, no nice-to-have-met-you's; another, a fresher and warmer body was waiting in the wings; and I had to freshen and warm up my own body during the cab ride to my next shot at self-promotion.

What was entailed in this sort of activity was, to adapt a phrase from Coleridge, a willing suspension of humanity—on both sides, on mine and on that of the journalist with whom I was dealing. This was a problem for me, though, because I do not suspend my humanity so readily. I don't for a moment wish to pretend that I am a beautiful person, but when I meet someone it is necessary for me to believe in the possibility of our getting on together and perhaps even becoming friends. The out-of-town talk-show or newspaper interview seems, somehow, to preclude this. It was all cash-and-carry, ten cents a dance, wham-bam, thank-you-ma'am, here's your hat, what's your hurry.

Still, in the service of simple greed, I probably could have got through it all right—in fact, I did get through it all right— my lovely integrity and shining spirituality intact. But I had the additional problem of not being able to take myself, as an expert in my subject, quite seriously. Mark Twain defined an expert as a guy from out of town. Today he's a guy who has written a book. Certain of the talk shows I went on featured what were referred to as "call-ins," in which listeners called in their questions to the guest. Having written a book on divorce, I was supposed to be able not merely to answer but to solve all sorts of marital problems: sexual hang-ups, emotional maladjustments, punch-ups, financial disasters. I found myself frequently leaning into the microphone before me and saying that I really had no solution to the problem—that I thought maybe the solution was to be found in professional help (which I didn't believe, either). Like anyone of a fairly complex nature, I had too much contempt for myself to pose as an expert in matters where I was quite as lost as everyone else. But of course I was traveling around the country selling myself precisely as an expert. Husband beating you? Sex repulsive to you? Children heartbroken? Hey, no problem, I discuss those things in my book.

Lighten up, bro. Lightening up brings me to my other difficulty, which is that during interviews, either giving or receiving, I am altogether too impressed with the artificiality, and hence the silliness, of the entire activity. I have written only one piece of journalism that required an interview, and that interview lasted less than five minutes. Many years ago I was asked to write an article about a local gossip columnist who was very big in the city of Chicago, a man whom my friends and I had made fun of for his clichés and pomposity since we were in high school. I knew that my article was less than likely to be admiring. The point of the article was to try to understand how this man with so little talent, natural or acquired, had made such a great success. At the time, he had a national television talk show, his column was widely syndicated, he kept a room in his luxury-laden apartment for Harry Belafonte when the great calypso singer was in town. Failure can usually be explained, but certain successes—and his distinctly seemed one of them—remain a mystery.

My subject put himself at my disposal. This was the age of the New Journalism, which, like everything called New, would soon die out. But under the New Journalism journalists hung out with their subjects, spending vast amounts of time in their homes, talking with their relatives, generally prying into their lives as much as was permitted—and then a lot more. My subject asked if there was anything he could do for me to make my job easier. He was, after all, a journalist himself. I thanked him, saying that I might like to sit in the studio during his weekly television program, and that if I thought of anything else, I should certainly be in touch about it. I suppose I could have asked to sleep in Harry Belafonte's pajamas.

I began the interview by asking what turned out to be my only question. "From where," I asked, "do you think your power derives?" He leaned back in the swivel chair in his office—his tie was loose—and, clasping his hands together behind his head, unloosed a flow of the dopiest fifth-hand clichés about the Fourth Estate I had heard in years. As he came to the sonorous conclusion of his answer—something about our fellow countrymen understanding the importance of a free press—I realized that to ask any further questions would be hopeless. It was all I could do, in fact, to ask if he showed slides with the answer he had just given me. His shield of pomposity, I sensed, could not be punctured, at least not by me.

Gathering up my non-notes, I told him that he certainly gave me a lot to think about and that I would get back to him if I had any other questions. I saw him only one more time, at a taping of his television show, where his wife, in the green room, suggested I try one of the cookies laid out for guests on the coffee table, cookies that, she averred, were "simply orgasmic," a phrase I couldn't resist using in my published article. When the article appeared, my subject, in his column, called it "a scissors and paste job," rightly claiming that I scarcely interviewed him for more than five minutes.

Since it may be far from clear, let me say quickly that in telling this story I am trying to let myself off the moral hook for being just another journalist thug. I'm not sure that I have. I do, though, think that I would have been in even worse moral shape if I had spent lots of time with my subject, sat through meals with him, talked with his son, hung out in Harry's room—and then blasted him. Instead, saving the shoe leather, I just blasted him without hanging out, basing what I had written on decades of reading his columns and watching (in amazement) his television shows. Janet Malcolm, the *New Yorker* writer, has written that "every journalist who is not too stupid or too full of himself to notice what is going on knows that what he does is morally indefensible." Quite a bit to it, I fear.

One of the chief differences between human beings and animals, I have come increasingly to feel, is that human beings tend not to learn from experience. So one gray autumn morning, when a soothing female voice called, asking if I was the man who had recently written a book of short stories, I allowed—shucks, ma'am—that I had indeed written those stories. She broke into an impressive and unrelenting fusillade of praise for my writing, ending by saying that, however much she liked my stories, which as I may have noticed was quite a lot, her mother liked them even more. When I thanked her for her generous praise and asked what I could do for her—I was ready to give her three, maybe four pints of blood—she asked if she could interview me for the newspaper for which she worked. I said, with less hesitation than Walter Cronkite discovers the perfect platitude, yes, certainly, sure, of course, whenever you like, absolutely, yes, hell yes, finally stopping lest I repeat the entire Molly Bloom soliloquy at the end of *Ulysses.*

I do not read either of the two main newspapers published in my city. I prefer the *New York Times,* not because I think it so much better, but because it carries more obituaries about people from the world of art and culture; and who dies seems to me the only real news—or at least the only news that stays news, which, I believe, is how Ezra Pound defined literature. I was later told that this woman, as a journalist, had a reasonably high reputation for her stiletto work. Not having read her before, I did not know. Nor, I have to report, did I inquire. What journalist in her right mind, when you get right down to it, could resist my sophisticated yet wholesome charm? Besides, her mother was already on my side. The only question I considered before going into the interview was a less-than-complex one: sport jacket or suit? Perhaps you will think me naive. But then I was still young—not yet sixty.

I fear that my previous paragraph makes it sound as if I were the victim of a hatchet job, blood and hair all over the walls. Not quite. I woke one Thursday morning and discovered, in a neighbor's paper, an enormous photograph of myself, in color, peering out from the front page of the *Chicago Tribune*'s Tempo section. The subhead on the piece read, "[Joseph

Epstein] is a bow-tied dandy with a street-kid muse." I read the piece, twice, in a fog of bewilderment. In it I figure as more than a little out of it; a great cultural snob; a man whose essays are "precious little things" ("an acquired taste, like marzipan"); smugly happy about my lack of fame, though maybe not so happy as all that. ("But obscurity doesn't bother him. Much.") Touches of physical description did not help. " 'Life is very strange,' says Epstein, who with his oversize head and ears and trim little body looks like an intellectual Pee Wee Herman." Zap! Whap! Wham! In for a penny, I always say, in for a pounding. My own self-vaunted charm seems not quite to have been entirely successful. Maybe I should have worn the sport jacket.

When Abe Hirschfield, who was briefly publisher of the *New York Post,* was asked how his interview with A. M. Rosenthal of the *New York Times* went, he answered: "He asked some questions, took some notes. I don't know what he's going to do with it. That's the gamble." And a gamble almost all publicity is, unless one is powerful enough to control it. By powerful enough I mean famous enough. Jacqueline Kennedy Onassis, for example, used to lay down strict ground rules before granting an interview, and these included: no tape recorders, no photographs, all questions limited to her professional life (as a book editor), approval of all quotations used, the prerogative not to answer any questions, and a trusted associate in attendance. If the journalist wanted the interview badly enough, he acceded. Vladimir Nabokov did not "give" an interview so much as "make" an interview. Questions were prepared for him, which he answered, not in conversation, but in careful prose. These less-than-impromptu interviews were only conducted, moreover, by people Nabokov trusted.

On the few occasions I have given interviews, I have tried to control them through seeming winning. (The fact that I might actually be winning was not allowed to get in the way.) I saw it as my job to make the person doing the interview think me an attractive and serious fellow who deserves to be treated with decency and respect. Once, on a rare occasion, when I had information that was badly wanted, I was able to require a journalist to show me all the quotations he planned to use in his interview with me, though in this case it didn't really matter, for the reporter was entirely sympathetic.

Sometimes I have chosen not to let reporters in the door. Many years ago, when I was director of an anti-poverty program in Little Rock, Arkansas, a writer of iconoclastic reputation from the *New Republic* called to say that he would like to come down to do an interview with me and write about the anti-poverty program in Little Rock. Even though I myself was a fairly regular contributor to the *New Republic* in those days, I told him that, if he arrived in town, I would do what I could to have him met and shot at the city limits, for I sensed that there was nothing he was likely to write that could do me or the job I was trying to do any good.

But why bother to control interviews? Why not dispense with them entirely? One is flattered by the request for interviews because interviews are taken to be an index of fame in the modern world. The more one is in demand for them, the more one can assume that there is interest in what one does. Writers seem especially vulnerable here, gratified at any evidence that such interest exists. The first writer to undergo extensive interviewing was, of course, Samuel Johnson; the interviewing was done by a freelance named James Boswell (also, by the standard of hanging around his subject, the first New Journalist). Goethe, who put up with the sycophantic Johann Peter Eckermann, was the next great writer to get the extended interview treatment. But Johnson and Goethe at least seemed to deserve such treatment; their views and opinions on their work and on nearly everything else were—and remain—permanently pertinent. Not many other writers merit such close attention, yet, when offered any attention at all, few seem able to resist it.

Joseph Conrad was one writer who was able to resist it. Desmond MacCarthy has written of Conrad that "he seldom parted with his signature in any cause, and he respected his own craft so sincerely that he did not think it necessary for his manhood publicly to express strong views on the problems of London, traffic, diet, or foreign exchanges." Because of this, MacCarthy felt, Conrad "missed many opportunities of obtaining cheap advertisement" and instead concentrated on his fiction. Conrad was high-strung and spoke English with a strong accent (pronouncing *these* and *those* as "thesea" and "thosea" and *good* and *blood* as "gut" and "blut") and so may have been all the more nervous around journalists and about public performance. When Conrad traveled to the United States toward the end of his life and was met in New York by hordes of journalists and photographers, he wrote to his wife: "To be met by forty cameras held by forty men that look as if they came out of the slums is a nerve-shattering experience." Zdzislaw Najder, Conrad's best biographer, believes that "Conrad harmed his popularity by holding himself aloof from the literary and journalistic milieu, avoiding interviewers and all forms of advertising." He may well have hurt his popularity, but he did have one powerful thing going for him that caused him to rise above this: this was that he happened to be Joseph Conrad.

Conrad was in any case not a great devotee of journalism or publicity. In *The Secret Agent,* he refers to newspapers "written by fools to be read by imbeciles." In *Nostromo,* the character Nostromo finds all his prestige in being well spoken of; publicity, not by press, but by word of mouth means everything to this heroic figure. Drugged on publicity is the way

Conrad thinks of this perhaps greatest among his fictional crea-
tions. What Conrad would have thought today while watching
Geraldo or Oprah is amusing to contemplate. The thought of
Conrad appearing on these shows to flog a new novel is too
painful to consider. The cynical among artists make use of publicity to serve
their own ends. But the serious always know how frivolously
ephemeral it all is. Maurice Ravel, writing to his friend Ida
Godebska, remarks that a Belgian journalist has written to ask
"where I spent my vacation, what my plans are for the winter,
on which days I take my medicine, and other similar matters.
It appears that this would keenly interest his readers. I'm replying that I took a cruise to the Indies, and this winter I'm going
to hunt grouse in Scotland and begin training for the interna-
tional car races." Philip Larkin, who cared about and guarded
his reputation, nevertheless was careful not to promote it
through hype.

On his famous postcard that began "Edmund Wilson regrets that it is impossible for him to . . ." Wilson listed, among
other items, "Give interviews," "Supply personal information
about himself," "Supply photographs of himself," and "Supply
opinions on literary or other subjects." Late in life, Wilson
took to publishing interviews with himself, one of which he
titled "Every Man His Own Eckermann"; under such an arrangement one is at least certain to be asked intelligent questions. A story used to be told—I do not know if it is true—that
Edmund Wilson turned down an opportunity to appear on the
cover of *Time* magazine, and this was in the days when to
appear on the cover of *Time* was an apotheosis of sorts, long
before that once-powerful journal began to put dinosaurs and
rock stars between its red borders.

Which brings me to the sad inflation in publicity. The low
quality of people who are nowadays the subject of interviews,

profiles, and publicity generally makes receiving any of these forms of public attention less than self-assuring. Proust said that in fashion and in medicine there must always be new names; he could add, were he alive today, that there must also always be new names in the arts, in the media, even among the wealthy. ("A man with a little money," says Lester Kane in Dreiser's *Jennie Gerhardt*, "hasn't any more privacy than a public monument.") But the publicity machine seems now too far ahead of the material out of which publicity, even by generous measure, ought to be made. Celebrity has thinned out beyond any possible persuasiveness. The *Paris Review* made a great splash when it began its once-famous series of interviews with writers (later published as books with the continuing title *Writers at Work*), but, though the series continues, roughly twenty years ago they ran out of first-class writers to interview. The *New York Times Magazine*, after doing profiles of many undeserving writers, has now come down to doing similar profiles of jittery, trendy academics who are forever discovering new secrets in literature. Getting publicity these days is rather like receiving an honorary degree along with a Mafia man who donated money to build the new gymnasium, a psychologist who is pretty obviously a crank, and a ventriloquist who has given lots of his free time to educate the public about carbohydrates. Such honors become less than a matter of degree.

It might be easier to take publicity seriously if one felt that the people who dispense it, the journalists themselves, took it very seriously. I am far from convinced that they do. I recall some years ago receiving a call from a young woman in *Time*'s Midwest bureau who wanted to know what my thoughts were about the twentieth anniversary of the assassination of Robert Kennedy, which was coming up the following week. I allowed as I hadn't any thoughts about it, nor was I likely to have. "Oh, really," she said, and then, not losing a stitch, she added, "Do you know anyone else in the Middle West who is likely to have an interesting opinion on this subject?" I was not long ago called by a reporter from the London *Daily Telegraph*, a man with a hyphenated name and a lovely accent, for my opinion about Maya Angelou. Again, I had to allow that I hadn't one, which was connected with the fact that I had never read her. Might I put the reporter in touch with someone who had read Miss Angelou? the reporter queried. I said that I didn't know anyone else who had read her, either, adding that I believed that Miss Angelou, like many another contemporary American writer, is not so much read as taught, which, I averred, was not at all the same thing. Beautifully accented laughter came over the phone. I believe that remark was used in his story.

For a time, when I was an active member of the National Council of the National Endowment for the Arts, I received a fair number of such calls from the press and radio and television talk shows. This was during the period of the Andres Serrano and Robert Mapplethorpe troubles, and the NEA was hot copy. Their purpose in calling me, I believe, was the pursuit of a small but perhaps vicious quotation to enliven their own pieces. I chose not to accommodate. If a member of the press called when I wasn't home, leaving a message on my answering machine, I would generally not call back, which was highly effective, for by the next day a newspaper journalist has his story already written and is no longer interested in what you have to say. But when a journalist would catch me in, our conversation might go something like this:

"Mr. Epstein, John Simpson, *Boston Globe*. I'm calling for your opinion on the flap at the NEA."

"Sorry, Mr. Simpson, but I haven't got one, or at least not one that I haven't already offered at meetings of the Endowment. Besides, why should I help you write your story by offering you a pert quip or two?"

"But what about the public's right to know?"

"Ah, the public. Next time you are in touch with the public, Mr. Simpson, please don't fail to say hello for me." Perhaps I should show more sympathy for journalists, these workers in the vineyard of public (but increasingly private) information. Their lives cannot be so easy. Flogging yet another of my books on a local radio station, I sat in the lobby of the studio, listening to the discussion then going on within, which was led by a psychiatrist with a strong German accent who was talking about eating disorders. Sitting there I felt a stab of pity for the host of the show, who had to talk, day after day, hour after hour, about all the social problems, social confusions, and various little madnesses making a claim for public attention. Do these talk-show chaps ever get confused, I wondered, and think they are talking to cross-dressing linebackers when in fact they are talking to abused sisters-in-law? Funny way to make a living. Funny way, come to that, to live.

In *A Child of the Century,* Ben Hecht reports that, in the let-'er-rip days of Chicago journalism in the first decade of this century, he had a beginning job on a newspaper as a photograph thief. Sometimes with burglary tools, sometimes with great ingenuity, always with impressive effrontery, the young Hecht would get into the homes of people who had recently been murdered or raped and steal a photograph—and, in one notable instance, a large oil painting—of the victim, which would be run in the next day's paper. Today we all bring in our own photographs, and, when asked, we provide a good deal more. It is one thing for me to know how Cher feels about younger men, or Mary Tyler Moore about her career after her emotional setbacks—this, after all, is part of the detritus of modern living—but why should I have to know that neither Gore Vidal nor Stephen Sondheim liked his mother, or that Susan Sontag dyes her hair, or that John Cheever was an alcoholic? Because all of them have chosen to tell interviewers these things. Some were asked, some volunteered the information. Every man and woman in our day is apparently his or her own Boswell; so many Boswells and, alas, no Samuel Johnsons whatsoever.

Were Karl Marx alive today, would he be the subject of a Dewar's Scotch profile (Last Book Read: Feuerbach's *Lehrbuch des gemeinen in Deutschland geltenden peinlichen.* Hobby: Class Struggle)? Would Napoleon be photographed in a turtleneck from The Gap? Would Marie Antoinette do a Rolex ad? One can imagine the talk-show possibilities: "Welcome, ladies and gentlemen, to *The Yesterday Show.* Our guests tonight are: Jesus of Nazareth, songwriter Franz Schubert, playwright and comic Oscar Wilde, and Germany's own Adolf Hitler." One can readily imagine the questions that, say, a Barbara Walters would have for Hitler—Barbara, who, the *New York Times Magazine* reports, goes not for the jugular but for the soft spots—or the roughing up a Mike Wallace would give to Jesus. Sad to think of all the splendid opportunities that these great names in history missed to let down their hair before journalists or on television.

I realize that writers who complain about being too famous are neither attractive nor believable. I hope an exception can be made in my case, if only because I am complaining without the actual fame. Not that I should at all mind being famous. I shouldn't in the least mind being prodigiously famous, just so long, you understand, as I remain not particularly well known.

Nicely Out of It

I have of late been feeling comfortably, luxuriously, really quite happily out of it. In wondering how this pleasing condition has come about, it occurs to me to ask an anterior question: Was I ever truly *in* it? Or, to keep my prepositions straight, Was I ever truly *with* it? I'll get to the meaning of that "it" presently, but the "with" speaks to a happy conformity, an almost total consonance, *with* one's own time. Carried to the highest power, being with-it calls for being a conformist just a little ahead of one's time, which is, come to think of it, a short definition of a trendsetter. I cannot say that I ever achieved such an exalted station, though I have the feeling that I might have had I stayed on the job. But I abandoned with-it-ry fairly early in life and hence, for better *and* worse, dropped out as a serious conformist.

I fear an air of put-down has crept into that paragraph, when all I intended was a mild whiff of self-congratulation. Let me attempt to make amends by saying quickly that I realize conformity, or living in spiritual consonance with one's own time, is no small pleasure. I myself last felt fully with-it nearly forty years ago, a period I often think of as the most pleasant in my life.

The "it" in "with-it" refers to life, life in its full and fine vibrancy, especially life lived at the very vortex of contemporary experience. To wear the clothes, to eat the food, to hum the tunes, to think the thoughts of one's own time, all perfectly unselfconsciously; to feel utterly at ease in the atmosphere in which one lives, without any complaint or fret; to be up to the moment, *au courant*, jollily, joyously with-it—all this is, no doubt about it, a delightful state in which to find oneself.

I was seventeen when last in this state. I thought that I knew pretty much all I needed to know about life, with only a little filling in required here and there. I picture myself as I was then, walking down the corridors of Senn High School, wearing a green-and-white letter sweater, Levi's, white sweat socks, loafers. At my side is a girl named Jackie, with a winning smile and a generous bosom draped in softest cashmere; in the background, the city of Chicago, which seems endless in the possibilities it offers a young man of adventurous spirit; ahead of me, an unclouded and entirely promising future. That happy fellow—me—now seems as distant, really quite as historical, as the head of a youth on an Antiochian coin of the second century B.C.

What would have been the reaction of that serenely thoughtless young man had he, around that time, drawn a fortune out of his cookie that all too accurately prophesied: "You will soon and forever after live at a self-consciously oblique angle—skeptically, critically—to the life of your times"? "Whaddaya, kidding me?" he would likely have replied. Had I, knowing what I know now, been on the scene, I would have implored him, "Struggle against it, kid. Escape your fate. Don't, whatever you do, travel to Samarra. Forget the fortune, eat the cookie, pay your check, fight to remain pretty much as you are." But such advice probably wouldn't have mattered. Fate isn't so easily eluded.

When young I not only thought it important to be, but

found no difficulty in staying, completely and cheerfully with-it. When I—not quite so young any longer—determined to become a writer, I fought manfully to stay up to the moment. By "up to the moment" I mean absolutely current in politics and popular culture. I felt under an obligation to know the key politicians as well as the popular songs; to go even to the bad movies; to listen to television talk shows; to glimpse most of the popular magazines, including the women's magazines, of the day. All this was done with deliberation and under the banner of keeping in touch with my country and its culture, which, as a writing man, I felt it incumbent upon me to do.

As best as I can date such an event, I believe I began to feel out of it roughly in 1966. Around that time the curtain fell, dividing the country between the young and the not-young, and I found myself, even though only twenty-nine, on the not-young side of that curtain. The student revolution had begun, and I—in taste, in temperament, in point of view—had *ancien régime* so clearly written all over me that I might as well have worn a powdered wig.

The unintelligible lyrics of rock music may have been the first inkling I had that I would fall further and further out of it. I continued occasionally to listen to country-and-western music with comic pleasure, learning that, as you yourself may not be aware, "God made honky-tonk angels" as well as that, what is perhaps more obvious, "everybody's somebody's fool." But listening to hard rock seemed more on the order of a punishment, and my desire to stay generally with-it, though still real, stopped short of masochism. (Masochist to sadist: Beat me. Sadist to masochist: No.)

I hope the following confession doesn't land me a job on the U.S. Supreme Court or even, God forfend, as President, but—you may as well know this up front, Senator—I have never smoked pot, another sign of my early out-of-it-ness. I have been in rooms where people seemed moronically happy puffing on the good stuff, as they called it; and I was once at a party where everyone sat in a circle and passed around a joint, but when it got to me I felt the whole ritual vaguely preposterous—your ironic man, poor chap, tends to eschew ecstasy—and passed it along without partaking.

Although I loved the movies of my youth, I found I couldn't take the movies of the 1960s and most of those that followed all that seriously. In fact, the more ambitious the intentions of these movies, the more they seemed like comic books to me. To prove my out-of-it-ness once again, in my pantheon Pauline Kael never came close to replacing Edmund Wilson.

I don't for a moment wish to give the impression that I live unrelievedly on the highbrow level of culture. I live there with a great deal of relief. In the realm of culture, I rather admire people whose standards are more stringent than my own. I was recently talking with a friend to whom I happened to mention the name Steve McQueen. He stopped the flow of conversation to ask who Steve McQueen was. I found it striking that a man in his late fifties could live all his days in the United States without having heard of Steve McQueen. I once asked this same friend, not long after I had come to know him, if he ever went to the movies or watched much television. "I consider the movies and television," he announced, "dog droppings" (I euphemize). Not even to allow these major American forms of entertainment the dignity of horse or bull by-products seemed to me perhaps further than I wished to go, but his distancing himself from the seductions of popular culture seemed to me impressive nonetheless.

I still watch lots of sports on television and go to five or six baseball games a year. I am well known at my local video-rental store, where I often ask for assurance that the movie I am about to rent isn't all shooting and screwing. (I am usually told, rightly, that it isn't: the movie generally turns out to be only about 60 to 80 percent so.) I nowadays steer clear of all talk shows and am proud to report that a number of currently famous people are at least still obscure to me. Nevertheless, by osmosis of a mystical kind, I know rather more than I wish I did about people with no possible relevance to my life and whose minds I find more than a jot less than fascinating. I feel I would be living a better, a more elevated life if I didn't recognize the names Burt Reynolds, Marv Albert, Madonna, Connie Chung, Willie Nelson, David Gergen, Regis Philbin, and Dan Dierdorf. But, alas, I do.

In the progressive stages of out-of-it-ness, I not long ago crossed the line from merely being mildly out of it to taking a small but genuine pride in being out of it. I'm not sure I can convey how pleased I am at never having seen an Andrew Lloyd Webber musical, or the television show *L.A. Law,* or Arsenio Hall, or the Whitney Museum Biennial. How regrettable that I didn't take a pass on the Robert Mapplethorpe show, the last episode of *Cheers,* or Jay Leno! I suppose one can't be perfect—one can't, after all, hope to miss everything. More and more, however, I have begun to feel that it would be nice to try.

I feel I am progressing nicely when, standing in the checkout line at the supermarket, glimpsing the grocery-store press (our version of England's gutter press), I don't recognize the names of people involved in scandals, or when I haven't a clue about the person on the cover of *People.* Yet there is no gainsaying that I do know the names Dolly Parton, Loni Anderson, and Tina Turner (not to speak of Keena Turner, the former San Francisco 49ers linebacker). So many, after all, are the old names I do not know enough about: Callimachus, Hypatia, Erasmus, Palestrina. I know, I fear, altogether too much about the Barbarians and not nearly enough about the Hellenes.

The names one must nowadays know to qualify as with-it lack not only quality but much in the way of staying power. In human typology, most are a little lower than I wish to go. If names there must be, let us have names of better quality. I even have a taste, come to that, for the gentle art of name-dropping. I wish I had a talent for it as sure as that of the late Ben Sonnenberg, the public-relations man, who specialized in what his son has called "the secondary name-drop." When asked if he knew George Gershwin, for example, Sonnenberg would reply: "*Know* him? I used to play gin rummy with his mother." He also once told an interviewer: "I know the difference between Irving Berlin and Isaiah Berlin, and I know them both." I shouldn't myself at all mind being able to say that I played Ping-Pong with their fathers—and beat both badly. I should mind this a lot less than having to confess, as I now do, that I know who Tommy Tune is.

One doesn't become out of it overnight. I happened recently to have been reminded that as long as fifteen years ago, when I was a mere slip of a youth of forty or so, I was called, by a book reviewer, "crankish" and "rearguard." This was distinctly not meant as a compliment, but, somehow, I didn't find myself taking offense. I even felt myself a touch precocious in being judged out of it so relatively young. If I lived to be eighty, there was no telling how far out of it I might eventually go; perhaps I could slip all the way back into the eighteenth century, which has always seemed to me a nice place to visit.

Apart from having a naturally conservative temperament, there are any number of reasons for falling out of it. One is that it might be part of some general personal breakdown. Staying with-it, after all, can be a terrible strain. When F. Scott Fitzgerald declared his crack-up—in *Esquire,* of all places—he was partially declaring his wish to be out of it, at least for a while. In a passage demonstrating that, even in the midst of a crack-up, he could continue to be charming, Fitzgerald wrote:

Trying to cling to something, I liked doctors and girl children up to the age of about thirteen and well-brought-up boy children from about eight years old on. I could have peace and happiness with these few categories of people. I forgot to add that I liked old men—men over seventy, sometimes men over sixty if their faces looked seasoned. I liked Katharine Hepburn's face on the screen, no matter what was said about her pretentiousness, and Miriam Hopkins' face, and old friends if I only saw them once a year and could remember their ghosts.

Another reason for falling out of it is that you don't much like your times and wish, either gently or brusquely, to slip away from them. I have often enough felt sufficiently at odds with our times to have to consider this as an explanation for my slipping gradually out of it, though I don't, in my own case, think this the chief reason. Yet when I consider what it would take today to be considered with-it, the prospect, so pleasing to some, is to me, to put it gently, problematic. To begin with, there is the geographical problem. One cannot really be considered seriously with-it in, say, Minneapolis, or Salt Lake City, or Milwaukee, or Sacramento. One could perhaps qualify while living in San Francisco or Los Angeles; or, from a specialized standpoint (in outdoor living, in politics) in Seattle or Washington, D.C. Abroad, London, Paris, Rome, Florence continue to strike the gong as with-it cities.

But the with-it capital of America, probably of the world, is New York—more specifically, Manhattan—a fact that in itself may be enough to discourage many from the demands of a thoroughly with-it life. A great many people stand ready to put up with the punishing quality of quotidian life in New

York—crime, filth, rudeness, high prices—in exchange for the reward of thinking themselves at the center of the action. I have known people who have left careers—in teaching, in publishing—rather than leave New York. What I believe alarmed them about the prospect was their sense that being out of New York meant, in the end, being out of it—and this, clearly, appalled. What price with-it-ry?

What, today, would a thoroughly with-it life look like? Much time, I imagine, would have to be spent at art galleries and shows looking at many doubtless extraordinary, mostly extra-aesthetic objects. Evenings would find one at a vast variety of new restaurants, tucking into all sorts of dubious delicacies. Either before or after dining one would be expected to buzz off to the Brooklyn Academy of Music for an evening of interminable avant-garde opera or to an unpleasant play on a terrifying subject Off-Off-Broadway. One would, as a man, be wearing the bulky, dark clothes of the kind I see advertised in *Gentlemen's Quarterly* or *Esquire*. One's hair would be pomaded and brushed back; a single earring as like as not would dangle from one ear. One would have to read a great deal of that journalism, companion sheets to the grocery press, that ought to go by the name of the with-it press: at a minimum, this includes *October, Details, Rolling Stone, W, The New Yorker, Vanity Fair, The New York Observer*.

As clearly as New York is the with-it capital of the United States, just so clearly is Chicago, my own city, nicely out of it. The pretensions of with-it-ry—in culture, in fashion, in social life—somehow don't seem to go down at all well in Chicago. Some people in Chicago do attempt to be with-it, but in the act of doing so they tend to seem faintly ridiculous. With-it clothes, for example, don't really succeed here. The characteristic male physique in Chicago is that of the Mayors Daley, *père et fils*, or the Brothers Belushi: chunky, short in the legs, thick in the chest, and not at all made for the clothes of the moment, or any moment that I know, except perhaps the Visigoth invasion of Rome. Chicago is a city where no one is going to look down on you if you are carrying around an extra twenty or thirty pounds. (The food of choice is pizza and Italian beef-and-sausage combination sandwiches, which tend not to conduce to that starved-to-perfection look that marks the with-it of our day.) Great cultural institutions exist—the Chicago Symphony, the Art Institute, the Lyric Opera—and a fair amount of serious art gets made, but, owing to the necessary exclusions of serious culture, it is understood that they are not as central to the city as are the Chicago Bears, Bulls, Cubs, White Sox, and Blackhawks.

But even in the fastness of Chicago, with its anti-chic spirit, it isn't always easy to turn your back on what the rest of the world construes to be with-it. A decade or so ago, for example, I discovered that I had ceased to read much contemporary fiction. Faster than you can say Italo Calvino, I had fallen two Malamuds, three Roths, a Bellow and a half, four Mailers, and five or six Updikes behind. I had let John Irving pass me by. So, too, Ann Beattie, Joan Didion, Gabriel García Márquez. Every book you read is a book you don't read, by my reckoning, and there were too many important non-contemporary books I had not yet read. Life, as everyone knows, is short, and it doesn't take long to learn just how damnably long inferior art can be.

Still, I had a bad conscience about not reading these novelists. Apart from the aesthetic pleasures it brings, the novel, I believe, is a great instrument of discovery. When it is going well, the novel brings the news—to my mind the only enduringly serious news—about what is going on in the human heart. So, attempting to quiet my bad conscience, and turn a few bucks at the same time, I signed on with a magazine to become its critic of contemporary fiction, thinking to catch up with all the Malamuds, Roths, Updikes, Beatties, Didions, Márquezes, and Mailers. And I did. On balance, I think I can report that it wasn't worth it. Either these writers had become worse or I had become smarter, perhaps a little of both, but I found they no longer spoke to, and certainly not for, me. As for the human heart, most of these writers turned out to be more concerned with organs four buttons below that.

I have begun to drop out again. I have taken a pass on what is promised to be the last of John Updike's Rabbit Angstrom novels: when Rabbit died, I failed to turn up at the funeral. I have not read Salman Rushdie's *Satanic Verses,* and don't intend to. I recently reached page 110 of Philip Roth's novel *Operation Shylock* and I called it quits, having decided that to finish his books you have to be at least as interested in Philip Roth as is the author, which isn't easy. There is an American novelist named T. Something Boyle. The Something is a complicated name beginning with a *C* and has three or four syllables. I am perfectly content to think of him as T. Congressman Boyle, not being sufficiently interested—or perhaps being too complacently out of it—to bother even getting his name right. This is the second time I have bailed out on contemporary novelists, and it seems to me increasingly unlikely that I shall bail back in. I may be beautiful, as the blues song has it, but I'm goin' to die someday, so, I now tell myself, how 'bout a little serious reading before I pass away?

If a loss of interest in the news is another sign of being out of it, I qualify here, too. Many years ago, living in New York, I used to read three newspapers a day. I now read one, the *New York Times,* and that I read reluctantly and, following the rule of prostitutes in Athens, never, never on a Sunday. I do not read a local paper, which renders me more than a little out of it in my own hometown. Not reading the *Chicago Tribune,* I usually do not know the names of the most recent serial killer in town, the most recently fired superintendent of schools, or the most recently traded hockey players. Somehow, though, despite this, I seem to get by.

I begin each day's *New York Times* by turning directly to the obituary page. This, I am told, is a standard old-guy's move. So be it. Who died seems to me the most important news. I am interested not only in famous deaths but in quaint ones, such as that of Ruth Ford, age ninety-two, who ran what sounds like a lovely store selling music boxes in Manhattan. The other morning I was surprised to find my own name on the obit page. Surely I hadn't become so out of it that I failed to notice my own death. I was relieved to discover that it was not I but a professor of philosophy at Amherst of the same name who had died. I hope my friends, reading this obituary, were similarly relieved. If my enemies were sorely disappointed, they should not worry: I promise to make it up to them eventually.

I next turn to the letters columns, looking for—and not very often finding—a man after my own heart. I glimpse the op-ed page, filled, as V. S. Naipaul once noted about a character he despised in his novel *Guerrillas,* with so many opinions that do not add up to a point of view. I read perhaps two editorials a week, usually not all the way through, but quickly turning to the last few sentences—the bottom line, you might say. I blaze through the foreign news, turning away with a wince from the standard stories of barbarity and natural disaster in the Third World. I read the national news for accounts of scandal, political squalor, decline and fall generally. I probably read the pages devoted to the arts—news and reviews of fiddlers and scribblers, daubers and dancers—more thoroughly than any others, though I come away from them no more satisfied for my greater effort. Like the eighty-year-old bachelor in a V. S. Pritchett story, I have begun to pick up each morning's paper searching for something that will annoy me—and, happy to report, I almost always find it.

Skimming the newspaper seems luxurious to me. Once, when I worked on a political magazine, I used to have to read the *New York Times* with great attention to stories that held no intrinsic interest for me. I had to note the exact spelling of the name of the latest ephemeral revolutionary party in Peru, the absence of N. V. Podgorny from the photograph of members of the Soviet Central Committee, the name and party affiliation of every member of the United States Senate. I was allowed to stop only at the prices of cocoa in Ghana.

Not long after I departed this job, letting natural interest be my guide, I began to eliminate entire categories of newspaper stories from my reading. Stories about agriculture went first. Space exploration followed. I soon ceased to read anything about central Africa. On the subjects of Latin America and the Indian subcontinent no one has ever accused me of being duomaniacal, and, based on my newspaper reading, no one ever will. I read stories about the environment only intermittently. I rarely read stories about the economy, contenting myself with knowledge at the headline level of detail; if professional economists can't understand the economy—as, clearly, they cannot—what chance have I?

I continue to read stories about blacks and Jews, murder and rape, the disgrace of politicians, the fall in educational standards, people making jackasses of themselves. I check the sports page, but, fortunately, the *New York Times* has so poor a sports page that it does not detain me long. My lapsed interest in the news might trouble me more if I didn't recall the novelist Isaac Bashevis Singer once telling me (I never played gin rummy with his mother, by the way) that he preferred the New York *Daily News* to the *New York Times*. "It's a vonder-

ful paper, the *Daily News,* Mr. Epstein," I remember Singer
saying in his strong greenhorn accent, "filled mid every kind
of moider, scandal, and disgusting act. Just poifect for a novelist."

Reading the *New York Times* in so glancing a way, I find
I no longer know many of the names of the paper's regular
reporters and critics, where once I knew every last Drew,
Brooks, Harrison, and Clifton among them. But then neither
do I know the names of the editors of *Time* or *Newsweek,*
where once I knew nearly the full mastheads of both magazines. I know a dentist who claims to have practically lost his
practice when he canceled his office subscription to *People,* but
in my dentist's office I am not even tempted by the rag. What's
the point? If the redoubtable Cher were to move in with an
elephant I suppose I would read about it, though before the day
is out I am certain to have forgotten the elephant's name.

As a result of all this inattention to the news, I am not sure
that today I can name more than twenty members of the
United States Senate, where once I knew them all. I know the
name of my alderman, but I had lately to be reminded of the
name of my congressman. I cannot tell you the names of the
prime ministers of Italy, India, or Algeria, among other countries. With the exception of Kurt Waldheim, I cannot tell you
the name of a secretary-general of the United Nations since U
Thant. What I chiefly remember about Mr. Thant is that he
allowed himself to be badly snookered by a New York land-
lord, and he wound up having to pay an outrageously high rent
on his apartment. This incident made me think at the time that
if you were ready to believe in the efficacy of the United
Nations, you might be interested in some real estate I could
show you.

I note, too, that I am less attentive to new slang and jargon
than I once was. Even when I learn what new phrases mean,

use them, except for comic purpose. I don't mean merely the obviously stupid language of political correctness—with its silly *isms* (fattism, ageism, classism) and *ableds* (differently, otherly, uniquely)—which only an imbecile would take seriously anyway. I never say "focused" and, myself, try to stay "unfocused." (A recent *New York Times* obit for a professor of French at Columbia carried the subtitle "A Focus on Diderot.") I blanch at the new use of *fun* as an adjective, as in fun couple, fun time, fun run. Sometimes I find I not only dislike a term—*graphic* novel, for example, for a novel-length comic book—but the very thing it describes. This category includes "dramadoc" and "docutainments"; also, while the bad taste is still in my mouth, "infomercials" and "infopreneurs." Let us not speak—you won't catch me doing so—of "foodies," "compassion fatigue," "cruelty-free," or "cocooning." Hey, dude, I tell myself once I get going on this subject, chill out.

Reading the with-it press often doesn't chill me out but merely chills me. There I see and instantly forget the names of movie starlets of whom I have not previously heard. I read about young entrepreneurs—usually designers, or gym-shoe manufacturers, or "infopreneurs," many of them—who seem to me empty of everything but the harsh emotions connected with the kind of ambition that has nothing behind it but the sheer desire to get ahead. I thumb through an issue of *Esquire* or *Vanity Fair* and nothing, not even the ads, holds any interest for me. In the pages of these magazines, as a line from an old song has it, "I just don't see me anywhere."

For the first time, I have begun to skim in my reading, often bottom-lining an article after giving it a three- or four-paragraph shot at arousing my interest. I bottom-line on the assumption that there is nothing useful I can learn from the article, or there is nothing sufficiently interesting to be worth stealing from its author's prose, or there is nothing in it that is going to stay in my mind anyhow. Skimming seems eminently sensible to me, but because it is something I never used to do—Justice Holmes claimed to finish every book he began and ceased to do so only in his seventy-fifth year—it also seems to me another sign of falling out of it.

Is this intensification of my out-of-it-ness no more than a sign of getting older? Getting older of course means—and here I do not euphemize—getting closer to death. In *The Sixties,* the last volume of his journals, Edmund Wilson, then in his late sixties and in poor health, comments again and again on how "the knowledge that death is not far away . . . has the effect of making earthly affairs seem unimportant. . . . And [it is] harder to take human life seriously, including one's own passions and achievements and efforts." Wilson attests to feeling "the *flimsiness of human life,*" where, "surrounded by the void of the universe, we agitate ourselves, one sometimes feels, to very dubious purpose."

Death, even the hint of death, has a way of making nearly everything else trivial. I was walking away from reading a petulant review of a recent book of mine, beginning to work up a temporary but genuine sulk about it, when I met an acquaintance who told me he had been discovered to have colon cancer. I'll take, I thought to myself, the bad review. Can it be that I am gaining a modicum of perspective, some distant hint of what is important and what is utterly beside the point in life? If so, this could be troublesome, for true perspective will put a person out of it faster than anything going. With perspective, one hears the dogs barking as the caravans hove out of sight and knows that future caravans will follow, each of them soon enough also to disappear. Why be one of the barking dogs?

As one grows older, there is, I suppose, something appropriate, even natural, about falling out of it. To be old and too much with-it, in the same way, can be quite unseemly. A man in his sixties ought not to write a book about Michael Jackson; a woman of seventy ought not to dress like Janet Jackson. (I wish I didn't know those two names.) The quickest way I know to be called Pops or Old-Timer is to show up at a rock concert wearing a ponytail when you're in your fifties.

I suppose a happy medium is possible in all this. I have friends in their seventies with a serious interest in the performing arts, who make it their business to see most movies, plays, and dance groups going—as sometime theatrical producers, they have a professional interest—and they do it with dignity and without any of the heavy breathing one generally hears when older people try to stay with-it. Edmund Wilson, too, attempted to stay with-it, within reasonable limits. He continued to go to the theater, to comedy reviews, to the movies, to the occasional nightclub (the tumult from which, he allowed, "stunned" him). But he reserved the right, sacred to the old, to find the young wanting, complaining at one point that he found it regrettable that so many of the young among the artists and intellectuals he knew in New York and Boston were in psychoanalysis.

In my own out-of-it-ness, though, I sense something more going on than my growing older and, hence, nearer to pegging out. I think a good bit about death, but do not do so, I believe, obsessively. While I have allowed that there is much about our time that is not to my taste, I am not in anything like the condition of Edmund Wilson's friend Dorothy Sharp, who, he says, "dislikes everything that is going on (but I and so many of my generation feel the same way). . . . It is plain that she is losing the will to live." A number of the acts featured just now in our cultural and political life may irritate me, but I still enjoy the show and have no intention of giving up my seat any sooner than I have to. No, something deeper is going on.

What it may be is a decisive change in sensibility, leading to a similarly decisive change in character, some of it generational, that makes it impossible for me to partake fully in contemporary culture. I have tried to formulate what is behind these changes, but without much success. Then, not long ago, I came upon the following interesting passage in an essay by Martin Amis, son of Kingsley. In an essay in *The New Yorker* in defense of the poet Philip Larkin, who had been posthumously under attack for improper opinions, Martin Amis writes:

Larkin the man is separated from us, historically, by changes in the self. For his generation, you were what you were, and that was that. It made you unswervable and adamantine. My father has this quality. I don't. None of us [persons in Martin Amis's own generation] do. There are too many forces at work on us. There are too many fronts to cover. In the age of self-improvement, the self is inexorably self-conscious. Still, a price has to be paid for not caring what others think of you, and Larkin paid. He couldn't change the cards he was dealt ("What poor hands we hold, / When we face each other honestly!").

I wish Martin Amis had gone on to say more on this point, especially about those "forces at work on us" as well as about those "fronts" too numerous to cover. He does not specify what they might be, but I suspect he is falling back on all-too-vague military metaphors for the struggle to stay with-it in a culture that changes so rapidly. One of the reasons it changes so rapidly, of course, is that so many people—friends of Martin Amis if not of Philip Larkin—are ready to go along with every change, lest, terror of terrors, they be found out of it.

Yet who wishes to be with-it if the price is an almost endless changing of one's personality to accommodate those "forces" and those "fronts"? There are—perhaps there always have been—those who are ready to go with the flow, with its quick current, not particularly minding swimming amidst all the detritus in those muddy and churning waters. Such people pride themselves on being exceedingly knowing, above the ruck, with the show, perennial insiders over whose toes nobody but nobody pulls the wool. The aesthetic tends to be the chief criterion for such people. What is taken for style or taste is generally the basis for all their judgments; and style and taste, in the end, are made to stand in for virtue. To have opinions not congruent with theirs—however often theirs change—is, somehow, poor style and in bad taste.

It is unclear to what end all this knowingness and aesthetic judgment is directed. It is equally unclear to what end the self-improvement Martin Amis refers to is to be carried on. (Endless self-improvement always reminds me of Santayana, in his eighties, remarking, apropos of a physician suggesting that he lose twenty or so pounds, that he obviously wishes to have him perfectly healthy in time for his death.) The with-it of our day, as Martin Amis suggests, see no reason to play the cards they were dealt. Instead they see themselves in a game that might be called endless draw poker in which you keep turning in your cards till you find a hand that you can work with, always with the proviso that this, too, can be turned in at a later time should the aesthetic winds shift and leave you shuddering out in the cold.

I prefer being out in the cold with my own well-worn but comfortably out-of-it notions. These include: that there are a number of unchanging ideas—none of them particularly stylish—worth fighting for; that honor is immitigable; that so, too, is dignity, despite the almost inherent ridiculousness of human beings; that one's life is a work of art, however badly botched, which can be restored and touched up here and there but not fundamentally changed; that, in connection with this, integrity includes coherence of personality; that elegance, where possible, is very nice, but there are many things more important than style, loyalty and decency among them; that a cello is a finer instrument than an electric guitar; and that a man ought to start out the day with a clean handkerchief. I hope I speak for others who are out of it when I say that we take these truths to be self-evident. And, as those of us who are out of it have learned, when it comes to most of the really important truths, no other kind of evidence is usually available.

Decline & Blumenthal

When a friend asked me what I was writing, I replied that I was planning an essay I intended to call "Decline and Bloomin' Fall." "That's interesting," she said, "but tell me, who is Blumenthal?" I have known no Blumenthals but two Blumenfelds in my life, both men: one is now in his eighties and in the jewelry business; the other is someone with whom I went to high school, who later went on to medical school, after which he repaired to Texas and, far from declining or falling, so far as I know has risen and continues to ascend. Still, "Decline and Blumenthal," which ought to be the title of a good Bernard Malamud story, is too fine to toss away, and so I shall retain it. Besides, it has just the right jauntiness for an essay on a subject that can use all the comic relief it can get.

Not long after the gift of this lovely title, I came across a piece of Australian slang that I had not previously heard: "He's lost the plot." I gather you say about someone who has gone off on a fairly long tangent, or who is just plain nuts, that he has "lost the plot." Something very useful about that phrase; something much better than the simpler "He's lost it" or other ways of suggesting that the next fellow is of course quite mad. Since the plot here has to do with a little entity called Western civilization—"Western Civ," as college students call it—and is a pretty complicated story, I suppose it is fairly easy to lose. If after reading this you think I've lost the plot, please send, in my name, a pint of Play-Doh and a thousand-piece puzzle of a serene landscape to your local insane asylum.

Let us begin with typographical errors, of which I hope none has cropped up thus far in this essay. In the last essay I wrote, such an error appears in my penultimate paragraph. Four people proofread this essay, I among them. In an essay of mine in another magazine, the word *the* appears twice in a row. In the postscript to a friendly letter, a correspondent notes that on page two hundred and something of my most recent book the word *shear* appears where *sheer* is wanted. Since I am one of the most fallible of proofreaders, I hire—and share the cost with my publisher for—the services of a professional proofreader. Not to sufficient avail, apparently.

I once heard it said that the *National Geographic* has never had a typographical error in its entire history. I heard this nearly twenty years ago. Not a regular reader of the magazine, I cannot say if the record is still intact. But if it was true then, I hope it's still true now, for every other magazine I read contains typos, as they are called in the trade, and so do most books, even from old and once-reliable English firms. Many writers, editors, and publishers blame this on the new computer printing. I am myself inclined to think otherwise. I am inclined, in fact, to agree with Evelyn Waugh, who once said that now that they no longer defrock priests for sexual perversities, one can no longer get any decent proofreading. What Waugh meant, of course, was that there were no longer people around with both the learning and the intellectual conscience to get such small but crucial details as proofreading absolutely correct. Decline, alas, and Blumenthal.

One run down in the ninth, we have men on first and

second with no outs. The man at bat earns an annual salary of $2.6 million, not counting, I am sure, bonuses. He is at the plate with instructions to bunt—a sensible act that will send the men on base down to second and third, making it possible to score the man on third with a sacrifice fly that will tie the game. Except that the man at bat, who is probably earning more for this afternoon's work than one of Evelyn Waugh's defrocked priests earned for a year of proofreading, immediately demonstrates that he hasn't a ghost of a hint of a clue about how to bunt. That laying down a bunt is something every boy in every schoolyard in America was once expected to know how to do and is one of the fundamentals of the game is probably not an argument that would be especially cogent to this guy. Learning a small but essential self-sacrificial act such as bunting is not, in any case, how he came to be earning $2.6 million a year. So on his second inept attempt at a bunt, he pops the ball up to the pitcher, who easily doubles the already running man off second. The next man up hits the requisite fly ball to left—a fly ball that might have tied up the game and taken it into extra innings—which depressingly ends the game. Our $2.6-million man will probably get a salary increase next year, bringing his earnings up, I should estimate, to not less than $3.5 million. Decline, I say, and Blumenthal.

I not long ago went with a friend to buy clothes at a store where I have shopped since college days. I had taken my sons to shop at this same store—not literally at the same store, but the same store in its previous location. My old salesman at the old location died, and I never go into the store without thinking of him: a beautifully turned-out man with white hair who lived for trips to Paris, where one of his children resided. My new salesman is a man who looks to be in his late sixties. I find him simpatico also. He once told me, not without chagrin, that he has a grandson of twenty-five who doesn't know how to knot a necktie. I suggested that he needn't worry, since most men of his grandson's generation will doubtless be buried in denim wearing baseball hats turned backwards. "Please," he said, "don't get me started." He is obviously a man with a decline-and-fall essay of his own that awaits writing.

My friend bought a suit, a sport jacket, and two pairs of trousers at this store. His bill came to a little more than $1,300. As I recall, they charged him extra for alterations—something I never remember happening in the past. When my friend gave his American Express card in payment of his bill, they ran a check on its validity in front of him. When we came back two weeks later, we discovered that none of the trousers was properly tailored and the suit coat rode badly on my friend's shoulders. Another trip, two weeks after this, revealed that they still hadn't got the trousers right. My friend agreed to take the sport jacket but asked for his money back on the other items. He was told that he couldn't have it just then, but that he could either wait for a check to be issued out of the firm's headquarters in New York or return later in the week and late in the day when they could reimburse him with cash. Four disappointing trips—having to pay parking-lot fees each time—for a single sport jacket, and one that, I am told, is not wearing all that well. I neglected to mention that this store had some years before been taken over by a famous firm of English discounters, whose name isn't but perhaps ought to be Decline and Blumenthal.

Typos, bad bunting, poor craftsmanship, wretched service—I am trying to start small here so as not to lose the plot. If one wishes to chronicle a decline and fall, how much better to be able to start as Edward Gibbon did: "It was at Rome, on the fifteenth of October, 1764, as I sat musing amidst the ruins of the Capitol, while the barefooted friars were singing vespers in the temple of Jupiter that the idea of writing the decline and fall of the City first started in my mind." It was at Wrigley Field, at Brooks Bros., while proofreading, that the idea for "Decline & Blumenthal" came to me. Unlike Gibbon's, mine is scarcely an original idea. Nearly everyone I know lives with the sense of serious decline if not impending fall. Our gains— chiefly in technology, medicine, and science—all seem so uncertain, our losses so absolute. Or so, when queried, do most people feel.

No, it is not at all easy to keep the plot straight. Apologies to Professor Heisenberg, but we have here a subject in which uncertainty becomes almost a principle. For one thing, in claiming a decline I have to consider my age, and whether good traditional old-timer's solipsism hasn't kicked in. No longer a "sprung chicken," as an immigrant woman I know once put it, am I seeing nothing more than my own decline writ large in my society and in all of Western civilization? Certainly, I would not be the first person to have done so. "The decent pleasures of life," H. L. Mencken wrote in his sixty-sixth year, striking the characteristic note, "have all diminished enormously in my time." At the close of *Before and After Socrates*, F. M. Cornford writes: "Then nothing remains but the philosophy of old age, the resignation of twilight that deepens over the garden of Pleasure and the hermitage of Virtue." I read that and wonder, Is England ever again to produce another scholar with the deep lucidity of F. M. Cornford? Seems, alas, unlikely.

Reading David Cannadine's study of G. M. Trevelyan, one discovers that Trevelyan himself had fairly early got into the decline-and-fall mood. Trevelyan's dates are 1876–1962, but as early as the end of World War I, not yet fifty, the historian writes: "I don't understand the world we live in, and what I understand I don't like." In his *British History in the Nineteenth Century*, Trevelyan, getting into the swing of things, noted:

"In the seventeenth century, Members of Parliament quoted from the Bible; in the eighteenth and nineteenth centuries from the classics; in the twentieth century from nothing at all." In the late twentieth century, it probably wouldn't surprise Trevelyan to learn, most politicians not only have ceased quoting but have had others, alas, compose most of their written and spoken utterances. (I see that I have already used up the legal limit of alases in this essay.)

Although I look gloomy, by nature—you're going to have to take my word on this—I am not. I don't think of myself as having much taste for declines or falls. I'm not a Wagner, Mahler, Hieronymus Bosch, Nietzsche man; I'm a Mozart, Ravel, Matisse, William James man. Where my taste runs to pessimists, it is the laughing pessimists I prefer: Karl Kraus, Justice Holmes, Mencken. I like a good joke maybe even a little better than the next fellow.

I'm an Apollonian kind of guy. I can't bear to think of those four horsemen of the apocalypse; I prefer instead the prospect of prancing pinto ponies wearing red cockades and ridden by smiling multi-racial kids. Joy, not sorrow, stimulates my imagination. A picnic lunch on the grass with friends, not solitary confinement in a Kafka novel, is my notion of a swell afternoon. I hope I haven't lost any standing in thus admitting to being, in effect, the intellectual equivalent of a Rotarian, but I feel the need to establish my bona fides in making plain that decline and fall is emphatically not my idea of a good time.

One day over the food of my people (Chinese), I asked my lunch companion, a retired businessman perhaps eight or nine years older than I, whether he thought we are living in an era of decline and fall. Lowering his chopsticks, he replied, "Well, look at it this way. When we were in high school, the great problems were gum chewing, talking or clowning in class, and (rarely) absenteeism. Today the problems are drugs, possession of guns, the safety of teachers, and teenage pregnancy. Yes, I'd say the argument for a decline can be made without too much trouble."

Of course, such horrendous behavior chiefly takes place in schools in the worst neighborhoods, and there are many—some would say too many—explanations for it. Over the course of twenty-odd years of university teaching, I have not found the quality of my own students to have fallen off greatly; on good days, when these students and I are truly humming, I actually think students are getting better and smarter. But then I am not someone who is shocked to learn from studies of student cultural ignorance that only a minuscule portion of seventeen-year-old students have read *Tess of the D'Urbervilles;* I haven't yet read it myself.

I teach at what is reckoned to be an elite school, so my perspective may not be trustworthy. Might it be that things are declining not, as is usually the case, from the top down but from the bottom up? Charting a decline can be a complicated business, and some people might not be convinced by words alone. I may need some visual aids here: a pointer, a couple of bar graphs, a few multi-colored pies, three or four Miró drawings, a Himalayan sprinkling of eraser dust on the shoulders of my teaching blazer. But the fact is—perhaps it would be more correct to say "the fact isn't," since I don't have many hard facts to present—that decline is something one feels in one's bones.

The omnipresence of crime and social sadness has had a good deal to do with this feeling. Big-city life now brings with it the distinct prospect of random death, and if that doesn't get you down, nothing much will. We may, in Daniel Patrick Moynihan's phrase, have "defined deviancy down," but we cannot convince ourselves that it is not a dreary part of all our lives. The daily press, the nightly news, our own eyes are there to remind us that we are living with major social problems from which perhaps protection but no real hiding is possible. In the past, people such as I believed that all was rectifiable by better education, social patience, and goodwill all around. It is becoming harder and harder to believe this and easier and easier to believe that we shall eventually be swamped by our ghastly social problems—it is becoming easier and easier, in other words, to believe we are living in a period of staggering decline.

The late Arnaldo Momigliano, in a brilliant essay entitled "Declines and Falls," quickly surveyed some of the theories by which declines of the past have been explained. Justus Liebig, for example, had the notion that societies declined when the mineral constituents of their soil were exhausted; Cesare Lombroso argued that great historical changes, declines among them, are brought about by madmen; Otto Seeck felt that social struggles, wars, and religious persecutions used up the best men, leaving opportunists and the dregs of societies to survive and help bring about decline. Other historical explanations for decline that Momigliano mentions include race mixture, climate change, body exhaustion. Spengler, Toynbee, & Co., partial though they were to cyclical theories of history, tended to feature decline.

The context for Momigliano's observations was a reconsideration of Gibbon's own views about the decline and fall of Rome. Cutting through all sorts of theoretical niceties, Momigliano maintains that "ultimately Rome fell because it was conquered. German tribes took over the Western part of the Empire. If we want a cause, this is the cause." But he then goes on to say that we do not want that cause "because we rightly feel that it does not make the situation meaningful; it is too obvious or too trivial really to explain what happened. . . . Anything which makes a situation meaningful can be turned into a cause, either in isolation or in conjunction with other elements." What made Gibbon so penetrating, in Momigliano's view, was that, in charting the decline and fall of Rome, he grasped, through the grandeur of his perspective, "that late antiquity meant the replacement of paganism by Christianity." Less interested in assigning causes, Gibbon understood an underlying situation.

One can assign causes aplenty to the feeling of decline in the air just now, almost all of them tenable, but none convincing unless tethered to a proper description of the general situation in which they are taking place. Why is it, for example, that I do not believe that men of the combined learning and good sense of Arnaldo Momigliano are likely to walk the earth soon again? Why am I dispirited at reading that in a small Texas town northwest of Houston, not only are four of fifteen of the local high school's cheerleaders pregnant, but the school board feels it would be legally hazardous—it fears litigation from women's and civil liberties groups—to ask them not to perform their cheerleading? My spirits aren't exactly lifted when I learn—thanks to the *New York Times Magazine*—that "kids know the names of more models than ex-presidents." But then an ad in the same paper carries a blurb for a novelist that reads, "Imagine Kathryn Davis as Henry James, only witty," which, since Henry James was probably the wittiest American who ever lived, causes me only to mutter, "Decline, my dear Blumenthal, everywhere decline."

"Gosh, honey," as Adam said to Eve on their way out of the Garden of Eden, "I guess we're living in an age of transition." Is there, in this feeling of decline I sense so poignantly, nothing more than the sense that the old world I loved is dying and a new world is aborning? How, after all, do I know that this new world isn't likely to be superior to the world it is replacing? If a new world is truly struggling to be born, ought not one—oughtn't I?—do one's best to help it along? What good does my complaining do? This past summer, outside the ballpark, the man from whom I usually buy my two-dollar bag of peanuts asked me how I was doing, and when I answered, "Could be better," he shot back: "How bad can things be when you're able to get away on a beautiful afternoon in the middle of the week to watch a ball game?" I told him he had a point, neglecting to add that I had tickets between home and first base precisely eight rows off the field.

No point in pretending that we have all only recently left Eden, even though those of us who are old enough can distinctly recall what we think was a splendid prelapsarian time. Real improvements have come about in my lifetime. I find no difficulty in coming up with a list of material items, from razor blades to computers, that have made life better. I once heard a story about a man, a Southerner whose family owned a vast cotton company, who on the night of Neil Armstrong's landing on the moon, asked his father if he thought he would ever live to see such a thing. "Son," his father is said to have replied, "I never thought I would live to see the day when I could relieve myself in my own house."

On the spiritual side, I can think of only a single item of improvement, and it is not a small one: the world seems more tolerant—or at least officially tolerant, and official is a lot—of minority groups of all kinds than it did when I was young. But this toting up of material and spiritual progress is apparently an old game. In *France, Fin de Siècle,* Eugen Weber makes the point that in his investigation of the end of the nineteenth century among the French, "the discrepancy between material progress and spiritual dejection reminded me of our times. So much was going right, even in France, as the nineteenth century ended; so much was said to make one think that all was going wrong."

A historical cliché has it that a century's end—any century's end—brings on a wave of general malaise, that old *fin de siècle* feeling. As Professor Weber writes: "The notion of end, somehow, goes with thoughts of decay and diminution."

It is the *fin de siècle,* the *fin de siècle,*
Ah life, where is thy snap, thy pop, and thy crackle?

A natural end-of-the-century tendency, too, is to see decadence on every hand. A critic of Rodin's sculpture of Balzac noted that people who see it "can know to what perilous degree of mental aberration we sank at the end of our century." Artists evidently felt differently. John Richardson, the biographer of Picasso, notes that the painters of Barcelona tended to believe "that the [new twentieth] century about to dawn would see the emergence of a glorious new art and the coming of a Messianic artist: a Nietzschean superman with a Dionysiac style." Leaving aside the question of whether that artist ever arrived—was he, as Richardson suggests, Picasso?—I think it fair to say that no one, among artists or anyone else, is expecting anything like such an artist to arrive in the twenty-first century.

One of the things that most strongly sends the decline vapors wafting into the air is what seems the absence of first-class men and women in positions of leadership. In this century we have known first financial and now human inflation. This is true not of America alone—"Europeans Fear That Leaders Are Not Equal to Their Task" ran a recent *New York Times* headline—but seems a worldwide phenomenon. I recognize that my plaint here about giants having walked the earth when I was young is scarcely a fresh notion. Tacitus, at the beginning of the *Annals,* speaks of the disappearance of "the fine old Roman character" of the kind found under the Roman republic. Yet the absence of serious people to fill serious jobs has never, at least to me, seemed so striking. A friend not long ago remarked to me that the newly appointed president of a university of great reputation was a man who, in the old days, would have made a middling-quality high-school principal. What applies to university presidents applies to cabinet officers, poets, baseball commissioners, novelists, and maître d's. Only athletes, auto mechanics, and maybe some chefs seem to have improved.

Part of the problem may be that there are men and women now in positions of real power who are younger than I, and they seem to me the thinnest of reeds. I know of men and women holding important judgeships and heading large federal agencies and billion-dollar foundations with whom I wouldn't even care to have to a cup of coffee. Perhaps there is nothing new in all this. As early as 1884, when he was forty-one, Henry James noted that "imbeciles [were apt] to be in very great places, people of sense in small." While on the speaker's platform, on a panel, on some academic board, or on the Council of the National Endowment for the Arts, I have thought of that deft Jamesian phrase and wondered if I myself had not become one of those imbeciles, even though these places are not all that great.

In an old joke, a successful young Englishman, wishing to thank his immigrant Jewish father for helping to put him through Oxford, arranges to have a splendid suit made for the old man at one of the best tailors in London. Two, three, four fittings, and the suit, a work of great elegance, is finally completed. The old gentleman puts on this magnificent garment, and straightaway begins to weep. "Papa," asks his son, "Papa, what is wrong? Are you crying because you are so touched by my gift?" "Not at all, my boy," the man says. "Now that I'm in this wonderful suit, I'm crying because we've lost our empire."

In connection with my own feelings about the decline, I

find myself a bit in the old gentleman's condition. I don't bemoan the loss of the British Empire so much as the enfeebled condition of Britain that followed from it. Owing to the splendid bravery of the English in World War II, which occurred during my young boyhood, I was an Anglophile right out of the gate. With the exception of its food, England stood for superiority on every front: ties, shoes, umbrellas, tennis racquets—everything English was of the best quality. G. M. Trevelyan, writing about England during the reign of Queen Anne, noted: "What men that little rustic England could breed! A nation of five and a half millions, that had Wren for its architect, Newton for its scientist, Locke for its philosopher, Bentley for its scholar, Pope for its poet, Addison for its essayist, Bolingbroke for its orator, Swift for its pamphleteer, and Marlborough to win its battles, had the recipe for genius." It would be too cruel to adduce contemporary counterparts to those names. The classicist Jasper Griffin, a man of my generation, has averred that an intensive education in the classics of the kind he received as a boy is no longer obtainable in England. Material things, spiritual things, nothing in England seems as good as it once was: the books, the clothes, the cars, not even the eccentrics, nothing compares well. All that is left to the poor English, it seems, are actors, journalists, and heavy irony. Thus it takes an Englishman, Alan Bennett, to remark, in his play *Forty Years On:* "Standards are always out of date. That is what makes them standards."

If England is no longer a model of much that is superior in life, the vistas are no brighter on the Continent. As a young intellectual and aspiring writer, I often found myself looking to Europe, with what I now think a useful feeling of cultural inferiority, for intellectual and artistic figures more impressive than those I thought our country could turn up. No longer. No André Malrauxs or Albert Camuses, no Arthur Koestlers or Marguerite Yourcenars, no Ignazio Silones or Primo Levis currently reside in Europe. The United States now exists on a level of at least cultural parity with Europe, which is not at all comforting, for it only means that Europeans are nowadays quite as unimpressive as we.

"Public Schools Are Failing Gifted Students, Study Says"—a characteristic headline over a characteristic newspaper story about a characteristic failure to cultivate the brightest kids in our schools. Two, perhaps three stories about the failure of education seem to find their way into the press every week: this or that collective test score is lower than last year's, Johnny can't write, spell, read, spit, you name it, poor damned Johnny, that knucklehead. Describing the great slide in education, these stories reinforce as strongly as any other kind of story one's belief in the decline of our civilization.

Because these stories are reported in the media, one is naturally dubious about them. With the exception of obituaries, nothing that appears in the newspaper, one assumes, can be wholly true. But in this realm, anecdotes from friends make one doubt even one's normal dubiety. Years ago a friend, asked to write a college textbook about modern art, was told that the word *bourgeois* was too complicated for undergraduate readers and that he should remove it from his text. (Instead he removed himself from the project, and a fine book went down the tubes.) A man with whom I exchange letters has recently reported to me that he has had to withdraw a manuscript he had submitted to a small university press because "a new editor there . . . eliminated very large chunks of it and rewrote the rest into language geared to retarded ten-year-olds." Such stories are becoming less and less uncommon, and in fact there is now even a name for the impulse at work behind them: it is called "dumbing down." You dumb down something by making sure it is accessible to the least intelligent portion of its potential audience.

This is not my memory of how education worked, or was supposed to work. As best I can recall, my teachers, far from dumbing things down, were regularly smartening things up on me. When I was a student at the University of Chicago—which, I am grimly pleased to discover, was recently named last in a list of schools where a lively party life and fun generally are to be had—I regularly felt out of my depth, over my head, intellectually about to drown. I sat in class worrying about humiliating myself by mispronouncing Thucydides' name: Suckadydes? "Bored and belittled," the story about the public schools failing gifted students reports, "the gifted students underachieve." "Frightened and embarrassed," might run a story about my own experience of education, "the underachievers become a bit gifted fairly fast."

But nowadays where are the teachers to come from who are capable of smartening up the curriculum? I haven't the least notion. The most serious teaching takes place in grade and high schools—there, as they say of surgery, is where lives are saved. In days of yore—excuse the archaic locution, for the time I am about to describe sounds as if it took place when Robin and his merry men roamed Sherwood Forest—the best grade- and high-school teachers tended to be women. Without a doubt, many of them took up such jobs because little of a putatively higher kind of work was available to them. These women are no longer available for essential work of this kind—and for this no one can, or I suppose even should, blame them. Modern feminism, I sometimes think, is about the right of women to spend their lives just as mediocrely as do men.

Here is what I meant when I wrote earlier that our gains in contemporary life all seem so uncertain, while our losses seem so absolute. The bright woman who fifty, forty, even thirty years ago taught school is now instead a lawyer, or a psychotherapist, or a freshly minted M.B.A. with a managerial job. Whether the world needs more lawyers, therapists, corporate managers is a question I am ready to leave open. That it needs more talented men and women teaching in the trenches is not an open question, and I just don't see where we shall find them.

I have of late had a certain amount of medical business in the city of South Bend, Indiana ("South Bend, sounds like dancing," says Katharine Hepburn to Jimmy Stewart in *The Philadelphia Story*), and could not help but notice the extraordinarily high quality of nursing care available in that modest-sized town. Some of these nurses have been men, but most have been women. The reason South Bend has so many good nurses, I have concluded, is that it is a small but not especially thriving city without lots of the false work that a larger city provides. Bright young women there do not have so many opportunities to do public relations or interior decorating, or to run fat clinics. The result is that many bright women go into such useful work as medicine.

People may argue about what is or is not useful work, but I, in my own social life, know almost nobody in the United States who *makes* anything. I exclude here the making of deals, or poems, or successful arguments. I mean palpable things: objects, products, commodities. Almost everyone I know is a lawyer, university teacher, writer, broker, editor, or shuffler of one kind of paper or another. At a dinner not long ago, I met a man who actually makes and sells pajamas and robes. I told him I found this startling. As a boy, driving up Western Avenue in Chicago, I saw a street filled with makers: tool and die, sausage, awning, and many other kinds of manufacturers. The sons and daughters of the men who owned these businesses are today probably sociologists, commodities traders, or psychiatric social workers. Is this progress, or is it decline? You tell me, my dear Blumenthal.

Progress, degress—this way to the egress. This Way to the

Egress was the sign P. T. Barnum put up to get suckers out of his sideshows; they thought they were on their way to see an exotic bird. Nowadays one reads the metaphysical equivalent of the egress everywhere. One has the feeling of a world done in, used up, played out. In what seems an almost unexceptional statement, the novelist-critic-translator-librettist-screenwriter Anthony Burgess wrote that "literature has had it. We have lost interest in language as an imaginative medium, and now we just write to communicate on the most basic possible level." The music critic Samuel Lipman has asked, "Who's killing our orchestras?" So much in contemporary visual art gives the feeling not merely of decline and fall but—I hope the phrase doesn't get around—of post-fall.

In politics, things are not much better. After winning the Cold War, we seem more depressed than exultant. Zbigniew Brzezinski writes of our suffering something he calls the "post-victory blues," adding that if they do not soon end, "the post-communist transformation will not only be much more painful and prolonged, but its outcome will be even more uncertain." We seem rather in the condition of the people in C. P. Cavafy's poem "Waiting for the Barbarians." The barbarians never arrive; it would almost be a relief if they had: "And now, what's going to happen to us without barbarians? / They were, those people, a kind of solution."

The pervasive feeling of decline and fall I have been attempting to describe is at bottom about demoralization. In good part, I believe, this demoralization is owing to the loss of belief in progress. The United States has always been a country whose underlying assumption has been that of progress—progress unstinting and unrelieved. I did better than my father, and my children will do better than I—this was the operating assumption. It no longer operates very successfully. For the first time, one hears talk of the downward mobility of children.

There are many who freely acknowledge that they will never do so well in the world as their parents. Will people really be content with this arrangement? I wonder. I find I do not easily reconcile myself to it. Nor would I if I were young.

"I realized," wrote Mme de la Tour d'Auvergne in her memoirs, "that the Revolution was inevitable when I noticed that the pâtissier was putting less butter in the brioches." Might one say something similar about the decline being inevitable when one discovers British politicians putting less grammatical English in their speeches, American tennis players less sportsmanship in their matches, Hollywood screenwriters less wit in their scripts? (William Goldman reports that he was asked to take a sardonic reference to Las Vegas as the Athens of America out of a screenplay because the producers were certain no one would understand it.) And what the devil is a brioche anyway?

Walking the streets of any large American city today one meets with the demented and with the hostile young, lending everything a heavy tone of sadness and menace. When I was last in Baltimore, a city I have always greatly liked, my overriding impression was that the whole place could use a paint job. I have begun a quiet campaign to change the sobriquet of New York from the Big Apple to the more fitting the Big Crazy, after the Big Easy, which New Orleans is called. On the Chicago El one bright Saturday morning, I rode from the Loop with a carload of young, my guess is unmarried, mothers, youth-gang members, two men selling a newspaper to help the homeless, and a thin, middle-aged transvestite who, I do believe, winked at me as he departed the train at Clark and Division. On the Howard-Jackson line, it was an A Train, but in such company the strains of Duke Ellington were not to be heard.

Twist the blinds, open the windows, for God's sake let in

some air. All this depression is beginning to get even me, its dispenser, down. Decline and fall is, after all, only a metaphor. When it comes to that, we have probably been on a fairly steady decline since the fifth century B.C. in Athens. History might be, in Gibbon's famous words, "little more than the register of the crimes, follies, and misfortunes of mankind," yet along the way there have been delights, splendors, heroism, and much joyous laughter. If we seem to be living in the bodeful night, if the world seems to be losing its principle of existence, if everyone seems to be rushing to blow out the trembling match of culture and leave us in darkness, if nothing less than a radical change of heart seems to be required to save us from further decline, then those who love life are under the obligation not to desert it—not yet anyway. Best not to concentrate altogether on the sycophancy, cowardice, and fraudulence of a society that feels as if it's in decomposition. Better to think instead of beautiful children in concentrated play, of Mozart's music for oboe and harp and flute, of Winesap apples and cold green grapes, of large-hearted men and women who refused to be daunted in much darker times than ours.

Boy N the Hood

Although after a while I'd like a chance to have a look at your insurance program, just now I'm curious to know if you own a cemetery plot. My guess is that if you're under fifty, you probably don't. As it happens, I do, but only because my father bought six such plots many years ago, when he himself was in his thirties. In those days people bought cemetery plots because they believed two things that I am not at all sure we believe today: first, that they were going to die and that this could happen at any time; second, that they would die in the very city where they were living, even though their death might be forty or fifty years away.

In our day, as is well known, through careful diet and exercise, death can be put off just about forever; one can live well into one's nineties and then settle back to enjoy the delights of slow cancers or fast dementia. As for dying in the city in which one has lived, a more preposterous notion scarcely exists. I, like you, shall doubtless die in Geneva, Paris, or Palm Springs, but surely not where I live now, not here, surely bloody not. Or so many of us think, doubtless quite wrongly.

I visit my cemetery plot, located on the rim of a lower-middle-class suburb northwest of Chicago, fairly often—ten, maybe twelve times a year. The drive takes thirty-five or forty minutes. My dead are buried there. I find the setting peaceful. Hungry though I am for life as the next fellow, sometimes I think that lying under the ground here would not be such a bad deal. My own plan is to be cremated, so "lying" isn't quite the right word; but I do intend for my "cremains"—to use the spiffy new funeral director's word that sounds like nothing so much as a substitute for real cream for one's coffee—to be set down here. The way I look at it is that this place figures to be my last neighborhood.

I have always lived in neighborhoods, so why not end up in one? Chicago, the city of my birth and upbringing, Chicago, that city of little villages known as neighborhoods, has turned me into a neighborhood guy, with some of the parochialism but also the quotidian pleasures the phrase implies. I like neighborhood comforts: familiarity, easy access to necessities, the feeling of slightly distant but nonetheless quite real community. I like the potential for friendliness in neighborhoods. I am someone who becomes friendly with shopkeepers, bank tellers, mailmen, and UPS and Federal Express deliverymen. I am on a first-name basis with my barber and am pleased to be known at local restaurants.

None of this, let it be understood, means that I'm not ready to move on fairly short notice. I am not quite in the condition of Philip Larkin, who wrote to his friend Monica Jones: "To people like me life is only bearable if they think they might move." Larkin was well into his thirties before he lived in his first unfurnished apartment, and when he did, the experience of buying furniture was more than a little daunting to him. At the same time that Larkin had no taste for what he called "abroad," he also yearned to be among the class of people I think of as permanent transients. To such people, a too-settled life is redolent of the stolid, the middle-aged, the spiritually inert, and it leaves them very edgy. "Next year in Jerusalem,"

Jews of an older generation used to say, lifting strong schnapps to their lips. "Next year anywhere else but here," the permanent transient thinks.

I used to think myself a permanent transient, at least in my soul, and at times I still do. My problem is that it is too easy to imagine myself living elsewhere: in Florence, in small towns in Nebraska, in British Columbia, just about anywhere, really, but the YMCA. I do so less and less, though, as the years go by. The feeling of familiarity that life in neighborhoods gives is congenial to me, even though I occasionally worry about growing too comfortable in it.

The first neighborhood I can remember was greatly circumscribed—it was, in fact, a hotel. During the early 1940s, before my younger brother was born, my parents and I lived in the Pratt Lane, a hotel on the north side of Chicago. (Living in hotels in those days must have been moderately fashionable. In *The Old Bunch,* a novel by Meyer Levin, a young Jewish lawyer's having begun to make it is shown by his moving into the Jarvis Apartment Hotel. Thirty or so years later, I myself briefly lived in the Jarvis, which was by then a bit down on its uppers.) At the Pratt Lane one received a fair amount of service: there was a switchboard; maids came in; and I believe laundry and dry cleaning were picked up and taken out to be done.

My first memories of the Pratt Lane go back to when I was four. I recall something resembling a regular social round in the hotel. My parents had a number of friends there. I must have been one of only a few children living in the hotel at the time, and I remember getting lots of attention. "Oh," I recall a chubby woman saying, bending to pinch my cheek, "this one's going to be a real heartbreaker." Like my father's prophecy that I would one day turn out to be a terrific salesman, this, too, proved to be untrue.

Not long after this, we moved a few blocks away to an apartment on Sheridan Road, a busy thoroughfare in a neighborhood that, though rather grand, still had an intimate feeling to it. In our courtyard building lived the sister of Barney Ross, once simultaneously the lightweight and welterweight champion of the world. Sam Cowling, a comedian on a then-famous radio show called *The Breakfast Club*, lived in the next building. But the great figure on the block was the pharmacist, Mr. Henry West, a tidy, compact man with rimless glasses and a salt-and-pepper mustache, whose smock lent him a certain authoritativeness. It was to Mr. West that one went for advice about minor ailments—a burn, a sore throat, a sprain—advice that he tendered with a measured sobriety. The soda jerk at West's Pharmacy was a boy named Jimmy Kogen; I met him again almost fifty years later and recognized him instantly by his wide and winning smile.

Although I remember walking with my mother to the butcher shop on Morse Avenue—with the war on and meat rationing enforced, it was a key location as well as a depot for neighborhood gossip—for the most part, my life was lived on the block. Lots of kids lived in the nearby three-story apartment buildings, and in the spring and summer evenings there were elaborate games of Kick the Can, Red Rover, Red Rover, and Capture the Flag. Lake Michigan was just a block to the east, and on occasion there would be evening beach parties where hot dogs and marshmallows were cooked on sticks over a fire. Sunday mornings men played softball on Farwell Beach, and on autumn afternoons the football team of Sullivan High School practiced on a field fronting the lake.

Because air conditioning was not yet available, on steamy summer nights my parents and I sometimes went to the movies. Often, as I remember, I went alone with my father; by then my mother was staying home with my baby brother. I don't believe we ever inquired about what movies were playing or when they began. We just went to the movies, and when we walked in in the middle of the film, we stayed to see the part we had missed. The neighborhood was rich in movie theaters: there were The Coed, The 400, The Northshore, The Howard, and, easily most impressive of the lot, The Granada, which, in its rococo exterior and Aladdinish decoration, was out of the Arabian Nights sired by San Simeon.

A joke of those days told about a little boy with a determined expression who was noticed circling his block over and over again. When asked why he was doing this, he replied that he was running away from home but wasn't permitted to cross the street. In fact, looking back, I am now impressed by the freedom I was given as a little boy. At age seven or eight—often, true, in the company of boys a year or so older than I—I was allowed to take a bus or the El to downtown Chicago or to a movie in another neighborhood or to a baseball game at Wrigley Field. Cities not only seemed but were less fearsome. Nuns in habit and priests in collar were part of the cityscape. Owing to all the priestly Bing Crosby, Barry Fitzgerald, and Pat O'Brien movies I saw, I took especial pleasure, on buses or on the El, in asking, "Would you like my seat, Sister?" I must have been attempting to pass myself off as a Catholic.

The neighborhood I have been describing seemed to be half-Jewish, half-Gentile, the latter half dominated, I retrospectively conclude, by Catholics. The large Catholic church in the neighborhood was St. Jerome's—never called Jerry's as St. Timothy's in the next neighborhood we lived in was called Timmy's. Catholic Chicagoans in those days often described their neighborhoods by the name of their parish. If you were not a Catholic but a kid interested in sports, you might describe where you lived by the name of the nearest public park and gym: "We live over by Chase Park." (Chicagoans have always been spendthrift with prepositions.) If you were a politician, you would describe where you lived by the number of your ward, possibly even your precinct.

When I was ten, we moved to a neighborhood that was changing. We, it turned out, were among the agents of change. The neighborhood was changing from middle-class German and Swedish to on-the-rise Jewish. If there was bad feeling about the change—and I suspect there was—we heard about it only fleetingly. The neighborhood was changing so quickly that Jews were soon, if not in, very close to the majority. Still, there was a decent mixture: I went to school with kids named Swenson, Christiansen, Duncan, and Maccaluso. On the way to school I passed a house with an elegant Japanese rock garden; a Dr. Varsabedian practiced medicine out of his home; a man named George S. May, an industrial engineer who is said to have had a collection of fifty-six Hawaiian sports shirts and who started the world's first big-money golf tournament at a country club called Tam O'Shanter, lived in a house across the alley from a three-flat building that he used as his office; in front of the house, a black chauffeur often polished one of May's series of dark blue Cadillacs.

The year was 1947, the economy was settling down, and things were beginning to look up after the war. The main shopping drag in the neighborhood—Devon Avenue, with the accent on the second syllable—seemed to grow more and more prosperous: filled with fine stores, none of them franchises, none of them owned by somebody living in Houston. Much new building of an undistinguished kind was under way. Perhaps owing in part to the infusion of so much new blood, there was a spirit of onward and upward about the neighborhood. Things were good, and nobody could give a compelling reason why they shouldn't get better.

Things had begun to look up for me personally. Ten years

old and in a new school, I was taken by my classmates to be
a superior athlete. I wasn't, but I was a very good mimic, and
I could imitate a good athlete, which at ten is pretty much the
same thing as being one. Suddenly I found myself a T-formation quarterback, a shortstop, the point guard (though the
position wasn't yet called that) on the basketball team. Since
sports were the only way of acquiring prestige among boys in
the neighborhood, I, clearly, had arrived. Later, at a high
school with roughly three thousand students, such athletic
prowess as I was thought to possess soon received a more
accurate measure, and the best I was able to play was frosh-
soph basketball and tennis. But the mark of high self-regard
had been permanently left: somewhere in my mind I still think
myself a T-formation quarterback, a shortstop, a point guard,
somehow or other a main player.

Two of my closest friends to this day grew up with me in
this neighborhood. In good Chicago fashion, one has returned
to the very block, the very apartment, where he grew up and
raised three children of his own. I have lived on very different
blocks since departing, yet if the veneer of worldliness were
scratched off me, I know that many of the ideas acquired in that
neighborhood would still be in place. From this neighborhood
I continue to draw on memories that have sustained me long
since moving away. Once, under a local anesthetic for a minor
operation and needing to divert my mind to pleasant thoughts,
I remembered myself at age thirteen, a football under my arm,
returning at dusk in late October to the 6600 block of North
Campbell Avenue, greeted by the fine smell of burning leaves
and the sight of orange flames flickering in the gutters along
the street.

Along with the public parks—Greenbrier was the name of
one, Indian Boundary another—restaurants were among the
neighborhood's chief social institutions. These tended to be

owned by Greeks (Kofield's) or Jews (Friedman's). Open around the clock, Friedman's Delicatessen was a place where, past my sixteenth year, I could depend on finding someone I knew at almost any hour. Fast food had not yet been invented, but fast talk had, and at Friedman's it was one of the *spécialités de la maison*. Everyone was a wise guy; everyone knew—or pretended to know—the score. Lots of talk about sports figures, crime, and fabulous deals floated, with the cigar smoke, to the ceiling all through the night. Men going off to early jobs stopped there for breakfast rather than wake their wives at five in the morning.

I don't know in what year Friedman's went out of business, but, if I were the local historian, I would mark the neighborhood's change from that date. I now live only a few miles from the old neighborhood, and I occasionally drive through it, flush with nostalgia and sadness. The eastern portion of Devon Avenue is now dominated by East Indian merchants—grocery, jewelry, sari shops. Westward, past California Avenue, there are Orthodox Jews in great number, many of them in Hasidic dress: little boys, earlocks flapping, clutch their bewigged mothers' hands. The last things I bought on West Devon, at a place called Lieberman Monument Works, Inc., were tombstones.

I have also gone back to eat at a deli on West Devon called The Bagel, where huge portions of forbidden food were provided—forbidden not by Jewish law but by contemporary medicine. In The Bagel one felt one could have been brought down by the secondary cholesterol; a sound health-care plan would call for such a restaurant to keep two cardiologists on the premises at all times. When I went there I took my life on my fork and ate enormous salami omelettes. But the clientele at The Bagel—no longer the dashing liars from Friedman's with their stories about stock-market killings, Cuban cigars, and great deals on cars—was elderly: tremors, walkers, toupees, patently false teeth were found at every table; to the dolorous music of time, the prostate shuffle was danced. The restaurant did a brisk—also brisket—lunch and Sunday-morning business, but very little in the evening. Finally, The Bagel packed up its artery-clogging calories and moved elsewhere, leaving an empty corner as a symbol of a neighborhood that has seen much better days. Its exit may have added a year or two to my life, yet I think of it with sadness. If I were a composer, I should one day like to write a Pavane for West Devon.

Old neighborhoods have not only a certain character but an archaeology. This archaeology, like the many layers of Troy, reveals different lives and ways of living. On the doorjambs of some of the apartments of South Shore, a neighborhood in Chicago that is now black, one finds the mezuzahs of former Jewish inhabitants. In a Mexican neighborhood one finds a stately Gothic Catholic church or high school named after an Irish or Italian saint. One day in Kenwood, out of a mansion befitting an industrialist in a Dreiser novel, I saw Muhammad Ali, the former heavyweight champion, emerge with an infant in his arms and an entourage in his wake.

The absence of a neighborhood feeling is what makes life in so many suburbs—and, to jump up my generalization a good bit, in much of the western United States—less than enticing to those of us raised in genuine neighborhoods. Perhaps the first qualification for a neighborhood is that one be able to travel it on foot, which eliminates most claims for neighborhood status for cities in southern California, Arizona, and Wyoming. A second qualification is individual ownership of retail establishments. The fewer the franchise restaurants and shops, the better. Neighborliness requires that the owners of shops and restaurants are on the premises and have a stake in the community. Much better that the restaurant you're eating in isn't owned by two guys in High Point, North Carolina, and doesn't serve meat that was half-cooked and frozen in Seattle.

A neighborhood ought to have something resembling regular rhythms: a flow of people going into and coming out of it, a weekday and a Saturday and then a quite different Sunday feeling about it. Institutions, whether they be churches, schools, libraries, public parks, saloons, or banks, ought to play a serious role in neighborhood life. A neighborhood does well, too, to have a few characters—make that more than a few characters. I sometimes wonder if I qualify as one of the characters in my own neighborhood.

I moved to a different neighborhood roughly five years ago. I had lived in my former neighborhood for something like eighteen years. (I even wrote an essay about it with the title "Unwilling to Relocate." As you can see, I was—willing to relocate, that is, about ten blocks to the north.) My current neighborhood is in central Evanston. Evanston is the first town north of Chicago. We have an apartment on the sixth floor of a building on the edge of what is called downtown. Two or so blocks to the east is Lake Michigan. Closer in are some very grand houses, many of them qualifying as mansions and a few selling for more than a million dollars, stately pleasure domes lived in by people who have mastered the tricks of moneymaking. From the windows of the room in which I work, which face south, I can see the side and portico of a retirement home, the backs of other apartment buildings, a Greek restaurant and some shops, a Christian Science Reading Room, the former office of Bell Telephone, the upper floors of a Holiday Inn (in whose sign the letter *i* doesn't light so that, at night, in green neon, I read Hol day Inn), and the slender steeple of a Baptist church where I used to go to hear ancient music concerts.

From my living-room window I can see the Evanston Library, which is less than a block away. Just beyond it is the Omni-Orrington Hotel. Across the street from our building, to the west, is a nearly block-long modern building that used to house the Washington National Insurance Company, once the largest employer in Evanston. Since the company has moved out, the building will soon meet the wrecker's ball and be replaced by a high-rise apartment building. My view to the north is of the red-brick, white-trim mansion of the Women's Club of Evanston; off in the distance, I can see the rounded top of the Baha'i Temple and the steeple of the Garrett Theological Seminary. Nearer by—less than a block away, in fact—is the Women's Christian Temperance Union, much made fun of by H. L. Mencken and others during Prohibition.

Sometimes I stand at my living-room window, a glass of wine in my hand, and, facing the WCTU's three recently rehabilitated cottages and its red-brick administration building, I drink to the memory of Frances Willard, the founder of the Women's Christian Temperance Union. ("Here's lookin' at you, kid.") I remember the Evanston of my boyhood as a town where Miss Willard would have felt quite comfortable—a town of white-haired (blue-rinse) dowagers and little tearooms serving genteel yet meager meals followed by rather pathetic cobblers for dessert. Evanston always had a large black population, historically there to provide servants for the rich suburban Northshore. Yet the feeling in the town was White, Anglo-Saxon, Protestant, and not a little boring.

In the age before malls and discount stores, Evanston was also the main shopping center for the suburbs and towns north and northwest of Chicago. If the town had unimpressive restaurants, owing in part to its issuing no liquor licenses, it did have good shops: a branch of Marshall Field's, superior men's and women's clothing stores, shops in which to buy china and silverware and fireplace equipment, furriers, and a superior grocery store with an excellent butcher shop called Smith-field's. All these shops from the *ancien régime* are now gone, with the exception of a book and office-supply store called Chandler's, which still sells Boy, Girl, and Cub Scout uniforms and runs a creaking elevator to its second and third floors.

Because of the Women's Christian Temperance Union, Evanston was a dry town. Students at Northwestern drove twelve or so blocks to Howard Street, the south side of which was in the city of Chicago, for the mild sin of a few beers. Today booze can be served in restaurants, and so there are a few bars in town connected to restaurants and even a couple of package liquor stores. No booze meant poor restaurants, which was regrettable, though, for myself, I did not greatly regret the absence of a bar life. I tend to go along with Heming-way, who, I believe, once said that bars were fit chiefly for finding fights or complaisant women.

In his brief essay "The Moon Under Water," George Or-well describes a perfect pub. It serves its beer in china mugs with handles, which he maintains makes beer taste better; its barmaids call everyone "Dear" but never "Ducks"; its clientele consists mostly of regulars who "go there for conversation as much as for the beer"; there is a garden out back in which children can play; it provides a solid lunch for a reasonable price; and it "sells tobacco as well as cigarettes, and it also sells aspirins and stamps, and is obliging about letting you use the telephone." The only problem with this pub, as Orwell reveals near the end of his essay, is that it doesn't exist. "The Moon Under Water," for such is the name of the place, is his fantasy of the perfect pub.

My own fantasy is of the perfect neighborhood Italian restaurant. As it happens, roughly a hundred yards from where I live there is an Italian restaurant. But its portions are too small and the food is not good enough; the owner unconvincingly addresses his customers as "Gumba"; and Verdi and Puccini tapes play much too loudly. None of this has kept it from being a fairly successful restaurant, but it remains far from my ideal plate of pasta. Other Italian restaurants in the neighborhood similarly fail to meet my requirements, which are that the food be flavorful, plentiful, and reasonably priced and that no pretension be observed in its preparation or serving. My perfect restaurant could be northern Italian, but it is more likely to be southern—a restaurant with tomato sauce at the heart of its menu and no hint of what a friend of mine calls "factory veal." The owner should be on the premises, a presence, but not be a distraction. I'll know this restaurant when I see it. The other day, out of town, I walked into such a restaurant and knew it when I saw the owner, a man in his early seventies, sitting on a chair near the cash register complaining about the waywardness of his children. "This place is going to have great food," I said, and it did.

But that, as I say, was out of town. In town, in my neighborhood, we do have an impressive variety of restaurants, ranging from Thai to Mexican, from Texas barbecue to Middle Eastern, from German to Vietnamese. At the best Chinese restaurant I am taken to my favorite table when it is available. Three Greek restaurants are in walking distance of my apartment, but I am partial to one, where I prefer to sit, a nonsmoker, in the smoking section, for a more interesting collection of customers assembles there. The waitresses are not actresses between jobs or poets awaiting grants, but full-time, professional waitresses, many of whom are of a certain age and who, having been around the track a time or two, show their mileage. I sometimes dine alone here, usually ordering two fried eggs, over, done fairly hard, and a side order of excellent ham; hash brown potatoes and toast come with the meal. Reading, cigarette smoke billowing around my head, ingesting heavy cholesterol, I exist in a condition of temporary contentment.

On my most recent trip, my pleasure was diluted by conversation between a waitress still in her twenties and a waitress perhaps in her early fifties as they took a cigarette break at a table near mine. The younger waitress, in tears, told the older waitress that her husband had been complaining about her getting fat and was being damn unpleasant about it. The older waitress blew up and told her not to take any such crap off him and to remind him that he married her not for her figure but for what was in her heart. She went on to report that she herself had had a number of operations, including a mastectomy. She began to warm to her subject—it's what you are, not what you look like, that matters—and instructed the younger waitress, who was softly crying, to put a stop to such behavior on the part of her husband and to do so right now.

I found this very impressive. More than impressive, I found it heroic; I wanted to stand and applaud. This eavesdropper's peek into the life of the restaurant made me understand it for the first time as a kind of family, where people turn to one another in troublous times, and it made me like it even more.

What the blue-rinse dowagers would make of the multiculturalness of current-day Evanston I do not know. But multicultural—without the offending "ism"—it surely is. A series of adjoining shops at which I have done business include, going from south to north, a shoe-repair store run by a recent Mexican immigrant, a compact disc shop run by a young black man whose assistants include a punky fellow with magenta hair who on occasion sports a nose ring, a photo shop run by a family of Middle Easterners, a shop selling eyeglasses run by Soviet Jews, an empty corner store, then, around the corner to the west, a jewelry and dress shop run by Sikhs.

The empty corner store was once a young women's clothing shop, which sold modestly priced blouses, skirts, jeans—what in the trade I believe are called separates. Its closing leaves a hole in the block; the effect is rather like a lost front tooth. Stores go in and out of business in the neighborhood with too great a regularity for my taste, not to speak of the taste—and fortunes—of the owners. The vast shopping malls to the west and north have taken a resounding toll on Evanston's shopping. Yet just when the game seems nearly done, someone new steps in to pick up the dice.

For a long while the closing of a discount drugstore left a key corner shop vacant; it was eventually filled by a Radio Shack. A Scandinavian furniture shop moved to a small location down the block, leaving another gaping hole, which, pleasing to report, was filled by a Barnes & Noble bookstore, a superstore. This has greatly bucked up the neighborhood, which is already rich in bookstores. I am in walking distance of five new- and six used-book shops. Of the new-book stores, Barnes & Noble is the main one. Its stock is large but not nearly as large as the tolerance with which it is run. At the front of the store, people stand for full half hours reading magazines set out on three racks. Nobody ever remonstrates with them. Upstairs, where children's books, paperbacks, and remainders are on display, coffee and pastries are sold, and a person can drink caffè latte and munch away on a fudge brownie while riffling through a seventy-five-dollar book on the French Impressionists. Nobody ever says a word. I tremble. One day, watching a young boy dribbling the crumbs from a chocolate-chip scone over a lavishly illustrated book on railroads and another illustrated book on baseball, I thought, Here, clearly, is a case of killing two books with one scone.

I sometimes meet a friend or student for late-afternoon coffee. I have come to prefer late-afternoon coffee to lunch, which Henry James used to call that "matutinal monster," because a socializing lunch had the effect on him, as it often does on me, of making a return to serious work difficult. Sometimes I have coffee at Barnes & Noble, sometimes at Starbucks. More often, though, I go to another coffee shop called The Unicorn, which is owned by a near contemporary who used to play basketball for Evanston Township High School and who reads my writing and treats me very kindly. At a corner table of The Unicorn one day I saw four other old Evanston hands, men also in their fifties who are former high school athletes and who never really left the neighborhood. Did the wider world never attract them? Or was the neighborhood, with its familiarity, as the *Rubáiyát* has it, paradise enow?

I don't read the *Evanston Review*—I don't read a Chicago newspaper either—so I cannot say whether crime is up or down in Evanston generally or in my neighborhood in particular. In my news bible, the *New York Times* (one of the books of the Apocrypha is closer to it), I read the results of yet another of those unnecessary surveys and learned that more than 20 percent of Americans do not feel safe walking in their own neighborhoods after dark. I am not fearful of being out after dark to pick up a VCR movie, a bottle of wine, or a prescription, or to return from a nearby concert. But nowadays, such is the tenor of contemporary life, one looks over one's shoulder even when opening the refrigerator.

Looking over one's shoulder in the streets of downtown Evanston, one is likely to see not a mugger but a beggar. Beggars, sometimes two or three of them, stand on the corner before the largest neighborhood drugstore. On this corner and others in town, a monthly newspaper called *Streetwise* is sold for a dollar to help the homeless. *Streetwise* vendors also await one outside neighborhood supermarkets. Young men in what seem to me impressive basketball shoes stand with Styrofoam cups asking for money outside coffee shops. A woman from a nearby halfway house has been asking me for "any change" for roughly five years now. Had I given her a half a buck every time she asked, the sum today would probably be in the thousands.

Apart from buying a monthly copy of *Streetwise*, I tend not to cough up. If I did, it would cost me five or six dollars every time I left my apartment. Occasionally, I will yield to a clever approach. "Excuse me," a guy one day asked me, "but are you an architect?" "No," I answered, "but why do you think I might be?" "I dunno," he said, "something about your tie. Got any change?" "For you, yes," I said, forking over a buck. Another time, while I was loading groceries into my car on a sunny afternoon, a very fit young man came up to me and, with a scowl, announced: "I'm just out of prison and I need any help you can give me." Something impressively menacing in that approach. What was he in prison for? I barely had time to wonder. Possibly for punching out someone who refused an earlier appeal for a handout. I forked over another buck.

I regret and—whether or not I am entitled to do so— slightly resent beggary as a feature of my neighborhood landscape and of cityscapes across the country generally. One can hand out a buck here and there, largely as a balm to one's own conscience. Clearly such handouts aren't much help to the people who are doing the begging, since in my neighborhood the same people seem to be at it year after year. But with begging endemic, one is always looking the other way; it is impossible to be lighthearted; a deep stain of hopelessness seeps through all of life.

At least there is no begging on my block. Instead there is a Guatemalan clothing shop filled with items of the richest colors, a beauty shop, a florist, a Chinese restaurant, a Dyn-o-Mite Copy shop, where I have more than once made my stale joke about Xerox never having come up with anything original. Easily the most going concern on the street is a health club. From this club emerge bulked-up young men, carrying thick weight-lifting belts, and an endless stream of women, most of them young, wearing spandex tights, their hair pulled back in ponytails, their faces flushed with exercise. A few doors down, the health club occupies a storefront, where, during the mornings, it offers a baby-sitting service; sometimes, when one passes, children are frisking in the window, rather like puppies in a pet shop. At other times the shop is used for instruction in karate, tai chi, and aerobics. Self-improvement is the theme of the health club, defiance of aging its larger meaning.

The block is dominated by the Northshore Retirement Hotel, whose clientele, along with being aged, seems preponderantly Jewish. Living so near such an institution provides more than a few intimations of mortality. On some mornings, upon waking, shuffling into the kitchen to get the coffee going, in the dark I see red lights blinking along my hall walls. The red lights are from a fire department's emergency vehicle, come to the Northshore to resuscitate—or to carry off—an older man or woman whose heart, lungs, or other major organ hasn't made it through the night. At the Northshore Retirement Hotel, any time is check-out time. A funny way to start the day, on a note of catastrophe for someone else.

Along with the fire department vehicles, there are ambulettes and other four-wheeled carriers of ill tidings that pull up before the Northshore Retirement Hotel. Sons and daughters, themselves no longer so young, often arrive to pick up an elderly parent for a holiday dinner or a Sunday outing. I do not go so far as Dorothy Parker, who, bemoaning her middle age, said: "People ought to be one of two things, young or dead." But, living near the aged, I more and more incline to the notion that the phrase "a happy old age" might just be an oxymoron.

A man of cheerful countenance makes his way around the block every morning, no matter how harsh the weather, with the aid of a walker. Many women regulars are out on rounds of errands, not letting osteoporosis or other of the depredations of old age blow them off the court—not yet anyway.

For a number of years, a small man, bald, neatly turned out, never without a tie and jacket or shoe shine, used to walk the neighborhood streets with quiet but impressive dignity. Once I sat across from him at a restaurant where he was having breakfast with a nephew and niece. The niece addressed him as Uncle Hy. My guess is that they were his only surviving family. Was he a bachelor—something about his appearance suggests he may have been a bachelor of the meticulous type—or a widower? What was his line of work earlier in his life? I have shifted into the past tense because I haven't seen him for a few months. Could it be that one of those fire department trucks that sometimes greets me upon waking was for him? If so, I hope his death, like his clothes, was tidy. He was a neighborhood guy, and, though we never spoke, I miss him.

As a neighborhood guy myself, I wonder where—and how—I'll end up. I hope decent health allows me to close out my book with dignity; I hope my spirit allows me to depart with courage. ("Courage is no good: / It means not scaring others," wrote Philip Larkin of death.) I hope I can avoid dying out of town, or even downtown. Ideally, I should prefer pegging out in the neighborhood in which I now live, and I should like to discover that the afterlife includes the best of the neighborhoods of my boyhood. I'd awake to find myself seated at Friedman's, a corned beef on rye, mustard, set before me as well as a side order of potato salad and a Pepsi-Cola. Old friends would be there. We'd talk about the great Chicago Bear teams of the past. We'd lie amusingly about our success in all realms of life. Wild laughter along with cigarette smoke would float to the ceiling. God, it would be heavenly.

Here to Buy Mink

Oedipus, schmoedipus, just so long as a boy loves his mother.

—*Old joke*

A few months ago my mother's youngest sister, my Aunt Florence, died, which put paid to an entire branch of my ancestry, a full generation on the maternal side. My mother's was a family of four sisters and one brother: in order of birth they were Ceil, Samuel, Belle (my mother), Sally, and Florence. All are now dead. Every family has its secrets, and many of my mother's family's secrets, which must have been manifold, died with this uncle and these aunts. I have been able to unearth only a few.

Here is one: There was no great abundance of money when my mother was growing up on the West Side of Chicago, yet the family had an English maid, a Cockney with the charming name of Minnie Tumbletee. Minnie sent me a dollar for my birthday every year until I was thirty, after which she must have concluded that I could make it on my own. Minnie was later married to a sergeant who was retired from the British army, a man whose air of cordiality was topped only by the complete incomprehensibility of his speech. But the puzzle to me was how my grandmother, who just managed to make do, happened to have an English maid right through the Depression.

It was sheer pretension, I thought, and it wasn't until I was past forty that I put the question to my mother. "What that was about," said my mother, in her matter-of-fact way, "was that my mother's sister in England had married a successful cap manufacturer in Leeds, whom she one day caught with his mistress. If he wanted to remain married to her and also keep his mistress, which he evidently did, my aunt set out a number of penalties for him. One of these was that he was ever after to send a certain sum of money each month to her sister in Chicago. My mother used this money to pay Minnie's wages."

I never knew my grandmother, who died when I was not yet three. She was an Eastern European Jew whose family at some point had settled in England. Consequently, she spoke with an English accent and her first two children were born in England. My mother, born in Chicago, was the first of her three daughters born in America. I have a photograph of my grandmother standing next to my mother, who is holding me, not yet a year old and got up in a bulky crocheted sweater and an ambitious hairdo featuring a large curl running down the center of my head. The pure type of the matriarch, my grandmother in this photograph is a stout woman with her white hair pulled back in a bun. She is wearing a print dress and holding a purse in a small but thick-fingered hand. Her nose is unmistakably Abrahamic (my mother's maiden name was, in fact, Abrams), and her mouth looks capable of witty but also, should the need arise, of fierce utterance. As I was only to discover after I turned fifty, it is also a face that must have camouflaged much suffering. "You was the apple of your grandmother's eye," Minnie Tumbletee told me any number of times, "for she loved you above all the grandkids." My mother's mother died before I came to know her, which I consider a genuine personal deprivation and a great sadness.

I never knew my mother's father either, and I often asked her about him, but never with satisfying results. My mother and I spoke with reasonable candor about many subjects, but her father was not one of them. Such information as she bestowed about him was sketchy at best. He was a nice man, she told me. He was not an outgoing man, she said. As for what he did, it was something in the clothing line, in the needle trades. Plainly, he was not hugely successful. How old he was when he died or what he died of were never revealed.

My mother died of cancer, of liver cancer specifically, and hers turned out to be a prolonged—over more than three years—and sad if not particularly painful death. One evening, during one of her several stays in the hospital, I dined in a dark Chinese restaurant with my father, and I asked him what he knew about my mother's father. I knew my maternal grandfather had died before my father met my mother, but I wondered what he had heard about him. "He killed himself," said my father, looking up from his egg roll. He named the source of his information, then added, "But your mother doesn't know that I know."

My mother and father were best friends, they lived together for fifty-seven years, and yet they never discussed the absolutely crucial fact that my mother's father had been a suicide. My father chose not to discuss it with my mother because he knew it would bring her pain; my mother, I assume, chose not to discuss it in part because it would indeed have been painful, in part because it might have been a source of shame, and in part because my mother was a strong enough woman never to have to convey her grief to anyone, not even to her dearest friend, her husband.

I am certain my mother did not share her grief with her

brother or three sisters. These were five people as nearly unlike one another as any group of five persons could be. My mother's older sister, who died in her forties and whom I never knew well, is said to have been extremely savvy. She was lean, looked severe, and married a man whom she so dominated that it wasn't until he was in his seventies that I first noted that he had a slight foreign accent.

My mother's brother, Sam, was a professional gambler, who, against all received wisdom on the subject, died very rich. It is said that as a young man he had to go on the lam because he owed Chicago mobsters some very long green. He lived extremely well in Los Angeles, owned a small percentage of the Riviera Hotel in Las Vegas, and, by my mother's careful count, at his death had no fewer than twenty-seven Ultrasuede jackets hanging in his closet. Sinatra, it is said, was at his granddaughter's wedding.

My mother's younger sister, my Aunt Sally, for reasons I shall never know, turned herself into a woman of the working class. She married a gentle, handsome man named Sidney, who had a thick black mustache, a serious stutter, and a drinking problem. A woman with huge reserves of affection, she never had children to expend it upon. She became the slightly mad aunt who seems to be a standard fixture at every Jewish wedding, usually found dancing the hora as if it were the closing moments of a stress test.

My mother's youngest sister, Florence, the aunt I loved, one day in her early thirties began crying and was unable to stop, with the result that throughout her days she was in and out of insane asylums, psychiatric wards, clinics, and other institutions. She was subjected to electroshock therapy, on and off every pill regimen, up and down every therapeutic roller coaster, but no one was ever able to relieve her sadness for very long. She died in her sleep at home, one of the few good breaks life afforded her, along with that of having a tender-hearted and faithful husband, who heroically looked after her through her many dark days.

Given all this madness and sadness, I have to report that my mother was one of the least neurotic people I have ever known. The very notion of the neurotic was alien to her. The only time I ever saw her thrown by life was when she was sick with cancer, whose cause she simply couldn't grasp—as, of course, neither could science—but whose effect left her feeling she had been poleaxed. "Did you ever imagine this would happen to me?" she asked me time and again. The way she phrased the question suggested that she looked upon her illness as a judgment, and I could never convince her that there is something arbitrary in the way most kinds of cancer strike and that her character or the way she had lived had nothing to do with her having cancer. Maybe it was this arbitrariness that threw her, for, though the word wasn't one she regularly used, my mother was deeply rational.

My final memories of my mother, of course, are those of her unequal fight—when is it ever equal?—against cancer. Her long course of chemotherapy, with its alternating rounds of hope and defeat, was psychologically hard on her. She was never, I believe, in great pain, but she was greatly weakened. So much so that one night during her illness I had to be phoned to help her out of the bathtub. I arrived to find her sitting in the dry tub, wearing a housecoat, looking both puzzled and slightly embarrassed. I remember, toward the end, driving her and my father to her chemotherapy sessions, which she always dreaded. My mother, seated in the front seat next to me, emitted short, panting breaths, which made me think of a wounded animal.

Cancer takes over one's life even more than does a demanding career. Physically and emotionally, there simply isn't time for anything else but the damned disease. So it became for my mother: all-consuming, all-absorbing, leaving her nothing else to think about but the changes in her body and the end that was ever more clearly in sight. Lying on her deathbed, holding my hand, she said, not particularly with relief, but coolly appraising her situation, "I won't be here much longer."

My mother will soon be dead three years, yet in all but fact cancer took my mother away three years before her actual death. After the awfulness of her last years, it is important to me to recapture the woman I remember.

A friend of mine, a woman, once said that my mother looked like a Spanish princess, and there was something to it. She was dark, handsome, stately, regal. She was not very tall, but she never seemed small. Another friend, who shopped at a fish market where my mother sometimes shopped, once asked the Italian owner if he knew my mother. "Oh, yes," he said, "she's a real lady." And she was.

Once, shopping at an outdoor fruit-and-vegetable stand, I watched a young Greek, from behind the counter, work up a fine rhythm goading his mostly female customers into quickly giving him their orders: "Okay. What next? What next? Let's go!" Then a woman of my mother's generation stepped forward and stopped this fellow dead by announcing, "Slow down, you got *me* now," and she proceeded to give him the most meticulous instructions along with her order ("Six bananas, they shouldn't be ripe before Tuesday, when my grandchildren are coming to stay with me"). This little tableau reminded me of my own mother, who was similarly formidable. She was a presence, my mother, a force, not someone to be taken as part of the crowd or masses. Something about her told people to slow down when they responded to her. She had impressive, really quite immense, dignity.

Where this inner strength came from is itself an interesting question. A girl brought up without any extraordinary advantages and some notable disadvantages—being poor, losing a father in an emotionally complicated way, having no real education—my mother became a woman never to be pushed around or otherwise fooled with. Perhaps her inner strength came from her mother, of whom she always spoke with warmth and admiration. Somehow life never frightened my mother. She found it amusing. She could take things as they were, play them as they lay. One of her great gifts to me, I have often thought, was that of confidence. My father reinforced this confidence by scoring a respectable business success. But it was my mother, in never showing the least trace of anxiety or even of nervousness in her dealings with the world, who taught me that there was nothing to be afraid of in life. Her being, her very bearing, suggested that life might even, within obvious limits, be mastered.

My mother had no cultural pretensions. The fact was that she had, in the large C sense of the word, no culture at all. She rarely attended plays or concerts, though sometimes she watched opera singers on PBS. Broadway musicals were the true boundary of her cultural interest, though I'm not sure she cared all that much even for them. She had been to Israel and she had flown to London on the Concorde, but travel really held no interest for her.

The truth is that my mother had very limited curiosity, except about people. This was the other side of her immense practicality. I never saw her read a book until her sickness, which depleted her energy and kept her indoors, and then she read a few of the Isaac Bashevis Singer and I. L. Peretz short-story collections I lent her. She read the newspapers only for local news—chiefly scandals and big crimes, of which Chicago has never had a short supply—and for obituaries. Among the many things she did not bother to read were her son's writings, with the exception of a single story I published that had a setting familiar to her. Near as I can tell, I believe she thought I got it right. I fear this makes me sound petulant, irritated that my mother ignored what I wrote. Not true. I never expected her to read what I wrote. I even think she was perfectly correct not to do so. She had better things to do than read her son on Chamfort, Santayana, and Italo Svevo.

My mother, I suspect, thought her older son a little crazy, though not at all dangerously so, and of course she was right to think this, too. She must have wondered why this son, who seemed smart enough, spent his days reading hopeless books and wrestling with sentences that were intended for a distinctly limited audience, when he could as easily have been a lawyer or a physician and commanded more obvious rewards. Every so often my mother would run into someone who had heard of her son, read something of his, or seen a review of one of his books in a local newspaper, and she would duly report this to me. But it was plain that she herself was not swept away by this. Having changed someone's diapers may tend to make you rather less impressed with him later in life.

Without setting out to do so, my mother served as an excellent ego deflater. I once called to inform her that I had been offered a job teaching English at Northwestern University. "Oh," she said, "that's nice—a job in the neighborhood," as if I had just got a job bagging groceries at a nearby supermarket. (And "a job in the neighborhood," it turns out, is exactly what my teaching at Northwestern has proven to be.) Another time I called to inform her that one of my books won a five-thousand-dollar prize from the *Chicago Tribune.* "Oh," she said, "we get that junk from the *Tribune* all the time. We throw it away without reading it." I chose not to explain further.

My mother went to Marshall High School in Chicago, where she took the commercial course and graduated at the age of sixteen. This meant that she learned typing, bookkeeping, shorthand—all the secretarial skills. She worked as a book-keeper as a young woman until she married my father when she was twenty-four. For the next thirty or so years she had no regular job, but then she went to work in her husband's business in her middle fifties. She was very good at it, which was no real surprise, for my mother was a quick study and extremely competent.

Not infrequently when I telephoned my mother, I heard a noise in the background. Sometimes while talking with me she would be typing a letter; other times she would be chopping vegetables or stirring a soup. She was one of those people who can do two or three things at a time—and do all of them well. Like lots of people with good minds and nothing theoretical or artistic to apply them to, my mother was an excellent cardplayer. She played cards in her thirties and forties—poker, then later canasta and a game called kaluki, but never bridge, a more suburban game—and she played to win, which she usually did. If she lost, it was never because she did anything stupid. She disliked cardplayers who complained, who, as she would put it, "cried the blues."

Vladimir Nabokov's mother, like mine, I was pleased to read in *Speak, Memory,* also liked poker. "She liked all games of skill and gambling," Nabokov reports. He loved his mother wholly and uncomplicatedly. "She cherished her own past with the same retrospective fervor that I now do her image and my past." John Updike is another writer whose mother seems to have loomed large, though Updike's relationship with his mother was, on the basis of his fictional mothers and from autobiographical references, rather more complex. This was so not least because the senior Mrs. Updike did not altogether approve of Updike's later writing. Perhaps it's better, after all, for a mother not to read her son's writings. Joseph Conrad adored his mother, but he lost her when he was seven—an irreparable loss. Tolstoy, too, was early orphaned. Elizabeth Bishop's mother went into an insane asylum when she, Bishop, was five years old and she never emerged. Hemingway had a tyrannical mother, who would really have preferred him to have been a girl. About the Proust kid and his mother, let us not speak.

My own considered view is that it is probably best to have a mother with conventional interests. To have a mother interested in avant-garde art, for example, would be a dreadful drag. Imagine being taken off by such a mother to see a Julian Schnabel exhibit or having to return home early from the playground to go to a John Cage concert. I am pleased as well to have had an entirely apolitical mother. I have a friend, a man of high achievement, whose mother gave his electric train to the Rosenberg children when he was done with it. She later told him, on his way to finishing at the top of his Harvard Law School class, that she wished he were rather more like Tom Hayden. My mother simply had no interest in my artistic, intellectual, or political development, for which I am supremely grateful.

My mother felt about politics as Raymond Chandler and his detective Philip Marlowe did; like them, she didn't give a hoot who was President because she knew whoever it was, he would be a politician. "They're all crooks, you know," she once said to me about politicians. My mother viewed professed idealism skeptically, which is of course the proper way to view it. She viewed abstraction in much the same way. She could only be persuaded by the firm, the factual, the particular. She would have been the last person to be susceptible to psychotherapy. I once told an acquaintance about my mother's having been psychologically stunned by her cancer. She suggested that there were many "support groups" for people with terminal cancer, and that one of these might be helpful to her. I never for a moment thought of mentioning it to my mother, for I could all too easily imagine her incredulous answer: "You mean you think I will feel better for having told my troubles to strangers? Thank you very much anyway."

None of the issues of the modern day meant a thing to my mother. She took the world, and herself, as they both were. The world wasn't soon likely to be changed; and, besides, it was an endlessly fascinating place as it was. Not to say that the world didn't have its scoundrels, creeps, and con men. Once, when my father was in the hospital for heart surgery, while the doctors—surgeon, cardiologist, radiologist, internist, anesthesiologist—were parading through his room, my mother, drinking a cup of coffee with me in the hospital cafeteria, set her cup down and with a smile announced: "What a pack of thieves and frauds they are!"

My mother had the street-smart knack for spotting phonies. She had a good sense of who liked her and who didn't and the reasons why. She herself displayed no snobbery. One of her best friends in her later life was a woman who had been in Nazi death camps and who had earlier done sewing and alterations for her. When my mother was younger, another of her dearest friends was a tall, freckled, unmarried woman named Marge, who was the aunt of a Quiz Kid of mathematical genius. She was the mistress for decades of a man who was said to be unable to obtain a divorce because his wife was Catholic. Whatever disrespectability might have clung to her friend's liaison was entirely ignored by my mother. When Russian Jews began emigrating to the United States, my mother befriended those she met, many of whom worked for her friends. She had a good instinct, my mother did, for spotting a generous heart.

No doubt she was aided in this by having such a heart herself. My mother never underestimated the usefulness of money—she may, in fact, have overestimated it—but I have never known her to smother a generous impulse. She put herself out for people. She did this for family naturally enough, at one point taking her sister Florence's young son in to live with us for five years, but also for those outside her family. A good part of the social life of middle-class Jewish women of her generation had to do with going to what my mother called "affairs," which weren't affairs in the adulterous sense, but luncheons for one charity or another: the Northwest Home for the Aged, the Home for Jewish Blind, Hadassah, the Cerebral Palsy Foundation. My mother used to sponsor one of these luncheons, which meant picking up the tab for lunch for 150 or so women and paying for an entertainer, which usually meant yet another (female) Barbra Streisand imitator. She was always suggesting to my father that he give someone who could use the extra money another hundred dollars for his birthday or Christmas or some other occasion. She knew money could do a lot of things, and helping people out was the best among them.

"I can stand a great deal of gold," Desmond MacCarthy reports that Henry James said on entering a particularly grand drawing room in England. This is perhaps the one sentiment—along with "Never say you know the last word about any human heart"—that my mother shared with Henry James. My mother had an enjoyment of wealth and a distinct taste for glitz. She used the phrase "rich-looking," entirely without irony, in pure approbation. She went to the beauty shop once a week and was a regular at the manicurist. ("For another seven dollars, I can be a lady," she would say.) She boggled at certain modern prices, but never at those for clothes—and she was always handsomely turned out, dressing with flair.

She liked to drive large and impressive cars. Her last was a Cadillac Seville, a maroon job, the last of the Caddies with a boxy back. I was in it with her once at O'Hare Airport when we ran into heavy traffic. I suggested that she put out her arm in the hope that someone would give her a break by letting her into the left-hand lane. "With a car like this," my mother said, casually, "they don't give you a break. They figure you've already had your break."

My mother was of the furs and diamonds generation. One of her last acts of generosity to her own family was to buy her two daughters-in-law mink coats. It was something she wanted to do, a kind of parting gift. Ill with cancer, my mother sat in a large wing chair, while her two daughters-in-law were courted by an amiable furrier who wore what seemed, in the context, a mouton mustache. My wife noted a coat and asked what it was. "That," said the furrier, "is sheared beaver." My mother, hearing this, stiffened and, sitting up in her chair, announced grandly: "We are here to buy mink." A great characteristic statement, I thought at the time, and think even more now.

In telling such anecdotes about my mother I seem in many ways to be describing the stereotype of Jewish women now in their eighties. In some ways, my mother fulfilled that stereotype. She urged people who dined at her table to eat vast quantities of her food. Her taste in decorating was sociologically predictable. Once when I had not called her in four days, she picked up the phone and, hearing my voice, replied, "Hello, stranger." "Mother," I asked, "are we in a Jewish joke here or what?" She laughed.

My mother didn't often tell jokes, but she had a genuine appreciation as well as a subtlety of comprehension for them. She had a lovely comic sense. All my life she reported amusing bits to me. One of the earliest I remember was of a woman with whom she played cards whose two young sons were so rivalrous that she gave up trying to stop their fighting and instead calmly instructed: "Fight nice." My mother once reported meeting a woman who, after her husband's death, claimed his estate was tied up, not in escrow, but in egg roll.

My mother's superior sense of humor was part of her natural feeling for language. She used phrases I had not heard elsewhere, always with considerable adroitness. When someone was lying, she would say that he was "full of hops." Although I never heard her otherwise refer to the Civil War—and I'm not even sure she could have told you when it took place—she sometimes used the simile "like Grant took Richmond"; sometimes, too, people were "fit to be tied." When people protested that she was doing way too much for them, my mother would pooh-pooh the matter by saying that "it was nothing and nothing." Too great a tumult she used to call, in what I take was an invention of her own, *roojie boojie.* An infant wandering about, clothes untucked, wearing clumpy diapers, she would invariably call "Orkey Cocker."

"I need that like a loving cup," she would say, making an English play on the Yiddish phrase *loch in kopf,* or hole in the head. My mother spoke little Yiddish around the house, but she had it in command when she needed it. She used it to communicate with Russian Jewish émigrés. Whenever I asked her for a translation of a Yiddish phrase, I was always impressed with the precision of her replies. "A *grauber yung,* " she said, "that would be an unlettered boor." "A *dreykopf,* " I remember her replying to another of my queries, "is a muddle-head." Unlike my mother's, my own Yiddish is good enough to fool the Gentiles but not good enough to speak to real Jews.

All her verbal talents were in her speech. On only a few occasions—when I was in the army and, later, when I lived in New York—do I remember receiving letters from her, and these were disappointing notes of the bread-and-butter variety. She used to open with an awkward sentence that she must have picked up in some business-letter-writing course, which ran: "Hope all is well with you as it leaves us the same." In person, she was always very well spoken. She spoke without grammatical error and never descended to dopey psychobabble or sociodrool: no nurturing, growing, lifestyle, identity-crisis talk passed her lips. In her company you knew you were in the presence of a serious and penetrating person, a woman of parts, whom you would do well not to attempt to con with obscurantist language.

One of my mother's great gifts to me was that she never put me in a position where the need to con her arose. She did this by granting me enormous freedom. Unlike the stereotypical Jewish mother, mine was not in the slightest a nag. I don't recall my mother ever yelling at me, and she never even came close to hitting me. I have no memory of my mother telling me to sit straight, go study, wear my galoshes, clean my plate, remember my gloves, mind my table manners, come in early, hang up my clothes, get a haircut, or any of the rest of the standard repertoire of mother-to-son communication that most boys undergo from the age of six until, defeated, they finally leave home in their early twenties. My mother must have assumed that I would know these things on my own, or that the world would soon teach them to me. If it was cold and I forgot my gloves, the pain that was the price for my forgetting them was likely to be reminder enough on the next cold day.

My mother asked so little of me. Beyond the age of ten or so, I don't think I asked much of her either, except a fairly high level of those services generally available, at great expense, at a very good hotel: dining at all hours, laundry and maid service, messages. No one is more solipsistic than an adolescent boy, and during these years my mother all but dropped out of existence for me. If I missed her, I also missed the normal Sturm und Drang of the good old parent-adolescent follies.

What a waste of time and energy that can be! People who have fought lengthy, serious battles with one or another or both parents seem to come away from these battles worn out and without much energy for anything else later in life. What good luck I had in never having to engage in them!

In *Six Exceptional Women,* James Lord, the biographer of Giacometti, illustrates that the most exceptional woman he has known is not Gertrude Stein or Alice B. Toklas or Marie-Laure de Noailles, but his own mother, to whom he pays a beautiful tribute. Louise Bennett Lord gave her son sympathy and understanding through such crises as life presented and stood by him in every instance, even when she disagreed with him. When she learned that her son was homosexual, at a time when this was not a talk-show subject, she greatly worried about it but did not in the least let it lessen her love for him. When he wished for a career as a writer, she and her husband, largely through her insistence, helped support him in the endeavor through many years when it looked as if this might be an egregious mistake. James Lord's mother was steadfast, reasonable, tolerant, kind, generous, good.

Lord's portrait of his mother, and of his relationship with her, is built from a large collection of letters he and his mother exchanged. They wrote as much as they did because Lord lived in Paris, his mother in New Jersey and Connecticut. What admirable documents their letters make—and enviable ones, too. In them, mother and son not only offered each other encouragement and solace when such qualities were most needed, but they were able to say, straight out and in print, how much they loved each other. After Lord returned to Europe, following a trip to comfort his mother during her husband's last days and to see her through the funeral, she wrote to tell him, "I wouldn't have thought that I could love you more than I already did, but now I do." Those are words that every son would like to hear.

A man assured of his mother's love, Freud somewhere says, is a conqueror. But mother love must be applied in careful proportions. Too much suffocates. A friend of mine jokes that his mother had such an elevated opinion of his talents that she would have liked him to accompany himself on the violin as he read from the Torah at his bar mitzvah. F. Scott Fitzgerald, who found his mother an embarrassment, in later life blamed her for spoiling him. People with a keen eye can sometimes spot men who seem to have had too much mother love: the chief sign is an extraordinarily high opinion of oneself accompanied by a slightly sad puzzlement that the world doesn't seem to share it.

I was always certain of my mother's love, yet in what I now think a usefully qualified way. Ours was not a family whose members went about hugging one another, exclaiming our love. My mother, though always immensely generous to her family, was not a woman who lived for her children. Nor, I hasten to add, would her sons have wished her to do so. She was an independent person, with a life of her own—she wasn't one of those mothers who drove her children to various lessons, insisted that everything she did was for her children, or claimed that being a parent was a full-time job—and she made it fairly plain that she expected us to live in the same independent way.

I think she also expected us to live by her standard. In high school, I went out with a girl who worked, after school, in a neighborhood shop. One day my mother told me she walked into the shop and met this girl. I waited for her pronouncement, which, when it came, stung: "You," she said, "can do better than that." Another time, when I was fourteen, my mother asked me if I had any money on me. When I told her I had a dollar or so in change, she replied, "A boy your age should have more money than that on him." Years later, when I was going through a divorce, I was surprised to learn that my mother thought I would move into a hotel, on the Near North Side, that was several notches above what I could afford. Perhaps these were occasions—and quite rare occasions they were—when my mother put herself in my place.

Many years ago, in the *New York Review of Books*, I accused Senator William Benton, the publisher of *Encyclopaedia Britannica* and yet another son of a strong mother, of not being the man his mother was. I have often wondered what kind of man my own mother would have been. Rather a dashing one I think. She probably would have been a businessman, and, I have no doubt, given her quickness and orderliness of mind and sound gambling instincts, a successful one: clever, daring, generous, a powerful moneymaker, a wheel, an operator, a very big deal.

My mother was quite without sentimentality or nostalgia. She almost never talked about the old days, good or bad, though I do remember her remarking on men selling sweet corn and sweet potatoes, warm and ready for eating, on the streets of the old West Side of the Chicago of her girlhood. Every year she would buy me a birthday gift, but it was never chosen with much care. Soon she took to buying me six pairs of undershorts one year, six T-shirts the next; and then, when I informed her that I had an overstock, she began buying me an annual dozen handkerchiefs—gifts that I received, it seems worth adding, in the bags they were brought home in, otherwise unwrapped.

I have seen my mother's feelings hurt and thought her at those times especially beautiful—dignified and very impressive in her subdued anger. These painful times were usually occasioned by what she felt was ingratitude on the part of others. Every family has its theme, and ours, for as long as I can remember, has always been ingratitude. Only late in her life did I see my mother cry, and, given her strength of character,

I was stunned by it. I was made miserable knowing there was nothing I could do to comfort her.

Rather late in my own life it occurs to me that, in retrospect, I am something of a mama's boy. I don't mean in the sense of having been tied to my mother's apron strings. She wouldn't have appreciated the encumbrance; and, besides, she didn't all that often wear aprons. No, it is more and more in the sense of coming to resemble my mother. I am coming to resemble her, first, physically. I have her high color, thin ankles, fleshy earlobes; the lid of my right eye is beginning to droop as did hers in her middle age. My view of the world, I sometimes think, is not so very different from my mother's either, though I once thought it was radically different.

My mother and I never told each other secrets or spoke of the things that stirred our souls. I shall go to my own grave not knowing essential things about my mother. Did she, for example, believe in God? (I suspect not, but I don't really know.) There were obviously bounds we both felt we could not cross. When I divorced, in my thirties, for example, she never asked me why; she only asked if I was sure it was absolutely necessary. It was understood that I would never in any way criticize my father, her husband, in her presence. From an outsider's view, it might appear that my mother and I were never intimate. In the conventional way, I suppose we weren't. We were instead beyond intimacy. We were at that stage of affection where we understood each other without having to explain much, where we knew we could rely on each other without any qualification, where we loved each other so much that we didn't have to display our love in outward endearments. I miss her, like mad.